Performance Analysis of the Indian Pharmaceutical Industry

Performance Analysis of the Indian Pharmaceutical Industry: A Global Outlook

BY

CHANDRIMA CHAKRABORTY
Vidyasagar University, India

AND

DIPYAMAN PAL
Bethune College, India

emerald PUBLISHING

United Kingdom – North America – Japan – India – Malaysia – China

Emerald Publishing Limited
Emerald Publishing, Floor 5, Northspring, 21-23 Wellington Street, Leeds LS1 4DL.

First edition 2025

British Library Cataloguing in Publication Data
A catalogue record for this book is available from the British Library

ISBN: 978-1-83797-744-4 (Print)
ISBN: 978-1-83797-743-7 (Online)
ISBN: 978-1-83797-745-1 (Epub)

Printed and bound by CPI Group (UK) Ltd, Croydon, CR0 4YY

INVESTOR IN PEOPLE

This book is dedicated to our Parents and daughter SHRINIKA

Contents

List of Figures and Tables

Figures

Tables

List of Abbreviations

(X-M)/Y	Net Export Intensity
2SLS	Two-Stage Least Square Method
AAGR	Average Annual Growth Rate
AE	Allocative Efficiency
AEMPS	Spanish Agency of Medicines and Medical Devices
AI	Advertisement Intensity
AIFA	Regulatory Framework of The Italian Medicines Agency
API	Active Pharmaceutical Ingredients
ASI	Annual Survey of Industries
BCC	Banker, Charnes, and Coope
BMI	Biennial Malmquist Index
CAGR	Compound Annual Growth Rate
CMIE	*Centre for Monitoring Indian Economy*
CRS	Constant Return to Scale
CSO	Chief Science Officer
D	Dummy Variable
DEA	Data Envelopment Analysis
DGCI&S	Directorate General of Commercial Intelligence and Statistics
DMU	Decision Making Units
E/L	Employee Per Production Worker / Composition of Work Force
EMA	European Medicines Agency
EU	European Union
FDA	Food and Drug Administration
FDI	Foreign Direct Investment
FGLR	Färe, Grosskopf, Lindgren and Roos
FGNZ	Färe, Grosskopf, Norris and Zhang
GAA	Growth Accounting Approach
GRM	Grand Mean
HFG	High Growth Firms
IDX	Indonesia Stock Exchange
IPI	Indian Pharmaceutical Industry
IPR	Intellectual Property Rights
K/L	Capital Per Production Worker/ Degree of Mechanisation
MF	Intermediate Inputs/ Firm Size
MFDS	Ministry of Food and Drug Safety

MI	Marketing Intensity
MLE	Maximum Likelihood Estimation
MNCS	Multinational Corporations
MOH	Ministry of Health
MPI	Malmquist Productivity Index
MS	Market Share
NHS	National Health Services
NXI	Net Export Intensity
OFDI	Outwards Foreign Direct Investment
PIAM	Perpetual Inventory Accumulation Method
PRC	People's Republic of China
R&D / R AND D	Research and Development
RBI	Reserve Bank of India
RDI	Research and Development Intensity
REER	Real Effective Exchange Rate
SEC	Scale Efficiency Change
SFA	Stochastic Frontier Analysis
SUR	Seemingly Unrelated Regression
SUS	Sistema Único De Saúde
TC	Technical Change
TE	Technical Efficiency
TEC	Technical Efficiency Change
TFP	Total Factor Productivity
TFPG	Total Factor Productivity Growth
TRIPS	Trade-Related Aspects of Intellectual Property Rights
VRS	Variable Returns to Scale
W	Real Wage Rate
WTO	World Trade Organisation
YOY	Year to Year Growth Rate

About the Authors

Chandrima Chakraborty is currently serving as an Assistant Professor in the Department of Economics, Vidyasagar University in West Bengal, India. Dr Chakraborty did her Post graduation in Economics from the University of Calcutta, India and then she obtained her M.Phil. degree and Ph.D. degree in Economics from Jadavpur University, India. Her major areas of academic interest include industrial growth, productivity and efficiency. She is also interested in environmental economics, gender issues, agricultural economics as well as health and economics of education.

Dipyaman Pal is presently serving as an Associate Professor in the Department of Economics, Bethune College, West Bengal, India. Dr Pal did his Post graduation, M.Phil. degree and Ph.D. degree in Economics from Jadavpur University, India. His major areas of academic interest include agricultural growth, productivity, volatility and efficiency. He is also interested in environmental economics and gender issues.

About the Foreword Author

Bishwanath Goldar is a retired Professor of Economics of Institute of Economic Growth (IEG), Delhi. He was a member of the National Statistical Commission and a National Fellow of the Indian Council of Social Science Research. He was a Professor at the ICRIER, during 2003–2004 and a Visiting Professor at the Centre for International Trade and Development, School of International Studies, Jawaharlal Nehru University, during 2012–2013. He is currently a Non-Resident Senior Fellow at the IEG. His areas of research interest include productivity measurement, industry, trade, foreign direct investment, energy use of industries, river water pollution, and rural water supply.

Foreword

India's pharmaceutical industry is one of the most important industries in the manufacturing sector. It is a high-technology industry, contributing significantly to India's merchandise exports. In contrast to petroleum refining, which is also a significant contributor to India's merchandise exports, manufacturing of pharmaceuticals is much more job-creating. The ratio of employment to fixed capital stock in the pharmaceutical industry is about 19 times that of petroleum refining. This ratio in the pharmaceuticals industry exceeds that in manufacturing computers, another important high-tech industry, and is about half of that in textiles, a highly labour-intensive industry.

In India's pursuit of becoming a developed country by 2047, a manufacturing-led growth strategy is at the heart of the development efforts. The expansion of India's pharmaceutical industry, alongside significant increases in pharmaceutical product exports, will play a crucial role in India's growth process in the next 25 years. According to *Economic Survey*, 2021, India's domestic pharmaceuticals market is expected to grow from about US$ 41 billion in 2021 to about US$ 130 billion by 2030. Enhancing the competitiveness of India's pharmaceuticals industry is essential for sustaining rapid growth, and a study of the efficiency and productivity of the industry, as done in this book, thus assumes great significance.

There are many challenges facing the Indian pharmaceutical industry. There is significant spending on research and development (R&D), but R&D intensity is relatively low compared to international standards. The number of patent applications in pharmaceuticals made with the Indian patent office increased from 2,741 in 2017–2018 to 5,622 in 2019–2020, and the number of patents granted in this area rose from 733 in 2017–2018 to 3,317 in 2021–2022. While there was a setback to the process of pharmaceutical patent applications in the years affected by the COVID-19 pandemic, the upward trend has probably resumed in the post-pandemic era.

India can produce low-cost generic medicine and provide it to the world, and it is recognised as a strategic partner in the drug discovery value chain. India has about 1,400 World Health Organization Good Manufacturing Practices (WHO-GMP)-approved pharmaceutical plants and about 250 European Directorate of Quality Medicines (EDQM) approved plants with modern state-of-the-art technology. However, many relatively small pharmaceutical plants have not been able to implement WHO-GMP. There is a problem of getting employees with requisite talent and skills, and the pharmaceutical industry is affected by a relatively high attrition rate. This factor has an impact on the efficiency and productivity of Indian pharmaceutical firms.

The book contains an excellent, careful analysis of the technical efficiency and productivity of Indian pharmaceutical firms using sophisticated econometric methodology. By examining several vital issues, the book enhanced our understanding of the performance of the Indian pharmaceutical industry and what is needed for performance improvement. Some of the interesting questions examined in the book include the impact of the product patent regime on firm performance and the state-wise differences in the productivity performance of pharmaceutical firms. The book will be of immense value to policymakers, industry experts and scholars. Post-graduate students and researchers will find the empirical applications of efficiency and total factor productivity measurement methodologies useful for their studies.

Bishwanath Goldar
Non-Resident Senior Fellow
Institute of Economic Growth, Delhi

Preface

Pharmaceutical industries have been a favourite sector for policy makers and academicians in both developed and developing countries. Indian pharmaceutical industry (IPI) is the major source of low-cost, quality drugs in the global market. It is imperative to assess its performance.

IPI has developed currently as the active as well as most eminent one, worthy of special consideration. IPI has emerged as the major source of low-cost, quality drugs in the global market. As medicines serve the population with safe well-being, it is favoured for policies in both the advanced and less advanced countries.

The scenario of IPI has changed over time. Till 1970s, about 70% of the Indian market was controlled by the foreign firms and the Patent Act of 1911 dominated IPI (Chaudhuri, 2005). Indian drug prices were very high. But with the modification of the Indian Patent Act 1970, medicine prices in the country declined. Fascinatingly after 1970, the global market recognised IPI with the introduction of process patents.

With the trade liberalisation and the signing of trade-related aspects of intellectual property rights (TRIPS) agreement, substantial changes occurred in the industry. IPI started a complete product patent regime since 2005. This enactment of the Product Patent Act is another milestone in this regard, which considerably changed the scenario and IPI became the frontrunners among the generic drugs producer. Thus, companies were unable to reverse engineer & produce new drugs invented abroad & protected by patents (Chaudhuri, 2005).

Therefore, to encounter the emergent challenge of global competition, enhanced efficiency and productivity of IPI are indispensable. The efficiency and productivity gained extraordinary prominence as in persistent economic slowdown only efficient firms are expected to withstand and develop.

The IPI holds a significant place in the global economy. The IPI is ranked 3rd in the world for producing medicines by volume. The country through the pharma sector is considered to be one of the most valuable nations.

Therefore, to encounter the emergent challenge of global competition, enhanced efficiency and productivity of IPI are indispensable. The efficiency and total factor productivity growth (TFPG) per se has assumed a very high importance in view of the fact that only efficient firms are likely to sustain and grow during a period of all pervasive economic slowdown.

The success of the pharmaceutical industry in India has allowed the country to not only meet these needs but also to export its expertise and knowledge to other countries, helping to improve global health and well-being. Overall, the growth and success of the pharmaceutical industry in India is a testament to the hard work and innovation of its companies and workers, and the important role they play in addressing some of the world's most pressing healthcare challenges.

The commitment to produce high-quality medications, while adhering to strict rules and regulations, using the expertise and innovation to address the healthcare needs of people everywhere has helped to achieve success in the IPI and to make a positive difference in the lives of people around the world.

This deserves analysis of efficiency and productivity of IPI, identification of different factors encouraging efficiency and productivity as well as the variables deterring efficiency and productivity. Also, it is needful to understand the global position of IPI in order to achieve growth and sustainable solutions for IPI around the world.

In view of the above perspective, the present book tries to touch upon a range of issues which may be considered as important as well as critical in analysing the performance of IPI in the context of global economy.

There are seven chapters in this book. Brief sketch of all the chapters is presented below:

Chapter 1: Introduction and the Relevance of the Study
Chapter 1 contains the introduction of IPI and its position in the global economy. Then the relevance of the present study will be discussed.

Chapter 2: Survey of Literature
Chapter 2 discusses survey of literature on pharmaceutical industry in India and across the globe. It discusses the existing study highlighting the gaps and presents the connection of the present study with the existing literature.

Chapter 3: Analysis of Efficiency and Total Factor Productivity Growth of Indian Pharmaceutical Industry Using Firm-Level Data
Chapter 3 estimates efficiency and productivity of IPI using non-parametric method of data envelopment analysis (DEA) approach. For doing that it measures output-oriented technical efficiency of IPI and total factor productivity growth considering each firm as a decision-making unit. Also, the factors behind the variation in technical efficiency and total factor productivity growth are identified using panel regression. Another important contribution of this chapter is that it verifies the presence of structural breaks, if any, in the total factor productivity growth series at firm level by using panel structural break methodology.

Chapter 4: Analysis of Efficiency and Total Factor Productivity Growth of Indian Pharmaceutical Industry Using State-Level Data
Chapter 4 investigates the performance of IPI using state-level data. It looks at the performance of pharmaceutical industries in major Indian states. It estimates technical efficiency and total factor productivity growth of Indian states. This chapter helps to compare the Indian states as well as to identify the position of the major states in terms of pharmaceutical industries. Also, the major factors responsible for variation in technical efficiency (TE) and TFPG of IPI are found

using a panel regression. Another important contribution of this chapter is that it verifies the presence of structural breaks, if any, in the total factor productivity growth series at state level by using panel structural break methodology.

Chapter 5: Total Factor Productivity Convergence in Pharmaceutical Industry Across Indian States
Chapter 5 tries to understand whether total factor productivity of pharmaceutical industry across the major states of India converges or not in terms of sigma and beta convergence by employing the conventional sigma convergence as well as the modern panel data approach of beta convergence.

Chapter 6: Moving Towards a Growing Indian Pharmaceutical Industry
Chapter 6 considers that IPI is one of the few industries which have been affected in a major way due to TRIPS agreement as from the year 2005 the existing process patent regime gave way to the product patent regime although the process of establishing a new patent regime in India started since 1995. In such an environment, it will be interesting to examine whether there has been any improvement in the performance of IPI after 1995, i.e. after the period of first version of the product patent regime. For this econometric analysis has been carried out for some selected variables like output, employment, productivity of labour, productivity of capital, capital labour ratio, export intensity, export price, import intensity and price by applying a recent development using unit root test to estimate the break point of these major variables using All India level data. This chapter clearly identifies the variables whose performance are satisfactory and other showing relatively poor performance and hence needs special attention.

Chapter 7: Position of Indian Pharmaceutical Industry in the Global Economy
Chapter 7 examines the performance of IPI and pharmaceutical industries of leading countries namely the United States, China, Germany, Japan, Ireland, Switzerland, France, Italy, Belgium, United Kingdom, Spain, Brazil, Canada, South Korea and the Netherlands. This chapter looks at the trends of three lead variables namely production, export and import of IPI and pharmaceutical industries of leading countries and tries to compare IPI with the other countries in terms of the above three variables and thus helps to identify the position of IPI in the global context. Also, this chapter verifies the presence of structural breaks, which may appear due to changes in economic regime over time, in the different series of production, export and import using panel structural break methodology.

Chapter 8: Summary and Overall Conclusion
Chapter 8 summarises the whole study and makes the concluding observations on each of the seven chapters and recommends some policies for the betterment of the pharmaceutical industries in the Indian states and for IPI as a whole.

The purpose of the study is to improve IPI and to raise awareness among the stakeholders and institutions, and among the Indian planners to take care to remove economic backwardness of the country and to make it a developed economy, equal development across different firms such that the people of weaker segments benefit from the country's economic progress. Thus, to reduce firm-level disparities the knowledge about the growth performance of different firms and the firms which are lagging behind are very much needed. Along with it state level analysis of Indian states will be helpful for interstate comparison and special care may be taken for the lagging states. The evaluation of IPI in the global economy, i.e. to understand the global position of IPI may lead to more developed IPI and sustainable one and may help to upsurge the rank of IPI with respect to the global economy.

We hope that the book will provide immense knowledge base to post graduate students, industry people, researchers and faculty members around the globe related to various subjects such as Economics, Industrial Economics; Medicine, Pharmacy, Health economics, Biotechnology, Microbiology, Business & Management among others. The volume will also be helpful for policy makers, multi-nationals and government officials as well as the general readers interested in the field.

Chandrima Chakraborty
Dipyaman Pal
The Authors

Acknowledgements

With extensive hard work on the stages from submission of the book proposal to final submission of the proposed book titled, *Performance Analysis of the Indian Pharmaceutical Industry: A Global Outlook*, it is an abundant pleasure for the authors as well as everyone related that the book is now published.

In carrying out the entire project, the help and support of different organisations, academicians and other members of the society who are directly or indirectly associated to the project cannot be forgotten.

First *and foremost,* we must acknowledge the cooperation and support of the Emerald Publishing Ltd. team for approving the proposal and continuously guiding us at all stages of developments of the book.

Secondly, we are highly grateful to Prof B. N. Goldar for his valuable contribution and adding to the existing literature through his foreword.

Thirdly, we are indebted to our little daughter, Ms Shrinika Pal for the support and sacrifice in carrying out this lengthy project.

At last but not in least, we would like to thank everyone who helped and motivated us to work on this project.

Chandrima Chakraborty
Dipyaman Pal

Chapter 1

Introduction and the Relevance of the Study

Abstract

This chapter introduces the development of the Indian pharmaceutical industry (IPI) in different phases such as till the 1970s, with the modification of the Indian Patent Act 1970, i.e. after the 1970s, with the trade liberalisation and the signing of Trade-Related Aspects of Intellectual Property Rights (TRIPS) agreement and in the product patent regime, i.e. since 2005. This chapter also discusses the position of IPI in the global economy along with the top medicine-producing countries in the world. The objectives of the present study are presented separately with the firm-level data, state-level data as well as All India and global-level data. All the research questions are also presented in this chapter related to the firm-level data, state-level data as well as All India and global-level data. Then the relevance of the present study in the existing literature is discussed considering each of the book chapters separately while outlining the structure of the present study.

Keywords: Indian pharmaceutical industry; Indian Patent Act 1970; trade liberalisation; TRIPS agreement; product patent regime; global economy

1.1. Introduction

Indian pharmaceutical industry (IPI) has developed currently as the active as well as most eminent one, worthy of special consideration. IPI has emerged as the major source of low-cost, quality drugs in the global market. As medicines serve the population with safe well-being, it is favoured for policies in both advanced and less advanced countries.

Performance Analysis of the Indian Pharmaceutical Industry: A Global Outlook, 1–7

doi:10.1108/978-1-83797-743-720251001

The scenario of IPI has changed over time. Till 1970s, about 70% of the Indian market was controlled by foreign firms and the Patent Act of 1911 dominated IPI (Chaudhuri, 2005). Indian drug prices were very high. However, with the modification of the Indian Patent Act 1970, medicine prices in the country declined. Fascinatingly after 1970, the global market recognised IPI with the introduction of process patent. With the trade liberalisation and the signing of TRIPS agreement, substantial changes occurred in the industry. IPI started a complete product patent regime since 2005. This enactment of the Product Patent Act is another milestone in this regard, which considerably changed the scenario and IPI became the frontrunners among the generic drugs producer. Thus, companies were unable to reverse engineer & produce new drugs invented abroad & protected by patents (Chaudhuri, 2005). Therefore, to encounter the emergent challenge of global competition, enhanced efficiency and productivity of IPI are indispensable. The efficiency and productivity gained extraordinary prominence as in persistent economic slowdown only efficient firms are expected to withstand and develop.

The economic reforms of 1991 further propelled the IPI onto the global platform by removing licencing restrictions. The IPI holds a significant place in the global economy. The IPI is ranked 3rd in the world for producing medicines by volume (Economic Survey, 2022-23). The country through the pharma sector is considered to be one of the most valuable nations.

As of 2021, India is the largest country for the production of low-cost generic drugs which is advantageous for exporting medicines to other countries. Therefore, the share of medicines in the global pharmaceutical export is 20% in terms of the generic pharma sector. It may provide a position of leadership to continue excelling and thriving through the help of a talent pool. This is possible through cultivating and promoting quality in pharmaceutical learning for formulation research within the country. The nation is the largest provider of generic medicines in the world and supplies medicines to many countries. The success of the pharmaceutical industry in India has allowed the country to not only meet these needs but also to export its expertise and knowledge to other countries, helping to improve global health and well-being.

The United States is the biggest pharmaceutical market in terms of consumption and import and the third largest in terms of export. The high level of healthcare spending alongside advanced healthcare infrastructure and a significant population plays an integral part in the strong demand for pharmaceutical products in the country. China has the distinction of being the biggest producer of pharmaceutical ingredients in the world. The most populous country in the world has a rising middle class, an increasing footprint of healthcare coverage, and an ageing population. Generic drugs and APIs make it the number one drug maker in the world in terms of volume. The country has a very tough drug approval process that takes significantly longer than other developed countries of the world. Germany is the biggest exporter of pharmaceutical products in the world and employs 143,000 people in the pharmaceutical industry. The country has the biggest pharmaceutical market in Europe and the fourth biggest in the world, with an annual consumption worth $64.6 billion. The significant level of pharmaceutical consumption in Germany is due to high healthcare spending and a large population. Japan is the third biggest pharmaceutical market in the world, with an annual estimated consumption of over $100 billion. The country is a key export market for pharmaceutical goods manufactured in the United States. Japan has an ageing population that is playing an integral role in the strong demand for pharmaceutical products. Ireland is the fifth biggest exporter of pharmaceutical products in the world. The country has established itself as a leading global centre for pharmaceutical manufacturing. Due to the low corporate tax in the country, numerous leading pharmaceutical companies like Pfizer among others have established their manufacturing facilities in Ireland. The country provides convenient shipping facilities across the Atlantic as well.

Coming to the pharmaceutical industry in India, its growth and success is a testament to the hard work and innovation of its companies and workers, and the important role they play in addressing some of the world's most pressing healthcare challenges. The commitment to produce high-quality medications, while adhering to strict rules and regulations, using the expertise and innovation to address the healthcare needs of people everywhere has helped to achieve success in the IPI and to make a positive difference in the lives of people around the world.

1.2. Objectives of the Present Study

Given the transformed situation of IPI, the following are the objectives of the present study:

With firm-level data:

- To estimate the extent of efficiency of the firms
- To identify the factors affecting such efficiency
- To find out the total factor productivity growth (TFPG) of the firms
- To break down TFPG into its diverse constituents
- To elucidate the causes of variation in TFPG
- To look at the common factors responsible for variation in efficiency and TFPG
- To verify the presence of structural breaks, if any, in the series of TFPG.

With state-level data:

- To estimate the extent of efficiency of the states
- To identify the factors affecting such efficiency
- To find out TFPG of the states
- To elucidate the causes of variation in TFPG of the states
- To examine whether total factor productivity converges in pharmaceutical industry across states
- To understand whether the total factor productivity (TFP) of the pharmaceutical industries across the 17 major states of India converges or not
- To check whether IPI is moving towards a growing industry or not
- To verify the presence of structural breaks, if any, in the series of TFPG.

Considering the data on leading countries along with All India:

- To test the growth performance of major selected variables of IPI at All India level
- To understand the position of IPI in the global economy in terms of production, export and import
- To make an inter-comparison of countries and their performance in terms of the above variables
- To verify the presence of structural breaks in the series of production, export and import.

Thus keeping in mind the above objectives, the following research questions can be framed:

Considering the sample firms:

- What is the efficiency score of the firms?
- What are the major determinants of the efficiency of IPI?
- What is the value of TFPG of the firms?
- Which component of TFPG dominates over the other?
- What are the determinants of TFPG of IPI?
- What are the common factors responsible for variation in efficiency and TFPG of IPI?
- Whether there exists any structural break in the series of TFPG?

Considering the sample states:

- What is the efficiency score of the states?
- What are the major determinants of efficiency of IPI?
- What is the value of TFPG of the states?
- What are the determinants of TFPG of IPI?
- What are the common factors responsible for variation in efficiency and TFPG of IPI?
- Whether total factor productivity converges in pharmaceutical industry across states?
- Whether IPI is moving towards a growing industry or not?
- Whether there exists any structural break in the series of TFPG?

Considering the leading countries along with All India:

- What is the growth performance of major selected variables of IPI at All India level?
- What is the position of India compared to other leading countries in terms of production, export and import?
- How the different countries performed in terms of the above three variables?
- Are there any structural breaks in the different series of production, export and import?

1.3. The Structure of the Present Study

The structure of the present study is as follows:

Chapter 1: Introduction and the Relevance of the Study
Chapter 1 introduces the development of the IPI in different phases such as till the 1970s, with the modification of the Indian Patent Act 1970, i.e. after 1970s, with the trade liberalisation and the signing of TRIPS agreement and in the product patent regime, i.e. since 2005. This chapter also discusses the position of IPI in the global economy along with the top medicine-producing countries in the world. The objectives of the present study are presented separately with the firm-level data, state-level data as well as All India and global-level data. All the research questions are also presented in this chapter related to the firm-level data, state-level data as well as All India and global-level data. Then the relevance of the present study in the existing literature is discussed considering each of the book chapters separately while outlining the structure of the current study.

Chapter 2: Survey of Literature
Chapter 2 discusses a survey of literature on the Pharmaceutical Industry related to efficiency, productivity and other issues in India and across the globe. Econometric theoretical literature on technical efficiency (TE) as well as econometric theoretical literature on TFPG are discussed in separate sections. Individual sections discuss studies on the performance of the pharmaceutical industries in the Indian context, studies on the performance of the pharmaceutical industries in the international context, studies on efficiency in the IPI, studies on TFPG in the IPI, other studies on IPI and also studies on the performance of the pharmaceutical industries in the international context (other than India). This chapter discusses the existing study highlighting the gaps and presents the connection of the present study with the existing literature in a separate section.

Chapter 3: Analysis of Efficiency and Total Factor Productivity Growth of Indian Pharmaceutical Industry Using Firm-Level Data
Chapter 3 estimates the efficiency of the IPI using non-parametric method of data envelopment analysis (DEA) approach. For doing that it measures output-oriented technical efficiency of the IPI considering each firm as a decision-making unit. Also, the factors behind the variation in technical efficiency are identified using panel regression. It also estimates the productivity growth of the IPI. For that, it measures TFPG considering each firm as a decision-making unit using non-parametric method of the DEA approach. Also, the major factors responsible for variation in TFPG of the IPI are found using panel regression. Also, this chapter compares the efficiency and productivity of the IPI, i.e. it compares TE and TFPG of the IPI. This chapter also tries to identify the common factors responsible for changes in these two performance indicators. Another important contribution of this chapter is that it verifies the presence of structural breaks, if any, in the TFPG series at the firm level by using panel structural break methodology.

Chapter 4: Analysis of Efficiency and Total Factor Productivity Growth of Indian Pharmaceutical Industry Using State-Level Data

Chapter 4 investigates the performance of the IPI using state-level data. It looks at the performance of pharmaceutical industries in major Indian states. It estimates technical efficiency and TFPG of Indian states. This chapter helps to compare between the Indian states as well as to identify the position of the major states in terms of pharmaceutical industries. Another important contribution of this chapter is that it verifies the presence of structural breaks, if any, in the TFPG series at the state level by using panel structural break methodology.

Chapter 5: Total Factor Productivity Convergence in Pharmaceutical Industry Across Indian States

Chapter 5 tries to understand whether total factor productivity of pharmaceutical industry across the major states of India converges or not in terms of sigma and beta convergence by employing the conventional sigma convergence as well as the modern panel data approach of beta convergence.

Chapter 6: Moving Towards a Growing Indian Pharmaceutical Industry

Chapter 6 considers that IPI is one of the few industries which have been affected in a major way due to TRIPS agreement as from the year 2005 the existing Process Patent regime gave way to the product patent regime although the process of establishing a new patent regime in India started since 1995. In such an environment it will be interesting to examine whether there has been any improvement in the performance of IPI after 1995, i.e. after the period of first version of the product patent regime. For this, econometric analysis has been carried out for some selected variables like output, employment, productivity of labour, productivity of capital, capital labour ratio, export intensity, export price, import Intensity and price by applying a recent development using unit root test to estimate the break point of these major variables using All India level data. This chapter clearly identifies the variables whose performance are satisfactory and other showing relatively poor performance and hence needs special attention.

Chapter 7: Position of Indian Pharmaceutical Industry in the Global Economy

Chapter 7 examines the performance of IPI and pharmaceutical industries of leading countries namely the United States, China, Germany, Japan, Ireland, Switzerland, France, Italy, Belgium, United Kingdom, Spain, Brazil, Canada, South Korea and the Netherlands. This chapter looks at the trends of three lead variables namely production, export and import of the IPI and pharmaceutical industries of leading countries and tries to compare IPI with the other countries in terms of the above three variables and thus helps to identify the position of IPI in the global context. Also, this chapter verifies the presence of structural breaks, which may appear due to changes in economic regime over time, in the different series of production, export and import using panel structural break methodology.

Chapter 8: Summary and Overall Conclusion

Chapter 8 summarises the whole study and makes the concluding observations on each of the seven chapters and recommends some policies for the betterment of the pharmaceutical industries in the Indian states and for the IPI as a whole.

Chapter 2

Survey of Literature

Abstract

This chapter discusses a survey of literature on efficiency, productivity and other issues related to pharmaceutical industry in India and across the globe. Econometric theoretical literature on technical efficiency (TE) as well as econometric theoretical literature on total factor productivity growth (TFPG) are discussed in separate sections. Individual sections discuss studies on the performance of the pharmaceutical industries in the Indian context, studies on the performance of the pharmaceutical industries in the international context, studies on the efficiency of Indian pharmaceutical industry (IPI), studies on the TFPG of the IPI, other studies on IPI and also studies on the performance of the pharmaceutical industries in the international context (other than India). This chapter discusses the existing study highlighting the gaps and presents the connection of the present study with the existing literature in the conclusion section.

Keywords: Pharmaceutical industry; technical efficiency; total factor productivity growth; Indian context; international context; literature survey

2.1. Introduction

Globalisation and the balance of payment crisis situations have influenced many developing countries to change their industrial policies from protected regimes to more open one and exposing domestic firms to global competition. The switch from a protectionist regime to global competition together with a stronger patent policy forced different industries to change their mechanism and take measures needed for long-term survival and growth.

Performance Analysis of the Indian Pharmaceutical Industry: A Global Outlook, 9–49

doi:10.1108/978-1-83797-743-720251002

In the process patent regime, Indian pharmaceutical industry (IPI), characterised by the strong processing skills of the indigenous sector, was permitted to reverse engineer and produce any drug under patent in the developed countries and sell it at very low prices. The Trade-Related Intellectual Property Rights (TRIPS) agreement, which was implemented in a phased manner starting in 1995, changed these conditions drastically by allowing product patenting for all the patented drugs. Economic reforms of 1991 coupled with TRIPS agreement brought about major changes to the IPI. India progressed to complete product patenting from 2005 in pharmaceuticals. As a result, competition increases manifold and the industry started using various cost-saving effective methods thereby becoming further efficient and competitive.

This chapter is structured as: Section 2.2 represents the survey of literature of the study. Subsection 2.2.1 discusses econometric theoretical literature on TE and TFPG. Sections 2.2.1.A and 2.2.1.B discuss econometric theoretical literature on TE and TFPG respectively.

Section 2.2.2 discusses studies on the performance of the pharmaceutical industries in the Indian context and studies in international context are discussed in Subsection 2.2.3. Subsection 2.2.2.1 elaborates on studies on efficiency in IPI and in Section 2.2.2.2 studies on total factor productivity growth (TFPG) in IPI are presented. Subsection 2.2.2.3 discusses other studies on the IPI. The connection of the present study with the existing literature is demonstrated in Section 2.3.

2.2. Survey of Literature

There exists huge number of studies on different aspects related to pharmaceutical industries in different parts of the world. Researchers have made an effort to gauge the activities of pharmaceutical industries under different time periods, following different methodologies and concluded accordingly.

However, since the major area of interest of the present study is confined to the analysis of efficiency and TFPG particularly of the IPI along with other countries' pharmaceutical industries, to keep out discussion within limit, studies on efficiency and productivity are mostly deliberated as well as other studies on IPI are discussed in Section 2.2.2. Studies on various issues in the international context (other than India) on pharmaceutical industries are discussed in Subsection 2.2.3.

2.2.1. Econometric Theoretical Literature on Efficiency and Productivity

2.2.1.A. Econometric Theoretical Literature on Technical Efficiency

2.2.1.A.1. Parametric Approach: Stochastic Frontier Production Function Approach. Solow (1957), under the assumption of Constant Returns to Scale (CRS), associates the production growth with neutral technical change and input growth. Later on, many studies focus on the efficiency change component, among which, the study by Nishimizu and Page (1982) is the first to introduce efficiency change as a source of productivity change.

A frontier definition of TE is provided by Koopmans (1951) corresponding to which Debrew (1951) and Farrell (1957) propose two measures of TE viz. the input-oriented measure and the output-oriented measure. The present study focuses on the output-oriented measure of Farrell (1957), which consists in comparing the observed output with the maximum potential output obtainable from the given inputs. A number of literary works follow Farrell's work. Aigner and Chu (1968), Afriat (1972) and Richmond (1974) estimated production frontiers using linear and quadratic programming techniques. However, this variety of literature is developed around the concept of deterministic production frontier, where the inefficiency is conceived as the only source of random disturbance in the production process. So, the random shocks lying outside the production unit's control are totally ignored in these models. To fill this gap, a set of analysis is developed with the publication of two almost contemporary papers – one by Meeusen and Van den Broeck (1977) and the other by Aigner et al. (1977). Shortly after these, a paper by Battese and Corra (1977) is published.

The subsequent literary development in this area differs as regards how to distinguish between two error components, the functional specifications used and also the distributional assumptions made about the efficiency term. Most of the studies (Aigner et al., 1977; Schmidt & Lovell, 1979) use single parameter distributions like half-normal and exponential (Jondrow et al., 1982). However, in some other studies, two parameter distributions like, Gamma or truncated normal distributions (Battese & Coelli, 1988, 1992; Greene, 1990; Stevenson, 1980) are used. Cornwell et al. (1990) introduce a flexible function of time in the production function to estimate the time-varying firm-specific efficiency levels. Kumbhakar (1990) also estimates time-varying firm-specific efficiency under a panel-data framework.

The variation in TE scores over time may be caused due to the presence of firm-specific factors. Some earlier studies (Kalirajan, 1981; Pitt & Lee, 1981) following a two-stage procedure, provide efficiency estimates in the first stage and then regress these estimates against a vector of firm-specific explanatory variables in the second stage. However, later studies (Battese & Coelli, 1995; Huang & Liu, 1994; Kumbhakar et al., 1991) use a single-stage approach to incorporate the firm-specific factors directly into the inefficiency error component.

The paper by Aigner et al. (1977) is one of the contributory papers with which the discussion on stochastic frontier analysis (SFA) originated. They define the composite error term as the sum of symmetric, normal, statistical noise and non-negative one-sided error components that capture the effects of technical inefficiency. They used the empirical example of the US primary metal industry of 28 states for 1957–1958. Test results indicate relatively small one-sided components of the disturbance, which actually suggests higher efficiency levels relative to the frontier.

Pitt and Lee (1981) extend cross-sectional maximum likelihood estimation techniques to panel data, while measuring technical inefficiency. Using data on 50 firms of Indonesian weaving industry for the years 1972, 1973 and 1975, they carry out an investigation of the sources of inefficiency following a two-stage method. The results reveal variation in the firm-specific mean TE from 60% to

70%, however, an alternative model with time-variant efficiency is found to be the most appropriate one for the selected sample of the study.

The paper by Jondrow et al. (1982) is the first to suggest a method of separating the error term of the stochastic frontier model into a normal error term and a non-negative inefficiency term. They estimate two models – one with TE error term following a half-normal distribution and the other with efficiency term following an exponential distribution. The distribution of the inefficiency term is conditioned on the estimate of the composed error term for each individual producer and thus obtained producer-specific estimates of TE.

Battese and Coelli (1988), using data on dairy firms in Australia for 1978–1981, estimate stochastic frontier production function under the assumption of non-negative and time-invariant technical inefficiencies, having a truncated normal distribution. The results report the best predictor for the firm-specific random variable and the appropriate TE of an individual firm under such specification.

Cornwell et al. (1990) incorporate a flexible function of time in the production function instead of making strong distributional assumptions for technical inefficiencies or random error terms. Using panel data on US airlines from the first quarter of 1970 to the fourth quarter of 1981, the study estimates time-varying and firm-specific efficiency levels.

Kumbhakar (1990), accommodating increasing, decreasing and time-invariant behaviour of technical inefficiency, specifies a model for TE estimation. Based on an assumption of cost minimisation, time-varying firm- and input-specific allocative inefficiency is also incorporated in the study.

Huang and Liu (1994), with the help of single-stage approach, measure production efficiency together with the firm-specific factors affecting the TE change. They propose a model of stochastic frontier regression different from the conventional model of Aigner et al. (1977). Huang-Liu's model combines a stochastic frontier regression and a truncated regression to estimate the production frontier with non-neutral shifting of the average production function. The truncated regression is used to identify the sources of efficiency. The study evidences non-neutral effects of a few firm-specific variables like the age of the firms, the export ratio and the expenditure on R&D on efficiency in Taiwan's electronic industry.

Battese and Coelli (1995), using a single-stage approach, define a stochastic frontier production function in which the non-negative technical inefficiency effects are assumed to be a function of firm-specific variables and time. Applying the model to 10-year panel data on paddy farmers from an Indian village, they show that the inefficiency effects are dependent on the farmer-specific variables and time of observation.

Kalirajan (1997), using firm-level data from South India, suggests a simple method to measure the economic efficiency of firms through returns to scale, when there is no data on price.

Kumbhakar and Lovell (2000) are concerned with the development of a modified econometric approach (SFA) to the estimation of productive efficiency. They associate proximity to estimated frontiers with the degree of efficiency with which producers pursue their objectives that can be purely technological or economic in nature. Along with the estimation of production frontiers, they are also concerned with the estimation of cost and profit frontiers. The frontiers are stochastic in nature because they continue to maintain the traditional econometric belief in the presence of external forces contributing to random statistical noise.

Wang and Schmidt (2002) contribute to the theoretical aspect of TE analysis by contrasting one-step estimation with the two-step method of estimation of TE. Analysing the properties of two-step estimators, they find very significant bias in the first step, when the inputs and firm-specific variables are correlated as well as when they are independent to each other. In contrast to two-step estimators, the one-step estimators, based on a correctly-specified model, are found to be asymptotically optimal. These estimators perform quite well in finite samples as compared to two-step estimators. The study evidences the severity of the bias of the two-step procedure with an extensive Monte Carlo experiment and suggests the use of single-step procedure.

2.2.1.A.2. Non-Parametric Approach: Data Envelopment Analysis. DEA is a Linear Programming Problem which can provide a mean efficiency within a group of organisations. The efficiency of an organisation is calculated relative to the group's observed best practice. Fried et al. (1994) argue that DEA can provide appropriate role models to serve as possible benchmarks for a program of performance improvement and also the most efficient production facilities. They also conclude that by DEA one can get the optimum scale and optimum size of output if all inputs are to perform according to best practice. So by DEA one can easily identify those inputs which are not efficient and those outputs which are inefficient.

In order to measure efficiency, one has to construct the production possibility set empirically from observed data. In parametric models, one assumes an explicit specification of the production function (in the single output case) or a transformation function (in the multiple output case) and uses appropriate statistical methods to obtain estimates of the parameters from sample data. But in the nonparametric approach of DEA, one makes some general assumptions about the underlying technology but there is no explicit functional form of the production function. Introduced by Charnes, Cooper, and Rhodes (CCR) (1978) and further generalised by Banker, Charnes, and Cooper (BCC) (1984), DEA allows one to construct the production possibility set empirically from observed data.

Both the input- and output-oriented measures of technical efficiencies in the case of single input and output, can be visualised in Fig. 2.1.

In Fig. 2.1, input x is measured along horizontal axis and output y along the vertical axis. Point A (x_0, y_0) represents the actual input-output bundle of a firm, A. Now $y^* = f(x_0)$ where y^* is the maximum output producible from input x_0. The output-oriented measure of technical efficiency (TE) of firm $A = \frac{y_0}{y^*}$ which is the comparison of actual output with the maximum producible quantity from the observed input. Now for the same output bundle y_0, the input quantity can be reduced proportionately till the frontier is reached. So, y_0 can be produced from input x^*. Thus, the input-oriented TE measure for firm $A = \frac{x^*}{x_0}$.

The TE score of a firm takes value between 0 and 1. A value of one indicates the firm is fully technically efficient.

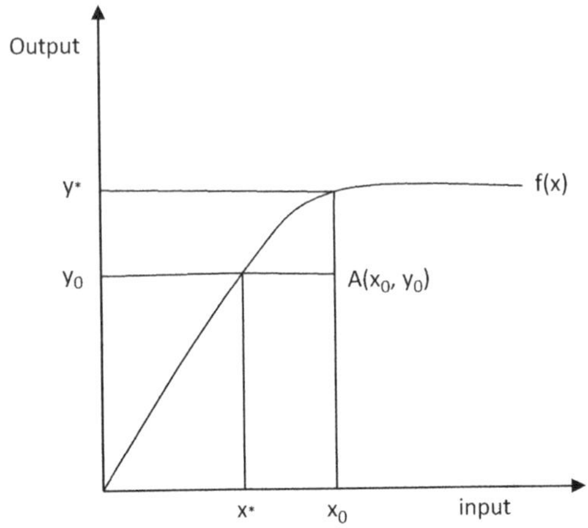

Fig. 2.1. Input- and Output-Oriented Measures of Technical Efficiency.

In DEA, a benchmark technology is constructed from the observed input–output bundles of the firm in the sample without any assumption regarding the production frontier. The general assumptions made about the production technology are as follows. (i) All actually observed input–output combinations are feasible. (ii) The production possibility set is convex. (iii) Inputs are freely disposable. (iv) Outputs are freely disposable. These are weak assumptions. These assumptions hold for all technologies represented by quasi-concave and weak monotonic production function.

Output-Oriented Measure

The concept of output efficiency basically deals with the question that is 'By how much can output quantities be proportionally expanded without altering the input quantities used?'

Following Banker et al. (1984), the output-oriented radial TE of a firm with an observed input–output bundle (x^0, y^0) under the variable returns to scale (VRS) assumption is obtained as:

$$\zeta_y\left(x^0,\ y^0\right)=\frac{1}{\Phi^*}$$

where $\Phi^* = \max \boldsymbol{\Phi}$

$$\text{s.t} \sum_1^N \lambda_j y^j \geq y^0;$$

$$\sum_1^N \lambda_j x^j \leq x^0;$$

$$\sum_1^N \lambda_j = 1 \text{ where } \lambda_j \geq 0; (j = 1,2,\dots N)$$

When CRS is assumed the restriction $\sum_1^N \lambda_j = 1$ is deleted from the equation.

Input-Oriented Measure

The input-oriented measure of TE of any firm t under CRS requires the solution of the following LP problem:

$$\min\theta \text{ Subject to } \sum_{j=1}^{N}\lambda_j y_{rj} \geq y_{rt} \quad (r=1,2...g)$$

$$\sum_{j=1}^{N}\lambda_j x_{ij} \leq \theta x_{it}; \quad (i=1,2...h)$$

$$\theta \text{ free}, \lambda_j \geq 0 \quad (j=1,2...N)$$

The input-oriented TE of firm t under CRS is

$$TE_{IN}^{ct} = TE_{IN}^{ct}(x^t, y^t) = \theta^* \in T^{CRS}$$

where $\theta^* = \min\theta : (\theta x^t, y^t) \in T^{CRS}$

Thus knowing θ^* input oriented TE of firm t can be determined. The input oriented measure of TE of any firm t under VRS can be determined by solving the above problem along with the constraint $\sum_{j=1}^{N}\lambda_j = 1$, taking into consideration the VRS frontier.

2.2.1.B Econometric Theoretical Literature on Total Factor Productivity Growth (TFPG)

TFPG can be measured by (i) Growth Accounting Approach (GAA) [i.e. by constructing either Solow Index (Solow, 1957), or Kendrick Index (Kendrick, 1956, 1961, 1973) or Translog-Divisia Index (Christensen & Jorgenson, 1969, 1970; Jorgenson & Griliches, 1967; Solow, 1957)]; (ii) Econometric (Parametric) Approach (i.e. by estimating production function or cost function); (iii) Non-parametric Approach (i.e. through DEA).

TFPG measures growth in output which is not accounted by growth in inputs. In order to get an idea regarding the extent of TFPG the following Fig. 2.2 is considered.

In Fig. 2.2, t = time period; $t_1 > t_0$ and x = single input and $f(x)$ = single output, $y_0 = f(x, t_0)$ and $y_0 = f(x, t_1)$ are the production functions at time period 0 and 1 respectively.

Production Function: $y = f(x)$, shows the maximum output y obtainable from a given input x. If (y', x') be the observed plan of the firm then the plan is technically efficient if $y' = f(x')$ and technically inefficient if $y' < f(x')$.

Measure of TE, E: $E = \{y'/f(x')\}; 0 < E < 1$

In the above diagram, AA' = inefficiency because with x_0 amount of input, maximum $f(x_0, t_0)$ amount of output can be produced by using the frontier but

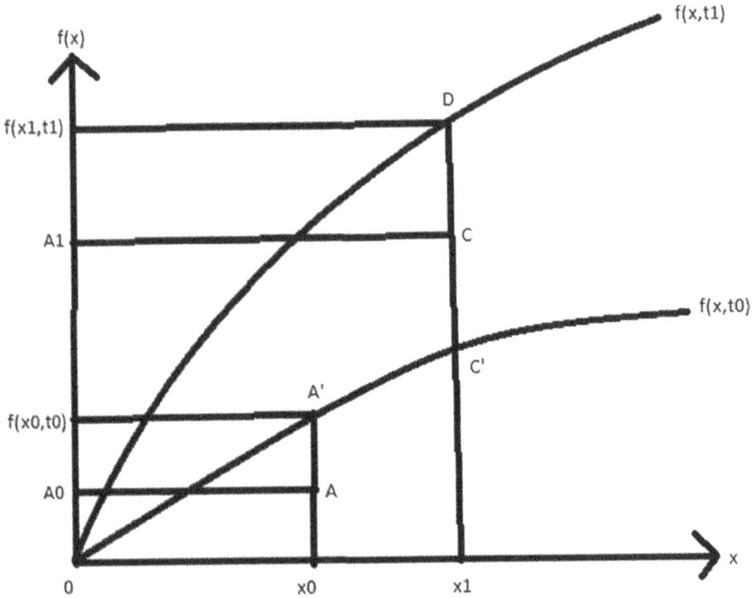

Fig. 2.2. Measurement of TFPG.

the entire input is not efficiently used that is why in reality only A_0 amount of output has been produced which is lesser than $f(x_0, t_0)$.

$$\text{Inefficiency} = \frac{\text{Actual output}}{\text{Maximum producible output}} = \frac{A0}{f(x0)}$$

Similarly, with x_1 amount of input, maximum $f(x_1, t_1)$ amount of output can be produced by using the frontier but the entire input is not efficiently used that is why in reality only A_1 amount of output has been produced which is lesser than $f(x_1, t_1)$.

$$\text{Inefficiency} = \frac{\text{Actual output}}{\text{Maximum producible output}} = \frac{A1}{f(x1)}$$

Movement from A to C = Movement from A to A' (Efficiency Change)
+ Movement from A' to C' (Scale Efficiency Change)
+ Movement from C' to D
– Movement from D to C (Efficiency Change)
where CC' = Technical Change = {Movement from C' to D – Movement from D to C}

The best practice level or a frontier is the production function giving the maximum possible output given a set of inputs. However, in order to reach the best practice level, knowledge of this level or the frontier is needed and also the distance from the frontier. In this context, it is also important to distinguish between technological progress and changes in TE. Technological progress occurs through the changes in the best practice production frontier. Total factor productivity (TFP) change is the sum of rate of technological progress and changes in TE. Thus, it is important to recognise that changes in TE affect TFP. In the literature, reference is made to allocative and TE. Allocative efficiency occurs when a firm employs its factors in the correct proportions. On the other hand, TE arises when a firm makes the best use of its inputs. TE is obtained by minimising the cost incurred at each level of activity (Ray, 2006).

2.2.1.B.1. Measurement of TFPG Using Growth Accounting Approach. TFP may be defined as the ratio of output to a weighted combination of inputs. Various TFP indexes suggested differ from one another with regard to the weighting scheme involved. In most empirical studies either the Kendrick index or the Solow index has been used.

A. Solow index
B. Kendrick index
C. Divisia index – Translog index

A. Measurement of TFPG Using Solow Index

This index is based on the Cobb–Douglas production function. Under the assumption of CRS, autonomous Hicks-neutral technological progress and payment to factors according to marginal product, the following equation is obtained:

$$\frac{\dot{A}}{A}=\frac{\dot{Y}}{Y}-\left[(1-\beta)\frac{\dot{L}}{L}+\beta\frac{\dot{K}}{K}\right]$$

where Y denotes output, L denotes labour, K denotes capital and β denotes the income share of capital. Dot stands for the time derivative.

The discrete form of the above equation:

$$\frac{\Delta A}{A}=\frac{\Delta Y}{Y}-\left[(1-\beta)\frac{\Delta L}{L}+\beta\frac{\Delta K}{K}\right]$$

$\frac{\Delta A}{A}$ is basically the extent of TFPG.

B. Measurement of TFPG Using Kendrick Index

Let us assume that there is one homogeneous output denoted by Y and there are two factors of production: capital denoted by K and labour denoted by L. Furthermore, let w_0 and r_0 denote the factor rewards of labour and capital in the base year. Then the Kendrick index for year t may be written as:

$$A_t=\{Y_t/(w_0L_t+r_0K_t)\}$$

Under the assumptions of CRS, perfect competition and payment to factors according to their marginal product, the total earnings of labour and capital in the base year is exactly equal output of that year; so that A_0 is equal to unity by definition. The Kendrick index may be interpreted as the ratio of actual output to the output which will be resulted from increased input in the absence of technological change.

For any $t \neq t_0$, A_t will differ from unity. The extent of TFPG is measured by the departure of A_t from unity.

C. Measurement of TFPG using Divisia Index – Translog Index

Consider an aggregate production function with two factors of production $Y = F(K, L, T)$

where Y denotes aggregate output, K denotes aggregate capital, L denotes aggregate labour and T denotes time.

The share of the factors will be $V_K = (rK/pY)$ & $V_L = (wL/pY)$

$$\Delta \log Y = V_K(\Delta \log K) + V_L(\Delta \log L) + VT$$

where $\Delta \log Y = \log Y(T) - \log Y(T\text{-}1)$
$\Delta \log K = \log K(T) - \log K(T\text{-}1)$
$\Delta \log L = \log L(T) - \log L(T\text{-}1)$

and $V_K = (1/2)\,[V_K(T) + V_K(T\text{-}1)]$ & $V_L = (1/2)\,[V_L(T) + V_L(T\text{-}1)]$

This expression for V_T is termed the average translog quantity index of technological change.

2.2.1.B.2. Measurement of TFPG using Parametric Approach, i.e. by Estimating Production Function or Cost Function

A. Estimation of TFPG using production function
B. Estimation of TFPG using cost function

A. Estimation of TFPG Using Production Function

Since TFPG measures the shift of the production function over time, in order to estimate TFPG using production function, we basically start with the assumption of any particular form of the production function and add time as an argument in that function.

The responsiveness of the production function (Y) with respect to time $\frac{\partial y}{\partial t}$ gives us the extent of TFPG. The researchers can assume different types of production function like Cobb–Douglas, CES, Translog, etc.

B. Estimation of TFPG Using Cost Function

$$\text{Cost Function is given by: } C = C(P_K, P_L, T)$$

where P_K = per unit price of capital, P_L = per unit price of labour and T = time.

If the coefficient of T is negative and statistically significant, then we have technical progress.

$$\text{Total factor productivity growth} = \frac{\partial \log C}{\partial T}$$

Negative of the coefficient $\frac{\partial \log C}{\partial T}$ gives us the extent of TFPG. To get positive TFPG, the cost function should fall over time.

2.2.1.B.3. Non Parametric Approach of Data Envelopment Analysis (DEA). The non-parametric approach of TFP growth measure differs from the other approaches in the sense that it does not require any explicit specification of production technology nor does it require any econometric estimation. Only a few assumptions about the production technology are needed. No assumption regarding market structure adds more flexibility to the analysis. This approach employs mathematical programming to measure TFP growth on the basis of actual input–output observations. A benchmark (or reference) technology is constructed on the basis of sample observations and this benchmark technology is then used to decompose the changes in productivity into its components like technical change, TE change and scale efficiency change. The most widely used measure of TFP growth is followed by constructing Malmquist Productivity Index (MPI). MPI scales output levels up or down radially with respect to the benchmark technology. Commonly the measurement of TFP growth using MPI is done through DEA. DEA is a 'data-oriented' approach for evaluating the performance of multiple decision-making units (DMUs).

In DEA, without explicitly specifying a production function, the maximum producible output is constructed using the sample observations and on the basis of a few assumptions like feasibility, convexity of the production possibility set, free disposability of inputs and outputs and also of CRS or VRS. In DEA, the efficiency frontier envelops all the data.

In the formulation of DEA by Charnes, Cooper and Rhodes (CCR) (1978, 1981), the data on market prices are not available. Shadow prices are chosen with the help of a linear programming problem so as to maximise the average productivity. Distance functions can be derived by suitably defining a non-negative scale factor. Productivity indices can be obtained from the distance functions. However, a later extension of DEA allows for reformulation of the original problem to take into account the market price.

CCR (1978, 1981) induce the method of DEA to address the problem of efficiency measurement for DMUs with multiple inputs and multiple outputs in the absence of market prices. However, the CCR-DEA model measures the TE of a firm under the assumption of CRS.

Later, Banker, Charnes and Cooper (BCC) (1984) make extensions of the CCR model by incorporating technologies exhibiting VRS.

Caves et al. (1982) show that for translog production function, Törnqvist output and indexes are equal to the mean of two MPIs. They introduce MPI as the ratio of output distance functions without any aggregation of inputs.

Färe et al. (1992) use mathematical programming to evaluate the distance functions that can be used in empirically measuring MPIs. Furthermore, they also decompose the measured MPI into technical change or 'shift in' production frontier and 'catching up' showing movements towards (or away from) the frontier, assuming CRS and any scale effect, by definition, is ruled out.

However, in a subsequent paper, Färe, Grosskopf, Norris and Zhang (FGNZ) (1994) follow an extended decomposition proposed by Färe et al. (1994) to further single out the returns to scale effect. FGNZ calculate a world benchmark frontier and compares each country with respect to this benchmark by allowing VRS. The model is applied to analyse productivity growth in 17 OECD countries over 1979–1988. The use of CRS and VRS by FGNZ within the same decomposition of MPI is later criticised by Ray and Desli (1997).

Schimmelpfennig and Thirtle (1994) apply Granger Causality tests and Cointegration tests to investigate whether any causal relationship between TFP and a few explanatory variables exists. To estimate the model, they use the data on agriculture for the UK, 10 EC countries and the USA. A long-run relationship is found between TFP and research spending.

Ray and Desli (1997) term the use CRS and VRS by FGNZ (1994) within same decomposition of MPI as not being consistent. They propose an alternative decomposition of MPI by using a VRS frontier as the benchmark and reach at the conclusion different from that of FGNZ.

Färe et al. (1997) provide a further decomposition of technical change index into an index of magnitude of technical change, an output-bias index and an input-bias index.

2.2.2. Studies on Performance of the Pharmaceutical Industries in the Indian Context

Over the years there are various studies that examined the performance of pharmaceutical industries in the different parts of the world under different time periods, following different methodologies. This section presents the studies on various issues related to IPI.

2.2.2.1. Studies on Efficiency in the Indian Pharmaceutical Industry (IPI)

There are studies on Efficiency in IPI due to Majumder (1994), Saranga and Phani (2003, 2009), Chaudhuri and Das (2006), Saranga (2007), Majumdar and Rajeev (2009), Mazumder et al. (2010), Fujimori et al. (2010), Saranga and Banker (2010), Chakraborty and Ghose (2014), Mahajan et al. (2014, 2018), Chakraborty and Ghose (2018), Chakraborty and Ghose (2019), Alam and Rastgi (2019), Chakraborty and Pal (2020), Mirmozaffari et al. (2022) among others.

Majumder (1994) studied TE of input-oriented type using DEA for a few pharmaceutical companies considering the capabilities and resource utilisation of nine large firms from the period 1987 to 1990 and inferred that the private sector firms are more efficient as compared to the public sector firms. Saranga and Phani (2003) gave an overview on cost efficiency using DEA for 44 companies that have persisted in the past one-decade. They established that in-house efficiencies played vital role for the existence as well as progress of the firms over the last one decade.

Chaudhuri and Das (2006) used the parametric method of SFA for estimating output-oriented efficiencies of IPI sector exploring data at firm level during 1990 to 2001. They concluded that average efficiency in the sub–period, 1999 to 2001 had settled compared to 1990–1998 and also big firms involved in export with international market have enhanced efficiency. Chaudhuri and Das (2006) analysed the efficiency of firms in IPI before and after the TRIPS agreement. The analysis reveals that the efficiency of firms has increased after the Indian legislature has passed the bill for accepting patent applications in early 1999. They found that R&D intensity and market share influence efficiency of firms. The impact of import intensity enhances inefficiency. Their result indicates absence of ownership effects after the Indian legislature had passed the bill for accepting patent applications. Saranga (2007) estimated efficiency of input-oriented type using firm-level pharmaceutical data employing DEA. Majumdar and Rajeev (2009) indicated that firms which are vertically integrated and producing bulk drug and formulation are more efficient and have higher technological invention. Saranga and Phani (2009) explored the effect of managerial and strategic parameters on the degree of operational efficiency achieved by a firm in the IPI using DEA. During the period 1992–2002, the relaxation of import restrictions and foreign direct investment (FDI), along with a major change in the regulatory norms, resulted in increased competition from firms with superior resources in this industry. The findings indicate that domestic firms, most of which are controlled by family-based governance structures, enjoy higher efficiencies than affiliates of multinational pharmaceutical majors. After controlling for firm size and initial efficiency levels, they find that firms with higher levels of innovation through higher R&D investments and older establishments are associated with higher efficiencies, when compared with their less R&D intensive and younger counterparts, respectively. Saranga and Banker (2010) studied the productivity change and factors driving this change in the IPI during 1994–2003, in the backdrop of economic liberalisation and change in regulatory norms using a non-parametric Data Envelopment based-methodology to estimate productivity change and decompose it into technical and relative efficiency changes. They find that, the long-term strategic measures by a section of innovative firms that foresaw the implications from competitive forces of globalisation and a change in the regulatory environment have sphere headed the technical change. Consequently, few innovative firms, characterised by greater R&D investments, transition into higher value-added products and businesses as a step towards more technically sophisticated new drug development have pushed the production frontier, increasing the technical and productivity gains. The higher technical and R&D capabilities and wider new product portfolios of multinational companies also have contributed to the positive technical and productivity changes in the IPI. Fujimori et al. (2010), using small scale IPI data, estimated stochastic frontier production function and concluded that the small-scale pharmaceutical industries (SSPI) are inefficient. They further proved that SSPI policies aimed at supporting progresses of TE to some level. Mazumder et al. (2010) found a negative trend for the output efficiency levels of firms and the evidence of efficient use of labour and raw material. They also found that research and development, export expenditure and imported technology use has negative impact in developing firms' TE. Mahajan et al. (2014), for large Indian pharmaceutical firms, measured the TE, super efficiency, slacks, and input/output targets by applying DEA approach. They found that private Indian and private foreign firms are more efficient than group-owned firms and suggested that ownership type affects the activities of a firm. Mahajan et al. (2018) determined the efficiency and its determinants of Indian pharmaceutical firms and found Product Patent action to have negative outcome on efficiency. They concluded that the enhancing factors are mergers and acquisitions' growth, shift in the direction of diversification, usage of progressive foreign technology, fixed assets' investment as well as thoughtful marketing activities' resource distribution. Alam and Rastgi (2019) using DEA assessed the efficiency of five Indian Pharmaceutical companies and suggested that the industry was efficient in utilising their resources to produce all the defined outputs. They indicated that India's transformed patent regulations are not harmful for the financial and general well-being of IPI. Chakraborty and Pal (2020) estimated TE and found out its enhancing factors employing firm-level panel data for the period 2000–2001 to 2015–2016. Output-oriented TE measure employing DEA and Panel Regression are used to achieve these objectives. Mirmozaffari et al. (2022) presented an artificial intelligence method composed of optimisation and machine learning. DEA is used to measure productivities and efficiencies of pharmaceutical companies during the COVID-19 pandemic using the additive model in window analysis, the BCC (Banker-Charnes-Cooper) model, and the CCR (Charnes Cooper-Rhodes) model. The three models are assessed using DataStream financial information with research and development (R&D) investment. The results indicated the additive model's superiority in window analysis, followed by the BCC and CCR models. In the end, some of well-known data mining algorithms, based on the suggested data, have been evaluated in various tools to find the most efficient tool and algorithm.

2.2.2.2. Studies on Productivity in the IPI

Some studies exist dealing with productivity in IPI. Some worth mentioning studies on the productivity of IPI are due to Pradhan (2006), Saranga and Banker (2010), Pannu et al. (2010), Kamiike et al. (2012), Ghose and Chakraborty (2012), Gupta and Kapoor (2017), Pal et al. (2018), Chakraborty and Pal (2020), Mahajan (2020), Hoque and Das (2021), Chandulal (2021), Vijayalalitha et al. (2022), Muthuswamy and Nithiya (2023) among others.

Pradhan (2006) found the trends in the global competitiveness of the IPI and also attempts to answer where does this industry stand when compared to global peers on pharmaceutical value-added, productivity, research and development and trade performance and also forwarded the new strategies that Indian pharmaceutical companies are adopting to become global players. It is found that strategic government policies were the main factors that transformed the status of the IPI from a mere importer and distributor of drugs and pharmaceuticals to an innovation-driven cost-effective producer of quality drugs. India emerged as one of the fast-growing pharmaceutical industry in the world with growing trade surpluses and exports. However, there are certain limitations that the government policies need to address, like low productivity and R&D intensity. A host of competitive strategies, like greenfield direct investment, overseas acquisitions, strategic alliances and contract manufacturing have emerged as favourites to Indian pharmaceutical firms recently. Saranga and Banker (2010) determined change in productivity employing DEA and also reasons driving the transformation for IPI over the period 1994 to 2003. They established that a small number of pioneering firms which are having superior Research & Development investments, changed to higher value-added products and businesses for more technically sophisticated new drug development, have shifted the production frontier thus raising productivity as well as gains due to technology. Also, they contended that positive technical and productivity changes in IPI are due to greater technical as well as Research & Development know-hows as well as broader new product portfolios of multinational companies. Pannu et al. (2010) with DEA and econometric models evaluated relative efficiency affected by Research and Development and innovation and change in productivity as well as performance of the firms over the period 1998 and 2007. A progressive effect of invention characterised through investment in Research & Development as well as productivity patents, share in market, exports and capability of attracting contract manufacturing amongst Indian pharmaceutical companies were found. Ghose and Chakraborty (2012) estimated TFPG by employing parametric approach during the period 1973–1974 and 2003–2004 after allowing adjustment for stationarity. They suggested Translog one as the better fitted production function and explained the variation in TFPG. Kamiike et al. (2012) employing parametric approach analysed the effect of industry dynamics on TFPG through 5 selected regions of India over the period 2000–2001 to 2005–2006. They established growth in productivity is comparatively greater in the agglomerated region. They also claimed that the growth in productivity due to plant dynamics is contingent on age and dynamism of agglomeration. According to Gupta and Kapoor (2017), pharmaceutical industry is an important and significant industry in India. The common practice by experts, would-be investors and stakeholders of a pharmaceutical firm is to observe the year-end or quarterly financial figures of a firm and then use them to assess the firm's future growth and competitive standing against rivals. However, over the past few years, there is a strange environment in which paid consultants and scamsters are making false and conflicting claims in terms of the performance and future growth of the companies. The researchers, however, have attempted, by means of DEA, to get past all this by benchmarking the companies based on the conversion from input to outputs.

Pal, Chakraborty and Ghose (2018) estimated firm-level TFPG over the period 2000 to 2013 using DEA and examined whether productivity of IPI has amplified after TRIPS. They suggested overall TFPG after TRIPS agreement increased and firms producing bulk drugs and formulations are less productive relative to only bulk drug or formulations producer.

Chakraborty and Pal (2020) estimated TFPG and to find out its enhancing factors employing firm-level panel data for the period 2000–2001 to 2015–2016. Biennial Malmquist index of productivity by DEA and Panel Regression are used to achieve these objectives.

Mahajan (2020) empirically studied the impact of product patent regime on the productivity of different categories such as ownership, R&D, size and product-wise of 141 Indian pharmaceutical firms using non-parametric DEA during 2000–2001 to 2014–2015. The results suggest that Indian pharmaceutical firms need substantive improvement in TFP by improving managerial and scale efficiency. IPI needs to improve productivity across the network and drive cost excellence initiatives across the spend base through operational excellence and digital initiatives.

Mahajan (2020) empirically studied the impact of product patent regime on the productivity of different categories such as ownership, R&D, size and product-wise of Indian pharmaceutical firms using non-parametric DEA. They applied Ray and Desli's MPI and its decomposition to measure TFP change, pure TE change, scale efficiency change and technical change under VRS technology assumption for 141 Indian pharmaceutical firms during 2000–2001 to 2014–2015. The study found the negligible impact of product patent regime on productivity. The technological change has played a positive role in the growth of productivity, whereas TE change depicts the judicious utilisation of resources for improving performance. From the results, it is found that R&D intensive firms depict better stability in the TFP than the non-R&D firms. However, Granger causality between R&D and productivity found no relationship. Productivity is more directly affected by investment in fixed assets rather than in R&D, which focusses on incremental value additions in a largely branded/plain generic product market. In case of ownership, private foreign firms found to have registered progress in TFP while others have recorded marginal regress, which probably could be attributed to the superior marketing and management skills of the foreign firms, besides possessing proprietary technology. Both small and large firms have shown positive growth in the new regime as compared to the pre-patent regime. These small firms are able to compete with large firms because of their up-gradation of the technological base by improving access to better foreign technology. TFP growth for all the firms can be attributed to improvement in technology, and innovation in terms of high capital-output ratio. Furthermore, the paper tried to identify the determinants of productivity from panel random effect regression, and it is found that export intensity, age and the new patent regime have negative and significant relationship with productivity, whereas other variables such as R&D, ownership, size and capital imports are insignificant. In the end, the results of sensitivity analysis have confirmed the validity of the selected variables.

Hoque and Das (2021) examined the trends in partial and TFP growth of India's pharmaceutical industry using industry-level time series data covering a period of 25 years from 1993–1994 to 2017–2018, which is further divided into pre-product and post-product patent periods. Three alternative indices of GAA viz., Translog, Solow, and Kendrick have been used to measure the growth of TFP with four input production framework. The results indicate significant increasing trends in capital intensity as well as labour, energy and material productivity and a significant declining trend in capital productivity over the entire study period. This study also finds a positive turn around in the TFP growth of Indian's pharmaceutical industry during the post-product patent era. The decomposition analysis confirms that output growth in the pharmaceutical industry is input-driven rather than productivity-driven as TFP growth contributes only 8.5% to the observed output growth.

Chandulal (2021) aimed to measure, analyse and compare the productivity performance of selected pharmaceutical companies in India based on secondary data on seven pharmaceutical companies selected as a sample based on paid-up capital of the year 2019–2020. The seven companies are selected for their higher paid-up capital, and the study period is seven years from 2013–2014 to 2019–2020. In this study, ratio analysis is used as an accounting tool in which four productivity ratios are employed. The one-way ANOVA technique of parametric test is used as a statistical tool to identify the difference among sample means. The major findings of the study indicate that in all the selected companies the performance of material productivity, labour productivity and overhead productivity show fluctuating trend. The overall productivity performance of all the companies is very close to each other during the study period of seven years. The result of the statistical tests revealed that in all productivity ratios drawn null hypotheses are not accepted. This means there is a significant difference in different productivity ratios among selected pharmaceutical companies during the study period.

Vijayalalitha et al. (2022) evaluated TFPG and its components using Malmquist DEA for the period of 2009–2010 to 2019–2020. The data are collected from CMIE-PROWESS for the firms that are having sales more than Rs. 100 Crores based on the year 2009–2010. Total of 96 firms were used for the analysis and are in-terms of rupees in Crores. Total sales, cost of raw materials, salaries and wages, cost of power and fuel, and cost of Advertising and marketing are used in the analysis. The analysis was carried out in four stages. In the stage I, all the firms were included, in the stage II the firms which are less than Rs. 500 Crores are included, in Stage III the firms which are between Rs. 500 to 1,000 Crores were included and in Stage IV the firms which are more than Rs. 1,000 Crores has been included. It is evident from results that the year 2017–2018 recorded highest TFP growth, which is due to TE. The year 2012–2013 recorded the lowest TFP changes, which is due to technological changes. It is also evident from the result that negative TFP growth is reported most of the firms during the study period. The main reason for lowest TFP growth is due to technological change in Indian pharmaceutical firms.

Muthuswamy and Nithiya (2023) aimed to increase the engagement and productivity of medical representatives and, in turn, assist the pharma industry in retaining their employees for growth by analysing the factors affecting their work life. This study examines the relationship between work quality and job satisfaction among medical representatives in the pharmaceutical industries in Salem and Erede districts. To meet the study's objective, a perceptual survey was conducted by collecting data from 161 medical representatives working in Salem and Erode districts using a structured questionnaire and analysing the data using statistical tools, including reliability, ANOVA, correlation and regression. The research contributes to formulating a policy that encourages the retention of medical representatives and boosts their productivity in the pharmaceutical industry.

2.2.2.3 Other Studies on the IPI

The survey of literature reveals that there are several studies, other than efficiency and productivity that analysed IPI under different issues and perspectives considering different time points and different methodologies. Some worth mentioning names are Lall (1974), Chandrasekhar and Purkayastha (1982), Chaudhuri (1984), Singh (1989), Chaudhuri (1993), Prasad and Bhatt (1993), Madanmohan (1997), Watal (1997), Srinivasan (1999), Agrawal and Saibaba (2001), Cullet (2001), Chaudhuri (2002), Lalitha (2002), Joshi (2003), Cheri (2004), Grace (2004), Pavcnik (2004), Srinivasan and Srikrishna (2005), Pradhan (2006), Rangnekar (2006), KPMG (2006), Mani (2006), Rangnekar (2006), Bhasa (2006), Kumari (2007), Basant (2007), Jha (2007), Chaudhuri (2007), Greene (2007), Chaudhuri (2008), Kiran and Mishra (2009), Dutta Chaudhuri and Kumar (2009), Mishra and Chandra (2010), Jha (2010), Institute of Economic Growth (2010), Srinivasan (2011), Kalani (2011), Chaudhuri (2012), Mathew and Unnikrishnan (2012), Shivdas (2012), Chaudhuri (2013), Parasiya et al. (2013), Goldar (2013), Horner (2013), Srinivasan and Phadke (2013), Sandhya et al. (2014), Tyagi et al. (2014), Srinivasan et al. (2014), Chakraborty and Ghose (2015), Tyagi et al. (2016), Chakraborty (2017), Atal et al. (2016), Vithalani et al. (2016), Reddy and Rao (2017), Chakraborty and Ghose (2017), Mukhopadhyay and Paul (2018), Kumar et al. (2020), Dhanora et al. (2021), Nandy and Sussan (2021), Kolte et al. (2021), Gupta and Gupta (2021), Singhal et al. (2022), Rosario and Mazumdar (2022), Festa et al. (2022), Singh and John (2022), Sharma et al. (2023), Saini and Agarwal (2023) among others.

Lall (1974) examined the main characteristics of the international pharmaceutical industry as it functions in the developed world paying special attention to the anomalies and distortions which exist because of the peculiar structure of the drug market and of the great oligopolistic power exercised by the leading firms and also the options open to the government of developing countries to reduce the cost of obtaining drugs. He concluded that in the long run, the best way to deal with the various and complex problems of the present international pharmaceutical industry as it operates in Less developed countries (LDCs) is to move in appropriate stage towards a socially owned indigenous pharmaceutical industry which copies for technology, bans brand names and markets the products through official agencies.

Chandrasekhar and Purkayastha (1982) in their paper, using the data on the major import of 29 foreign drug companies in India, attempted a tentative estimate of the average extent of outflow of profit due to transfer pricing during the period 1972–1976. Chaudhuri (1984) calculated the actual market share of formulation sales by the different sectors and concluded that the indigenous sector had technology to produce at least 76.8% of the value of bulk drugs produced by the transnational corporations in India during 1976/76-77 and 1977/77-78 and at least 97.5% of the value of formulations sold by the transnational corporations during 1977 and 1978. He suggested constraints of several types like financial, entrepreneurial, etc. but technology will not be a blockage for substituting many manufacturing activities of transnational corporations. Singh (1989) analysed the intensity of export, import as well as net import of pharmaceutical firms in terms of size of operations, foreign ownership, the degree of foreign ownership, relative size of foreign collaborator and the technology for the period 1973–1974 to 1976–1977. Chaudhuri (1993) discussed India's introduction of patent Act, 1970 in the face of tremendous resistance from the transnational companies and their countries of origin. He further pointed out that India will be a net looser and acceptance of the Dunkel Draft will result in a drastic change in its patent laws. Prasad and Bhatt (1993) examined the factors behind the current demand for strengthening the Indian patent system and the effect of such strengthening on Pharmaceutical sector. Madanmohan (1997) looked at plant exit data in IPI for recognising firms' role in the exit process and suggested that larger and low cost plants have higher profitability of survival in IPI and the characteristics of firms also had important influence on plant closing and also the decision of the firms owning many plants to close down is not related to relative production costs. Watal (1997) pointed out India's impossibility to obey TRIPS Arrangement. She suggested that the government of India is to make the acceptance of product patent application in pharmaceutical and agricultural chemicals – legal and transparent and then begin the more comprehensive and legislative exercises. She further pointed out that given the time constraint in complying with the majority of the TRIPS provisions within two years ago, it would seem prudent not to lose any more time and to begin the process of weighing all the available options immediately. Srinivasan (1999) discussed in his paper that government intervention led prices of Indian medicine to be escalating and different Pharmaceutical industry sectors have responded dissimilarly to the strategies. According to Agrawal and Saibaba (2001), major changes in IPI can be expected due to TRIPS and India will be required to start product patents and this will likely lead to sharp rise in prices of newly patented drugs. They concluded that TRIPS Agreement is not in the national interest and should be renegotiated.

According to Cullet (2001), South Africa and Brazil have both successfully adopt provisions in their respective patent legislations that indicates that there is scope for flexibility in TRIPS implementation. India too needs to redraft its patents (second amendment) Bill that takes into account more fully the needs of the people, especially their right to health and access to drugs.

Chaudhuri (2002) examined whether correction of Indian Patents Act, 1970 has taken benefit of TRIPS, and looked at exclusion, omission as well as compulsory licencing requirements in pharmaceuticals. Lalitha (2002) pointed out that the various options that are available to IPI in the new plant regime are R&D and new product development, contract research or manufacture, patent product and compulsory licencing, production of drugs using process capabilities and production of off patented products. Joshi (2003) anticipated the chances of Indian and foreign manufacturers in the product patent regime in 2005.

Cheri (2004) answered the policy-relevant questions like How is implementation of product patents in India and China affecting access to medicines? And Will generic copies of patented medicines have to be withdrawn from the market? Will prices rise? Will the domestic industry disappear? Will MNCs become more interested in working with domestic firms? What are the implications for donors?

Pavcnik (2004) suggested that India may understand a greater economic shock due to TRIPS, on the other hand may gain due to future domestic innovation and these countries can continue producing generic substitutes of patented drugs via compulsory licencing and necessitates confirmation of TRIPS rules appreciation and a reasonable licence fee payment to the patent-holders. Srinivasan and Srikrishna (2005) argued that task force report on creating life-saving medicines accessible at sensible prices is adequately upbeat to the country realisms and asserted that price guideline would be essentiality of the drug and strategic considerations based.

The well-known report by KPMG (2006) noted that soaring costs of R&D and administration are persuading drug manufacturers to move more and more of their discovery research and clinical trials to the subcontinent or to establish administrative centres there, capitalising on India's high level of scientific expertise as well as low wages. It also pointed out that India's current Good Manufacturing Practice (GMP) and US FDA compliance level is an important advantage for off-shoring.

Grace (2004) although highlighted the impact of intellectual property on FDI, trade and firm strategy, with inevitable consequences for industrial development, this study is not primarily about the pharmaceutical sector's role in economic development in India and China. A wide literature exists debating the positives and negatives of the introduction of patent laws on the development of the pharmaceutical industry, technological development, and economic development in emerging markets. This study is primarily about what will happen to important sources of low-cost quality medicines coming from India and China, an analysis which requires looking at the probable strategic scenarios and options available to firms in these countries (with inevitable implications for the industries as a whole, and for economic development). It must be recognised that the paper's focus on pharmaceutical supply and pricing is only one part of a multi-faceted system determining levels of access to medicines. For example, WHO advises that rational selection, sustainable financing, reliable systems and finally, affordable pricing are all necessary components in achieving better access to medicines.

Pradhan (2006) investigated that strategic government policies were the key reasons that altered the status of IPI but there are definite restrictions that the government strategies require to address such as little productivity as well as R&D intensity.

Rangnekar (2006) suggested that the limits to implementing TRIPS are equally on account of ambivalence within the government with respect to intellectual property and the changing self-interest of sections of Indian pharma and that despite a favourable international climate in the area of intellectual property, patent reform in India has been doubly constrained by the narrow agenda and domestic factors.

Mani (2006) argued that invention system has the competency to grow new chemical objects and Government Research Institutes and the enterprises do not have every necessary ability for bringing a fresh medicine in the market.

Bhasa (2006) empirically investigated the efficacy of ownership groups in enhancing firm performance by analysing 103 firms in the pharmaceutical industry during the period 1995–2001. Firm performance is measured both in accounting terms and also using a market related measure viz., market-to-book ratio. Overall the results suggest that there exists a relationship between ownership structure and firm performance. They found mixed evidences of the impact of different ownership classes on firm performance and also evidence that markets reward generously to firms that have higher concentrations of insider holdings and foreign shareholders. Firms, with high concentration of corporate bodies, were found to be punished by the markets. Except for the market metric of performance, higher concentration of insider holdings was found to have a negative or an insignificant impact on the other performance metrics. Retail shareholders were found to defy the monitoring hypothesis by having either no or insignificant impact on firm performance. Foreign-controlled firms were found to perform better than Indian-controlled firms.

Greene (2007) noted that with the re-introduction of product patents, many of the smaller firms would exit and many of the remaining would move away from plain vanilla generic production and turn towards contract manufacturing, contract clinical trials, outsourcing, and other forms of tie-up with multinational companies.

Kumari (2007) tried to recognise causes responsible for imports of firm technology in IPI on the basis of data at firm level from 1995. They found bigger sized and older firms importing more technology and profits as insignificant in determining technology imports. They argued that foreign equity participation firms have higher technology imports relative to their domestic complement.

Basant (2007) argued that a weak patent regime combined with policies to reduce market concentration, curb monopolies and encourage bulk drug production, initially through public sector investments, and the size of the Indian market could have led to development of indigenous process capabilities in India. Meanwhile, in Pakistan, the same patent policy was not combined with policies adopted in India and since the market size is much smaller, it did not have the same effect.

Jha (2007) argued that with the shift to a strong patent law, Indian pharmaceutical companies are rapidly shifting their focus to the generics market of the developed world but even as India has become a net exporter of pharmaceuticals, import dependence on active pharmaceutical ingredients (APIs) has steadily increased over the last 10 years. He further stated that the shares of both the APIs and formulations are declining and their investment preferences have shifted towards financial securities and a process of consolidation through mergers and acquisitions has been underway, which apart from increasing market concentration, has been a key element of firm strategy to tap business opportunities along the value chain in the domestic as well as the overseas markets. Also, he pointed out that in the field of R&D, with no Indian pharmaceutical company being equipped to take a potential drug from the investigational stage to the stage of final market launch, collaboration with multinational corporations is the norm, resulting in biases in the choice of therapeutic areas towards lifestyle-related diseases.

Chaudhuri (2007) examined a paradox that although India is recognised as a low-cost producer of high-quality drugs in the world, it has added to availability of medicines outside the country as well as reveals robust innovative abilities India developed but maximum Indians lacks steady contact to indispensable drugs. Chaudhuri (2008) pointed out that to cope in a world after TRIPS, some large Indian firms followed the dual approaches of a bigger internationalisation of generic drugs sales as well as an attention to R&D as subordinate associates of worldwide monsters. Kiran and Mishra (2009) examined the effect of new Patent Act in IPI specially on R&D and try to gauge the performance of few leading Pharmaceuticals specifically in terms of their abbreviated new drug application (ANDA) filings and consents and Drug Master File (DMF) filings with USFDA after the implementation of TRIPS. In their paper, Dutta and Kumar (2009) looked at the Price-Earnings ratios of many key companies during 2006–2008 and concluded that the market opine that they can bear the alteration successfully. They also found that over these years, cost of raw materials as proportion of sales has declined, which has facilitated to increase profitability. Mishra and Chandra (2010) using company information for 2001 to 2008 examined the significance of M&A to enlighten the firms' profitability in IPI. They pointed no indication of significant effect of long run M&A and also internal R&D as insignificant in determining profitability.

One major study was done by Institute of Economic Growth (2010) on the effects of new patent regime of drugs and pharmaceutical industries in India. They argued that the introduction of TRIPS agreement resulted in reduction in the proportion of the multinational pharmaceutical companies in Indian drug market and the prices charged by foreign producers could go up, on average by about 250%, of the foreign firms have full freedom in pricing their product and the government does not resort to compulsory licencing.

Jha (2010) concluded that in product patent regime and when the competitive pressures are restricted, the requirement for checking of prices and regulation would be larger for therapeutically superior medicines and as well as medicines leading in their class for definite symptoms must be scrutinised. Srinivasan (2011) estimated providing free and quality medicines cost at all stages of public healthcare as well as offered recommendations about the action to be taken. Kalani (2011) pointed out that IPI has made remarkable improvement in most recent times, making global recognition and are recognising numerous approaches like implementation of Information Technology tools to escalate productivity, efficiency as well as attain regulatory compliance, etc. Chaudhuri (2012) found that the MNCs in full swing are promoting Indian new patented medicines at an excessive price mainly for life-threatening illnesses and the performance of MNCs from the 1990s in terms of manufacturing and importing bear a close similarity to that before 1970s.

Mathew and Unnikrishnan (2012) pointed out that the horror of pollution due to IPI has held the consideration of researchers worldwide. They pointed out that the enormous Western pharmaceuticals outsourcing made India a prey of uncontrolled opportunism.

Shivdas (2012) using data of 116 India pharmaceutical companies for the year financial year 2013–2014, find that R&D expenditures are statistically significant along with expenditure on physical and human capital in explaining the sales performance. They also present an alternative framework based on resource utilisation for mapping and measuring the performance of a firm and its competitors. Their study shows that the average TE for the Indian pharma firms is low and there is also wide variation among the firm. They conclude that resource optimisation is a key for the long-term sustainable growth of any firm.

According to Parasiya et al. (2013), India is one of the developing countries. A substantial proportion of population of this country is largely exposed to the drug market whose purchasing power is extremely low. Around 42% population of this country lives under the National poverty line ($1.25 per day). Vital issue concerning them is to access the health care facility at an affordable cost. Medicine is a part of health care cost and it costs to around 70% to 80% of the total cost. Thus, the cost of medicine is a governing factor of health care system especially when it comes to price control of health care facilities. To bring down the cost of health care facilities, government spends money for health care facilities. A comparative expenditure made by the state government is depicted in this article. NPPA (National Pharmaceutical Pricing Authority) is the Indian pharmaceutical pricing regulating authority and it achieves its objectives by implementing the DPCO (Drug Pricing Control Order). In spite of existence of the DPCO, drastic price variation is observed between the products of same API and several factors are responsible for the same. To overcome the stated problem and monopolistic trade practice by patent holder/brand manufacturer, TRIPS (Trade-Related Intellectual Properties Rights) provides Compulsory Licenses which has its unique role to play in affordability of medicines. Essential medicine is a basic requirement of health care system to serve their customers and hence an effective and overt price control on drugs is the need of present. This study thus tried to justify the need to bring NLEM (National List of Essential Medicine) under DPCO.

Chaudhuri (2013) argued that the Supreme Court judgement on the Novartis-Glivec case is notable and has put substance under an economic and political standpoint and the deeper consequence of the decision is to reject patents when incremental invention is minor as in Glivec but the decision has highlighted the significance of country definite situation for determining suitable patent regime.

Horner (2013) commented that the recent decision in the Novartis-Glivec case continues a long-established tradition of India contesting a Northern agenda on patent laws and this key global role, arising from the exceptional combination of a vibrant domestic pharmaceutical industry with civil society awareness of the public health implications of patents, has been accentuated by recent developments and has continued relevance for the global South.

According to Goldar (2013), the export intensity of Indian pharmaceutical firms has increased substantially in the period after 1995 when the new, more restrictive patent regime was introduced in India. The hike in export intensity has been accompanied by an increase in R&D intensity of Indian pharmaceutical firms. The results of the econometric analysis presented in the paper indicated that increased R&D efforts of Indian pharmaceutical firms were responsible in a major way for the observed increase in export intensity. The econometric results suggest that the impact of R&D intensity on exports depends on the level of productivity already reached by the firms.

Srinivasan and Phadke (2013) pointed out that the National Pharmaceuticals Pricing Policy 2012 has a new technique for defining price ceiling, and is difficult, to say the least as can produce the misapprehension of regulating prices without really doing so. They further said that it will decrease certain top brands prices and will leave so many tertiary care beneficial life-saving medicines beyond price control basket.

Tyagi et al. (2014) examined the trends in exports, imports, R&D performance and patenting activities in regard of the Indian drug and pharmaceutical industry for the period 2000–2012. Although most of the analysis, drawing upon different databases, is of descriptive nature, it also estimates the functional relationship between exports as a dependent variable and patents granted and R&D expenditure as independent variables. The study found that lagged R&D expenditure and lagged total patents granted affect exports positively and significantly. It suggests encouragement to public–private R&D partnership in the realm of basic and applied research, which could be commercially harnessed by the interested private sector partner(s).

Sandhya et al. (2014) attempted to provide a quantitative picture of FDI inflow for R&D from 2003 to 2009. They commented that use of FDI in R&D is restricted to information technology, pharma or biotechnology as well as automotive segments and this FDI inflow has not instigated growth, rather has raced growth-oriented areas. Srinivasan et al. (2014) pointed out that the Drugs Price Control Order, 2013 led to much irregular playing field, with numerous ceiling prices, which is not fair for consumers who are already dealing with illogically priced market.

According to Atal et al. (2016), rising cost of medical therapy is a major concern for patients, and there is high variability in the prices of numerous branded medicines available in India. Drug Price Control Order (DPCO) 2013 was implemented by the Government of India with the aim of bringing down the cost of essential medicines. This cost analysis study was carried out to assess the brand price variation in major classes of common drugs under price control; thus assessing the impact of DPCO and analyse issues related to it. Latest price list of available brands for cardiovascular drugs, antibacterial, analgesics, drugs for diabetes, asthma, arthritis, convulsions covered under the DPCO, was procured from a leading commercial drug directory. Unit prices of drug formulations available as different brands were compared. Maximum–minimum prices and average prices were found. Price variations between brands were calculated and expressed as percentage variations. Assessment of existing pricing policy and quality norms was done. Significant inter-brand price variations were found for the majority of formulations. These variations ranged from more than 100% from average to more than 500% between maximum and minimum brand prices for drugs like amlodipine, atorvastatin, diclofenac, amoxicillin-clavulanic acid, clopidogrel. Out of 60 formulations observed, 40 showed price variations in excess of 50% from average price and 23 showed variations greater than 200% between the costliest and cheapest brands. Despite the implementation of price control, brand price variations still exist widely for commonly used drugs. Re-assessment of pricing policy and implementation of quality norms is needed.

Tyagi et al. (2016) analysed the R&D profile of Indian drug and pharmaceutical industry during the period 2000–2013, and the factors that influence a pharmaceutical firm's decision to undertake R&D activities. The study period from 2000 to 2013 has been characterised by a rapid growth in industry's R&D expenditures, as part of the strategic shift, induced by the Patents (Amendment) Act, 2005. Using the real financial data for the top 91 publicly listed Indian domestic pharmaceutical companies, the study provides new evidence on drivers of R&D intensity in Indian drugs and pharmaceutical industry. A panel data random effects Tobit model along with OLS model using firm fixed effects are applied to identify the factors affecting the R&D intensity of the sample firms. The empirical findings of the study reveal that firm's size, past year profitability, past innovative output, leverage ratio; past cash flow; export and import intensities of the firm tend to significantly impact the R&D intensity. While firm size exhibits a non-linear relationship, cash flow, past innovative output shows a positive and significant relationship with R&D intensity. Furthermore, patent count and firm's overseas presence, considered as additional important determinants of firm-level R&D intensity, influences R&D positively. Lastly, the global orientation of Indian pharmaceutical firms has been found to impact R&D activities considerably.

According to Vithalani et al. (2016), the Indian pharmaceutical sector is highly fragmented with more than 20,000 registered units. The pharmaceutical industry in India meets around 70% of the country's demand for bulk drugs, pharmaceutical formulations, chemicals, tablets, capsules, orals and injectable. There are two major things coming out, firstly, IPI is growing in output, value, volume, number of units – steadily and showing resemblance to the entire growth story of Indian Economy. Secondly, there is a major change occurring to the very basic system of pharmaceutical business in India. By issuing the patent ordinance, India met a WTO commitment to recognise foreign product patents from 1st January 2005, the culmination of 10-year process. In this new scenario, the Indian pharmaceutical manufacturers would not be able to manufacture patented drugs which they have been doing since long although by another process. This study has been undertaken for critical assessment of pharmaceutical industry of India. The study period is of 10 years from 2004–2005 to 2013–2014 to analyse the profitability performance of leading pharmaceutical companies and comparison amongst them.

Reddy and Rao (2017) attempted to study the need of various digital tools available for different domains of pharma industry to become successful in global markets. Researcher has adopted an empirical study to conduct this research using primary and secondary data. Primary research was done by identifying target participants from the pharma industry and adopted a purposive sampling technique to collect the data online through a structured and validated questionnaire. Data were extracted, analysed, and interpreted using graphical analysis. The results of this study found that in all the questions in questionnaire, majority of the participants were in favour of adopting digital tools in the pharma industry irrespective of size and type organisation. Based on the outcome of this empirical study, it was established that there is a clear need of domain based digital tools for Indian pharma companies to compete and sustain in global markets.

Chakraborty and Ghose (2017) attempted to recognise the main causes behind IPI output growth employing state-level information during 1983–1984 to 2007–2008. Large firms, exact combination of work-force as well as wage rate upsurge and export intensity, import intensity and net export intensity are found to enhance growth of output. Mukhopadhyay and Paul (2018) aimed to disclose inequality in health in India by exploring the Indian pharmaceutical and biotech sectors' growth as well as looked at justness matters like gender, health and health costs of poor consumers.

Dhanora et al. (2021) argued that technological innovations are positively associated with firms' market performance. It aimed to examine the impact of product and process innovation on the market power of 168 Indian pharmaceutical firms during 2000–2013 by generating product and process patent stock to capture firm-level innovation activities. The findings of this study suggest that both product and process innovation positively influence firms' market power and also reveal that MNEs enjoy more market power in the IPI. It also highlights that there is a differential impact of firms' product group on market power and concludes that patenting is a positive source of firm performance in the IPI.

Kumar et al. (2020) tested whether the Indian pharmaceutical companies support efficient market hypotheses (EMH) and examine the efficiency of the Indian stock market in three forms, i.e. the weak, the semi-strong, and the strong form of market efficiency. For testing the weak form of efficiency, researchers collected stock price data of 10 listed pharmaceutical companies for the past 6 years, from 2012 to 2017 from the NSE website, and conducted a run test. To test the efficiency of semi-strong form, researchers collected data on the announcement of events like buyback, stock split, rights issue, dividend, bonus issue. They conducted an event study on the data. For testing the strong form of efficiency, researchers collected data consisting of NAV of some mutual funds (pharmaceutical funds) and the returns of a benchmarking index to compare. The study concludes that the pharmaceutical companies and Indian stock market is efficient in the weak form of EMH and not efficient in the semi-strong and strong form of EMH.

According to Kolte et al. (2021) in India, drug prices are controlled and are commonly known as Drug Price Control Orders (DPCO) issued under the Indian Essential Commodities Act of 1955. It is governed by the National Pharmaceutical Pricing Policy (NPPP) and accordingly, a National List for Essential Medicines (NLEM) was formulated. DPCO is useful for controlling the prices of life-saving drugs that are essential in the current scenario of healthcare and diseases. All the essential drugs are included under DPCO and a ceiling price is formulated. Drug prices cannot exceed the limit stipulated by DPCO. They have studied DPCO and discussed its impact on the pharmaceutical sector. The present research paper encompasses the brief history of DPCO, its contents, objectives, etc. Effects of DPCO on foreign trade is also analysed in this paper. They have attempted to find the effects of drug price control and its implications on the industry as a whole. They have also attempted to gaze future prospects for the pharmaceutical industry.

Gupta and Gupta (2021) take into account the regional aspects of IPI, based on various reports and unit-level data of Annual Survey of Industries since 1991 to 2011. In the year 2005, IPI came under the obligation of Trade-Related Aspects of TRIPS. Simultaneously, Indian pharmaceutical firms were also required to comply with GMPs of World Health Organization (WHO-GMP). The descriptive evidences depicted that with the introduction of TRIPS and WHO-GMP number of firms and man-days employed declined across the states during the introductory period of TRIPS; whereas net value added and gross capital formation remained constant for the same period. But in the post-TRIPS period, most of the states reported greater performance, especially in terms of net value added and gross capital formation.

According to Nandy and Sussan (2021), the relationship between R&D spending and export is not clear. Filling this gap of knowledge, this paper investigates the longitudinal performance of IPCs in terms of their export and R&D spending, the relationship between their R&D intensity and export, R&D intensity as a function of firm size and age, the comparison of innovation between IPCs and top global pharmaceutical companies, and the comparison of the innovations of major IPCs. Data on export, R&D intensity, and patent filing at both the industry and firm levels from year 2000 to 2019 were collected. The results show that export revenues and R&D intensity have not increased significantly from 2012 to 2019. However, R&D intensity is positively correlated to export. The age of IPCs is inversely related to their R&D intensity. Compared to global pharmaceutical companies, IPCs show significantly lower R&D intensity. The results have nuanced implications for managers.

Singh and John (2022) aimed to describe the pharmaceutical market environment in India and throughout the world. Additionally, it covers the important difficulties that are present. It also considers a few indicators that show the pharmaceutical sector in India has a promising future.

Singhal et al. (2022) investigated the relationship between an organisation's Intellectual capital (IC) and its health. A new model – Modified Extended Value-added Intellectual Capital Coefficient – was also proposed. The findings were compared with the two existing models, namely, Value Added Intellectual Coefficient and Modified Value Added Intellectual Coefficient. Panel data regression is used to assess the performance of 25 Indian pharmaceutical and drug companies throughout the period 2010–2019. Human capital efficiency (HCE), structural capital efficiency and relational capital efficiency have been proven to have a substantial positive correlation with return on assets (ROA). In addition, a negative yet significant link exists between organisational capital efficiency and a company's profitability. Under the Value Added Intellectual Coefficient, human capital and structural capital efficiency do not affect the market value to book value. The market value-to-book value, on the other hand, is positively impacted by capital employed efficiency.

Rosario and Mazumdar (2022) employed the measure of value-added intellectual coefficient (VAIC) to assess impact of IC on the profitability and market valuation and to assess the growth of VAIC and its components among the companies over the years selected for the study. The study uses 22 pharmaceutical companies listed in the Bombay Stock Exchange for a period of 12 years from the financial year 2008–2009 to 2019–2020. By using path analysis, the study demonstrates that the components of VAIC have an impact on the Return On Capital Employed (ROCE) and market value, which has only grown as compared to earlier studies & years. The study also demonstrates that high sales and profits need not necessarily result in high VAIC.

Festa et al. (2022) aimed to access, analyse and highlight opportunities and problems of the Indian pharmaceutical sector in the broader national healthcare industry. The recent changes in the field, at the institutional and corporate levels, have placed India in the spotlight of the global pharmaceutical market, but several threats and weaknesses could limit this expansion. Descriptive and inferential analyses have been based on empirical data extracted from authenticated data sources. Subsequently, a narrative strength, weaknesses, opportunities and threats (SWOT) analysis was performed based on the results of prior investigations and on qualitative data that were retrieved from a marketing intelligence examination to generate an overall scenario analysis. Indian pharmaceutical companies have faced several challenges on various fronts. In the home market, drug prices are controlled by the drug price control order; therefore, there is strong pressure on revenues and subsequently on costs. In the international market, threats derived from pharmaceutical multinational companies are emerging as tough obstacles to overcome.

Sharma et al. (2023) aimed to comprehensively elucidate how Industry 4.0 has played a significant role in sustainable development (SD). Industry 4.0 in sustainability decreases the research efforts and examines the research sector's opportunities. This research also discusses the impact of Industry 4.0 on SD. Industry 4.0 constructs a bridge between industry and sustainability leading to SD. Sustainability can be achieved by adopting innovative techniques of Industry 4.0 in manufacturing. Moreover, Industry 4.0 provides potential benefits for enhancing pharmaceutical production concerning flexibility, expenses, standards and safety. It is noticed that Industry 4.0 has a beneficial impact on SD by implementing advanced technologies leading to flexible manufacturing processes.

Saini and Agarwal (2023) focused on the different difficulties that arise when developing a pharmaceutical company in India. The study uses secondary data and is descriptive qualitative in nature. According to the findings, the main obstacles to launching a pharmaceutical company in India include registration and licencing, resource requirements, investment issues, business plan formulation, availability of raw materials, and qualified labour and workforce optimisation.

2.2.3. Studies on Performance of the Pharmaceutical Industries in the International Context (Other than India)

The survey of literature reveals that there are several studies on pharmaceutical industries in the international context (other than India) under different perspectives considering different time points and different methodologies. Some worth mentioning names are Chilingerian (1995), Yeoh and Roth (1999), Scherer (2000), Jacobzone (2000), Feinberg and Majumdar (2001), Berndt (2001), De Carolis (2003), González and Gascón (2004), Bottazzi and Secchi (2005), Kaplan and Laing (2005), Epstein (2007), Hashimoto and Haneda (2008), Gagnon and

Lexchin (2008), Zhang and Li (2009), Demirel and Mazzucato (2010), Enyinda et al. (2010), Chan and Daim (2011), Hanggraeni (2011), Kesič (2011), Ngwuluka et al. (2011), Sorte Junior (2012), Rasekh et al. (2012), Basuki and Kusumawardhan (2012), Karamehic et al. (2013), Nouraei Motlagh et al. (2014), Jiankang (2014), El-Akhdar et al. (2015), Mazzucato and Parris (2015), Wakeel and Ekundayo (2016), Muratoğlu (2017), Gascón et al. (2017), Kazzazi et al. (2017), Ho et al. (2017), Al Ayouty (2017), Safari et al. (2018), Obukohwo et al. (2018), Shin et al. (2018), Minangsari et al. (2019), Ponce (2019), Yoo et al. (2019), Kian et al. (2020), Endri et al. (2020), Liu and Lyu (2020), Hussain et al. (2020), Osorio et al. (2021), Feng et al. (2022), AlMomani et al. (2023) among others.

Chilingerian (1995) reported on a 6-month study of the clinical efficiency of 36 physicians in a single hospital. Both technical and scale efficiency are analysed using DEA and a multi-factor Tobit analysis is conducted to see which variables are associated with higher levels of physician performance. DEA identifies 24 inefficient physicians. The slack associated with these physicians supports the hypothesis that a substantial amount of money could be saved if every physician practiced medicine as efficiently as the most competent physicians. The Tobit analysis revealed two categories of technically efficient physicians: those who (1) belong to a health maintenance organisation (HMO), or (2) specialise by diagnostic related groups (DRGs). Estimates of most productive output scale suggests that locally decreasing returns to scale set in at higher output levels for physicians who treat higher proportions of high-severity patients. The results illustrate how blending DEA with censored regression can sharpen an analysis of best practices.

Roth (1999) tested a model of the relationships among firm resources, firm capabilities, and sustained competitive advantage between 1971 and 1989. Sustained comparative advantage was captured by two variables: therapeutic differentiation and global New Chemical Entity (NCEs). The results show that R&D and sales force expenditures have indirect and direct effects, respectively, on sustained competitive advantage. Firm capabilities were differentiated into component and integrative capabilities. Component capabilities were captured by the firm's internal R&D efforts and therapeutic market focus, while integrative capabilities were concerned with the firm's ability to obtain FDA approvals and to develop radical new drugs.

Scherer (2000) surveyed the extensive body of research on the economics of the pharmaceutical industry (with peripheral attention paid also to regulated medical devices). According to him, pharmaceutical is one of the world's most research-intensive industries, generating a continuing steam of new products that save lives and raise the quality of life. The discovery of new drugs has evolved over time from a decidedly empirical process to one based to a considerable degree upon fundamental scientific knowledge. Rich linkages have emerged between profit-seeking manufacturers and basic research performers such as universities and national laboratories. The safety and efficacy of new pharmaceutical products are stringently regulated in most industrialised nations, adding to clinical testing costs. Because of high expenditures on research, development, and clinical testing and because new products, once proven, might be imitated easily, patent protection is unusually important. The extension of patent protection to third-world nations under Uruguay Round Treaty mandates has precipitated vigorous policy debates. Patents, first-mover advantages, and the lack of good substitutes for significant new drugs often give rise to substantial monopoly power, against which many national governments have counterpoised a diverse panoply of price control mechanisms. When patents expire, however, generic substitutes often introduce vigorous price competition. The extent to which generics capture market share from the branded original drugs depends upon government regulatory policies, the reimbursement strategies of health care insurers, and the organisation of health care provider institutions.

Feinberg and Majumdar (2001) examined whether knowledge spill-overs from MNCs' local R&D activities benefit domestic firms in the IPI from 1980 to 1994. In a policy environment that restricted FDI and provided weak intellectual property protection, they found that only significant R&D spill-overs in the Indian pharmaceutical sector were between MNCs and each other. They explored the implications of their findings in light of India's economic and industrial policy goals and implementation.

Berndt (2001) focuses on four factors that have increased utilisation, even as cost containment efforts have flourished: the importance of being unimportant; increased third-party prescription drug coverage; the introduction of successful new products; and aggressive technology transfer and marketing efforts by pharmaceutical firms. He also considered the roles that these four factors are likely to play in the future.

Carolis (2003) addressed two research questions: First, does technological competence enhance firm performance. Second, does competitor imitation of firm knowledge hurt performance. The relationships between technological competence, imitability and performance are basic premises in the resource-based view, yet there has been little empirical testing of them. Measures of technological competence and imitability are developed. These variables, together with measures of marketing and regulatory competence, are tested for their impact on firm performance in the pharmaceutical industry. Imitability has a negative and significant impact on accounting and market-based performance measures.

González and Gascón (2004) analysed the evolution of the productive patterns in a sample of 80 pharmaceutical laboratories that operated in Spain from 1994 to 2000. They estimated MPIs and decompose them into four sources of productivity change. The results suggest that pure TE change and the scale change of the technology explain most of the productivity growth observed during the period. The contribution of technical change to productivity growth is negligible, indicating a poor result from R&D activities at least in the groups of small- and medium-sized labs.

Kaplan and Laing (2005) summarised the issues surrounding local production from a policy and public health viewpoint. It provides four brief country-level case studies, and reviews the evidence supporting the industrial policy assumptions underlying the goal of local production. In brief, in many parts of the world, producing medicines domestically makes little economic sense. If many countries begin local production, the result may be less access to medicines, since economies of scale may be lost if there are production facilities in many countries.

The document concludes by providing a research agenda specifically designed to test assumptions about local production of pharmaceuticals.

Bottazzi and Secchi (2005) presented a description of the growth and diversification patterns of the top firms in the worldwide pharmaceutical industry. They applied parametric and non-parametric methods to the analysis of firms' size distribution and its dynamics. Their study confirms the results of previous empirical analyses of the growth dynamics of firms but also reveals structural features of the pharmaceutical industry that have never been investigated before. Using firm sales at a high level of disaggregation, they are able to analyse the diversification structure of the firm and study its relation with the aggregate firm size.

According to Epstein (2007), the global economy is being transformed by an explosion of information unleashed by the internet, the digital revolution, communications and increased international mobility. This transformation is manifesting in many ways, including the rapid development of countries such as China, commoditisation of public services, mobilisation of workforces, shifting of market control from suppliers to consumers, interlinked rises in product demand and customer expectations, and problems regulating international business competition. As Asia is home to half of the world's population, and offers both a large relatively low-cost workforce in some countries and a potentially huge retail market, this region could be central to the future of the global economy. Like other industries, the pharmaceutical industry faces a new array of Asia-specific opportunities and challenges. Success in meeting these challenges will go to those pharmaceutical companies that best understand the unique strengths and constraints of Asia's diverse cultures, talents and markets.

Gagnon and Lexchin (2008) calculated a new estimate from which appears that pharmaceutical companies spend almost twice as much on promotion as they do on R&D. These numbers clearly show how promotion predominates over R&D in the pharmaceutical industry, contrary to the industry's claim. While the amount spent on promotion is not in itself *a* confirmation of Kefauver's depiction of the pharmaceutical industry, it confirms the public image of a marketing-driven industry and provides an important argument to petition in favour of transforming the workings of the industry in the direction of more research and less promotion.

Hashimoto and Haneda (2008) presented a DEA/Malmquist index methodology for measuring the change in R&D efficiency at both firm and industry levels. Letting each of 10 firms in each year be a separate DMU, and employing 1 input and 3 outputs in a DEA case of R&D activity input–output lag, they measured 'total factor R&D efficiency' change of Japanese pharmaceutical firms for the decade 1983–1992 as defined by the period of R&D input. Decomposing the Malmquist index into catch-up and frontier shift components and using 'cumulative indices' proposed in this study, they evaluated R&D efficiency change for each firm and empirically showed that R&D efficiency of the Japanese pharmaceutical industry has almost monotonically gotten worse throughout the study decade.

Zhang and Li (2009) analysed the relationship of high-performance work practices and firm performance in a sample of pharmaceutical companies in China.

They found that the human resource management index composed of high-performance work practices such as extensive training, participation, detailed job definition, result-oriented performance appraisal, internal career opportunities, and profit sharing as reported by the human resource or finance managers was significantly related to firm's market performance as evaluated by the firm's general managers or marketing directors. Results also showed that the positive effect of the Human resource management (HRM) index on firm's performance was influenced by innovation strategy in the negative direction. Results extend our knowledge about strategic human resource management theory and suggest the need for further studies to identify other contingencies that may attenuate the universalistic nature of these valued practices.

Demirel and Mazzucato (2010) studied the dynamics of firm growth and firm size distribution in the pharmaceutical industry from 1950 to 2003. Growth dynamics are studied in the context of how the size composition of firms changes, how innovation patterns change, and how location leads to growth differentials among US firms. It is found that the growth advantage of small pharmaceutical firms increased after the 1980s as small firms became more active in patenting and their patenting activities became more 'persistent'. Location is found to affect growth differences only for the most innovative firms (that is, for non-innovative firms, location does not matter).

You et al. (2010) measured the efficiency of pharmaceutical firms and identify their determinants using Korean and American samples from 1992 to 2004. They documented some stylised facts in the patterns and sources of efficiency change in Korean and American pharmaceutical firms. The evidence showed that ownership structure can substantially influence the efficiency of pharmaceutical firms. Especially, institutional ownership rate affects corporate efficiencies negatively, corroborating the myopic institutional investor hypothesis. The hypothesis is supported by both Korean and American samples. However, they find evidence that foreign ownership in Korea promotes the efficiency of pharmaceutical firms. It is shown that R&D intensity is positively related to contemporaneous largest ownership rate and prior foreign ownership rate in Korean pharmaceutical firms.

Enyinda et al. (2010) worked on the empirical findings of the quantification of risks that decision makers consider most important when deciding on a risk portfolio to mitigate and the manner in which risks are prioritised according to their importance. The empirical findings suggest that decision makers attached great importance to counterfeit, Food and Drugs Board, and exchange-rate fluctuations. With respect to risk-mitigation strategies, risk reduction is considered most important, followed by risk avoidance. Dynamic sensitivity analysis with respect to a change (increase) in the Food and Drugs Board did not result in any change in the ranking of risk policy options, while a change (increase) in counterfeit resulted in a change in the ranking between risk reduction and risk avoidance.

Hanggraeni (2011) using DEA models analysed efficiency and productivity change in the Indonesian pharmaceutical industry between 2006 and 2011, listed in the Indonesia Stock Exchange (IDX) and also supported by applying efficiency financial ratio. This study finds that the decision for the most relatively efficient company is different using DEA compared to efficiency financial ratios, yet DEA has better measurement of efficiency. It is proven by one of State-owned Enterprises has been evaluated underperformed by the financial ratio analysis, unexpectedly is efficient using the DEA approach. This study has also proposed and tested a hypothesis on the average efficiency to check if the domestic and foreign pharmaceutical companies differ in their efficiency but the result implies that there is no significant statistical difference among them. This study indicates that firms having dominant contribution in selling over the counter medicines are more efficient than selling ethical medicines. Lastly, technological change contribution has more influence to productivity change instead of pure TE change in Indonesia pharmaceutical companies.

Chan and Daim (2011) analysed the Chinese pharmaceutical sector through three levels: policy level, enterprise level, and technology level. The results indicate that China is emerging in the biopharmaceutical industry. While there are several steps to be taken at different levels, including policy, enterprise, and technology, the country is presenting a potential for the future. The paper outlines the gaps in each area. The paper provides a very good outline against which any emerging economy could review its potential in the pharmaceutical industry.

Kesič (2011) studied on the strategic development trends in the world pharmaceutical industry in the period 1996–2006. They aimed to find that mergers and acquisitions prevail as a vital strategic development option in the world pharmaceutical industry. The research examines the exploratory hypothesis that the intensive globalisation process, increased competitiveness and changed structure of competitors, strongly influence the consolidation development trends in the world pharmaceutical industry which result in an increased number of mergers and acquisitions.

Ngwuluka et al. (2011) indicated that like its counterpart industry in other countries of the world, the Nigerian pharmaceutical industry generated both hazardous and non-hazardous wastes. However, the wastes were not categorised, poorly managed by 91.2% of the respondents, while 58.8% of the health and safety personnel had little or no modern knowledge of waste management. Furthermore, 73.5% of the respondents claimed that they were aware of the regulatory requirements on waste, but no adherence was observed. The industry did not benefit from the strict supervisions of regulatory agencies. Pharmaceutical waste was improperly disposed and all the secondary manufacturers (79.4%) discharged wastewater without removal of pharmaceuticals. This study highlighted the urgent need to train personnel in the pharmaceutical industry and regulatory authorities. Management of waste should be planned, documented, implemented and sustained.

Basuki and Kusumawardhan (2012) investigated empirically the impact of value-added physical and IC efficiency on a company's financial performance. This research uses Nazari and Herremans (2007) Extended Value Added Intellectual Coefficient as the efficiency measure of physical and IC. The data drawn from 3 out of 10 pharmaceutical industries listed in the IDX for the years 2003–2009 was analysed using linear regression analysis. This research contributes to extant IC literature by evidencing the IC components' impact on company performance as well as the actual implementation of the extended VAICTTM method in the empirical study. It is shown that IC components impact the profitability of the pharmaceutical industry in a significant and positive manner. Furthermore, it is found that whilst physical capital employed shows a significant positive impact on profitability, the impact of IC components on productivity is not significant.

Sorte Junior (2012) examined the use of governmental purchasing power and public laboratories to stimulate domestic production and research and development (R&D) activities in the Brazilian pharmaceutical industry. Three main areas in which public laboratories can play an important role are identified: (1) large-scale production of essential medications; (2) production of strategic drugs to reduce the trade deficit in the health sector; and (3) in-house research efforts and stimulation of R&D in the private sector through public–private partnerships (PPPs). The analysis of the production and R&D structure of the Brazilian pharmaceutical industry tends to show that the Ministry of Health (MOH) purchasing power can be used to nurture the growth of public laboratories and generate positive externalities for the private sector.

Rasekh et al. (2012) evaluated R&D activities of pharmaceutical companies, and also highlighted critical factors which have an influential effect on the results of these activities. To run this study a valid questionnaire based on literature review and experts' opinion was designed and delivered to 11 pharmaceutical companies. Empirical data show there are no acceptable situations considering the factors that should be taken into account by managers including: management commitment, human resource management, information technology and financial management.

Karamehic et al. (2013) showed the present conditions and future trends of the pharmaceutical industry in the US methodology. This paper represents a thorough literature review of the multifaceted sources including studies, books, peer-reviewed journals, US government sources (i.e. US Census Bureau, US Bureau of Economic Analysis, etc.). They concluded that numerous blockbuster drugs will be coming off patent in the next few years, opening the way to generics and eliminating a major source of the industry's profits. Still, there is plenty of room for improvement in the medications people take while there is no shortage of human suffering to alleviate. It is doubtful whether big pharmaceutical firms will be able to pursue these goals within the old model of developing exclusive new drugs that can be sold further in the future. In the past, medicines for the ailments that were never before addressed, like anti-cholesterol or anti-depression drugs were developed. Currently, and in the future, it is expected that only blockbuster modifications will be developed. This phenomenon is expected to create market saturation, which will significantly reduce profits. The business model that drove the major drug makers' success is not working anymore. Pharmaceutical companies must create new ways and to bring new ideas. The survivors will be those that market strategies supported by innovative approaches and winning capabilities.

Jiankang (2014) analysed the market structure, enterprise conduct and performance of biological pharmaceutical industry in China. It is suggested that the government to speed up the industrial restructuring, to optimise the industrial structure, to encourage the similar innovation, to optimise approval procedures of biological generics, etc.

Motlagh et al. (2014) aimed to identify the patterns and demand-inducing factors of drug consumption in Iran. The time series data of pharmaceutical expenditures was acquired from the yearbooks of Iranian Ministry of Health and Medical Educations. The time series data of the medicine price index and per capita income were obtained from the documentation of the Central Bank of Iran. Pharmaceutical demand was modelled as a function of economic variables using the logarithmic transformation of Cobb–Douglas demand function, and the function's coefficients were estimated, using regression analysis. While per capita income and government's commitment to insurance showed positive relationship with pharmaceutical expenditure, the price of medicines showed a negative corresponding correlation. The elasticity of price and income was found to be less than one, suggesting medicine is an inelastic and normal good. Their results highlight the notion that an accurate formulation of a pharmaceutical insurance package is crucial for preventing the irrelevant increase of pharmaceutical expenditures.

El-Akhdar et al. (2015) estimated a photograph of this sector and conducted the study by the adoption of the combined matrix SWOT at tool PESTEL for the external diagnosis and the approach by resources for the internal diagnosis. This analysis made it possible to reveal the strengths, weaknesses, opportunities and threats of this industry.

Mazzucato and Parris (2015) explored under what conditions Hepatocyte growth factor (HGF) matters for translating R&D investments into economic growth and how this depends on firm-specific and industry-specific factors. They used quantile regression techniques to study the R&D–growth relationship in HGF compared to low-growth firms. Unlike previous studies, they paid particular attention to whether this relationship depends on the particular period in the industry's life cycle. They focussed on the US pharmaceutical industry from 1963 to 2002 and found that the R&D–growth relationship is sensitive to the changing competitive environment over the industry's history, which suggests that innovation policy must focus not only on firm attributes but also on competitive structures.

Wakeel and Ekundayo (2016) focused on the relationships among market structure, efficiency and performance of the Nigerian Pharmaceutical industry. It employed market share and operational efficiency to determine the efficiency of the industry, pre-tax return on assets to measure performance, Herfindahl-Hirschman index to measure market structure. In addition, earnings per share (EPS) was used in the study as a control variable. Data were obtained from the Nigerian Stock Market Factbook covering 1996 to 2010. The panel ordinary least squares technique was employed in estimating the data. Thus, over the course of the study, both fixed and random effect results clearly showed that the efficiency hypothesis does not hold in the case of the pharmaceutical industry in Nigeria. Rather, it is shown that it is a structure that determines performance. Consequently, the study recommended that necessary structures must be put in place by the Federal Ministry of Health to enhance the capacity of local pharmaceutical firms in producing the desired quality and quantity of drugs needed in the country. It was also recommended that efforts should be geared towards eradicating totally the importation of fake drugs into the pharmaceutical industry.

Al Ayouty (2017) based on Egypt, knowledge production function estimation using firm-level panel data indicates weak R&D performance in pharmaceutical firms. At the micro-level, in-depth interviews with selected pharmaceutical firms reveal a low R&D intensity, in addition to an inconsistent pattern of spending over time. Firms undertake piecemeal research projects, thus lacking a long-term research vision. They put greater emphasis on R&D of the 'development' rather than the 'basic' or 'applied' types. Other symptoms of weakness are: modest collaboration with universities in research; modest collaboration with other firms in research and/or intellectual property; and a poor capacity to innovate. At the macro level, the public R&D system lacks good governance and sound coordination between research institutions. At both micro- and macro-levels, R&D efforts hinder innovation, thus hindering Egypt's SD and integration in today's knowledge-based economy.

Muratoğlu (2017) aimed to analyse the relationship between pharmaceutical industry exports and GDP. In this context, firstly the Revealed Comparative Advantage Index of all countries in pharmaceutical industry exports are calculated. This index revealed that 27 countries in the world are specialised in pharmaceutical exports by 2014. Then, panel data models are specified to test the relationship between pharmaceutical industry exports and GDP & GDP per capita in these countries for 2000–2014 period. Results indicate that pharmaceutical exports of these specialised countries effect both GDP and GDP per capita positively. High levels of export competitiveness in this particular industry which heavily relies on the discovery and production of new drugs/medical products also contribute to the advancement of economy.

Gascón et al. (2017) evaluate the relative efficiency of a sample of 37 large pharmaceutical laboratories in the period 2008–2013 using a DEA approach. They describe in detail the procedure followed to select and construct relevant inputs and outputs that characterise the production and innovation activity of these pharmaceutical firms. Models are estimated with financial information from the data stream, including R&D investment, and the number of new drugs authorised by the European Medicines Agency (EMA) and the US Food and Drug Administration (FDA) considering the time effect. The relative performances of these firms – taking into consideration the strategic importance of R&D – suggest that the pharmaceutical industry is a highly competitive sector given that there are many laboratories at the efficient frontier and many inefficient laboratories close to this border. Additionally, they used data from S&P Capital IQ to analyse 2071 financial transactions announced by their sample of laboratories as an alternative way to gain access to new drugs, and we link these transactions with R&D investment and DEA efficiency.

Kazzazi et al. (2017) addressed the priorities for negotiations by collating the analyses of professionals in the field, leading companies and non-EU member states. A government healthcare policy advisor and Chief Science Officer (CSO) for a major pharmaceutical firm were consulted to scope the paper. In these discussions, five key areas were identified: contribution, legislative processes, regulatory processes, research and outcomes, commercial risk.

With a thorough investigation of the literature, they proposed four foundations for the advancement of negotiations. These prioritise: negotiation of 'associated country' status, bilaterally favourable trade agreements, the minimal interruption to regulatory bodies and special protection for the movement of workforce in the life sciences industry.

Ho et al. (2017) examined the effect of FDI on domestic innovation based on a data set covering the pharmaceutical industries across 29 provinces in the People's Republic of China (PRC) over the period 1998–2007. They showed that there is a negative horizontal spill-over effect of FDI on domestic innovation when the intellectual property rights (IPR) regime is weak. This spill-over effect became more positive when the IPR regime strengthened after the PRC's accession to the World Trade Organization) (WTO) in 2001. They also show that there is a positive upstream spill-over effect of FDI on domestic suppliers of pharmaceutical intermediates. Taken together, their findings provide important policy implications on why developing countries should encourage FDI and strengthen the IPR regime together to enhance domestic innovation for promoting productivity and economic growth.

Safari et al. (2018) reviewed the different pharmaceutical industries around the world and propose a model for the context of Iran. This is a qualitative as well as a comparative study. In the first stage, using the World Bank website, countries were divided into four groups of low-income, lower-middle-income, upper-middle-income, and high-income economies. Then, four countries of Afghanistan, India, Brazil, and Canada were chosen from these four groups, respectively. Secondly, data gathered from these countries were given to two 12-member expert panels. Finally, using the articles and the results of expert panel groups, useful and effective policies were extracted for the growth and development of Iran's pharmaceutical industry.

Obukohwo et al. (2018) analysed empirically, the efficiency of the pharmaceutical sector in Nigeria. Employing a balanced panel of 20 pharmaceutical firms between 2012 and 2016, the paper uses a non-parametric technique (DEA) to analyse the firms' efficiency under the CRS and VRS assumptions. The results obtained show inefficiency in the pharmaceutical sector as it operates under a decreasing return to scale. This calls for an appropriate policy mix to stimulate the efficiency of the pharmaceutical sector in Nigeria by enhancing research and development (R&D) as well as regulations within the sector.

Shin et al. (2018) divided 701 US pharmaceutical companies according to their open innovation (OI) strategies to measure and compare their R&D efficiencies between 2001 and 2016. They analysed the deal data of companies by first dividing them into four groups (inside-out, outside-in, coupled, and closed) to calculate R&D efficiency using stochastic and meta-frontier analyses. In the first group analysis, the coupled group shows high TE, but in an overall comparison, the inside-out group achieves the highest efficiency values. These values increased between 2005 and 2010, when the R&D crisis in the industry was great at its highest. They thus identified the characteristics of each group based on our results, and presented extensive analyses using a time-series comparison and enterprise-level analysis. They claim that pharmaceutical companies can still cope with the current R&D crisis by implementing different OI strategies.

Yoo et al. (2019) reviewed and evaluated the national drug formulary system used to improve patient access to new drugs by making reimbursement decisions for new drugs as part of the South Korean national health insurance system. The national health insurance utilises three methods for improving patient access to costly drugs: risk-sharing agreements, designation of essential drugs, and a waiver of cost-effectiveness analysis. Patients want reimbursement for new drugs to be processed quickly to improve their access to these drugs, whereas payers are careful about listing them given the associated financial burden and the uncertainty in cost-effectiveness. However, pharmaceutical companies are advocating for drug prices above certain thresholds to maintain global pricing strategies, cover the costs of drug development, and fund future investments in research and development. The South Korean government is expected to develop policies that will improve patient access to drugs with unmet needs for broadening health insurance coverage. Simultaneously, the designing of post-listing management methods is warranted for effectively managing the financial resources of the national health insurance system.

Minangsari et al. (2019) investigated the efficiency of the pharmaceutical industry in Indonesia. The data used in this study are secondary data from 2000 to 2015 obtained from Badan Pusat Statistik. The method of study is the quantitative approach to use the Stochastic Frontier Approach. The finding results indicated that the pharmaceutical industry in Indonesia from 2000 to 2015 technically did not have optimal efficiencies, seen from the result of reaching an amount of 0.96455986. The capital variable has a negative and significant effect on the output produced by the producer in the pharmaceutical industry, while the labour variable has a positive and significant effect on the output produced. Limited human resources professionals will make the development of innovations to make the pharmaceutical industry as a priority industry in the Industrial Revolution4.0 will be inhibited so that the pharmaceutical industry is not achieving optimal efficiency.

Ponce (2019) study is a synthesis of the three main drivers that are exerting influence on the global pharmaceutical industry, mergers and acquisitions, R&D changes, and a new pricing context. During the last decades, there has been a revolution in drug discovery and development thanks to pharmacogenomics, proteomics, molecular biology, bioinformatics, biomarker-driven studies, systems therapeutics, drug-target interaction prediction and artificial intelligence. However, there are signs that a problem of excessive pricing of prescription pharmaceuticals is creating awareness among stakeholders that this situation is unsustainable with clear consequences for the global pharmaceutical industry's predominant business model.

Kian et al. (2020) identified the main dimensions and components of enforcing the pharmaceutical industry by the illustration of selected countries to stand against economic shocks. This is a comparative study which was carried out in 2019. Compared Selected countries are separated into two main classifications. The first category is referred to Turkey with similar characteristics to Iran. The other group is consisted of pioneer countries in pharmaceutical industries. USA,

Britain and Ireland. Data analysis was based on a framework analysis. The findings of the study indicated that Iran needs to allocate more funds to the R&D unit to obtain self-sufficiency and strengthening accommodated with building centralised infrastructures which coordinate these centres.

Endri et al. (2020) aimed to evaluate the financial performance of a pharmaceutical company that has been listed on the IDX. The sample objects that the authors use in this study are nine pharmaceutical companies listed on the IDX during the 2014–2018 period. The method of evaluating financial performance that they use is to use financial ratio analysis consisting of; liquidity ratios, activity ratios, solvency ratios, and profitability ratios which have been supplemented by DuPont analysis. The results that the authors get in this study prove that all financial ratios during the observation period experienced quite fluctuating changes. The liquidity ratio shows a high enough number which means that under the company's ability to pay off short-term liabilities, it is quite strong.

Liu and Lyu (2020) employed a dynamic network DEA model for measuring the innovation efficiency of the Chinese pharmaceutical industry. The results show that the reason for innovation inefficiency in the Chinese pharmaceutical manufacturing industry is the inefficiency of pure technology and scale, but pure technical inefficiency plays the main role. The contribution of knowledge innovation to innovation efficiency in the pharmaceutical industry is greater than that of commercialisation.

Hussain et al. (2020) investigated the outwards foreign direct investment (OFDI) trends of companies from European Union and Asian countries whereby focusing on the pharmaceutical sector particularly. Moreover, it is noteworthy that there is a rapid growth in pharmaceutical industries around the world due to advanced technology and infinite amassed need for treatment and cure options. Therefore, current study targets three European Union countries and three Asian countries, including both developed and developing nations, and investigates the OFDI patterns of pharmaceutical sector of countries. The results reveal that EU states are effective in both attracting FDI and making investments abroad and in domestic markets; however, the Netherlands among the three states has the highest performance in FDI inflows and outflows patterns. The analysis of Asian countries indicated that they are less effective in terms of their FDI flows compared to EU states. This is because of their developing stage and less economic growth stages. However, among three countries, Turkey presents the highest performance in attracting FDI from international markets, while Israel has the highest performance in making investments abroad among three countries.

Osorio et al. (2021) systematically reviewed literature with different food loss and waste by-products such as animal feed, cosmetic, and pharmaceutical products that strongly contribute to the paradigm shift to a circular economy. Additionally, this review compiles studies related to the integral recovery of by-products from the processing of fruits, vegetables, tubers, cereals, and legumes from the food industry, with the potential in SARS-CoV-2 disease and bacterial diseases treatment.

Feng et al. (2022) aimed to identify if and how patents, as essential indicators of innovation, generate financial performance measured by SMEs in the pharmaceutical sectors. Patent data are a vital source of competitive intelligence.

A positive association was found between annually added patents and gross sales. Many other patent indicators, such as the number of forward citations and patent transfer, were statistically significant. Moreover, the results suggested that there was a one-year lag between patent publication and financial performance. A series of patent quantity and quality indicators have shown significant effects on the financial performance of Chinese pharmaceutical enterprises.

Al Momani et al. (2023) examined the relationship between IC and the financial performance of Jordanian pharmaceutical companies (JPCs) using secondary data collected from six JPCs, listed on the Amman Stock Exchange (ASE) over the period 2012–2016 to measure the Value-added intellectual coefficient (VAIC™) model, which is used to measure IC and its components, including an additional element, namely Relational Capital Efficiency (RCE). EPS and Asset Turnover Ratio (ATR) were used to measure financial performance. The results indicated no significant relationship between IC and the financial performance of Jordanian Pharmaceutical Companies. Further regression analysis on the individual components of IC showed that only HCE had a significant positive relationship with financial performance indicators, EPS, and ATR. The findings imply that JPCs have utilised their human capital resources efficiently, and this component is vital for their competitive advantage.

2.3. Conclusion

The literature survey proposes that not much effort has been taken to analyse the problems of efficiency and TFPG of IPI at firm level and also at the state level. So, the analysis of IPI is very essential both for the academics and policy perspective. Also, the study on efficiency and TFPG of IPI covering extended time period spanning from 2000–2001 to 2019–2020 which covers both pre-product patent regime, i.e. 2001 to 2004 and post-product patent regime, i.e. 2005 to 2020 is practically lacking in the literature. Also, there is hardly any study understanding the global position of IPI and also there in no study on the growth of IPI along with the leading countries growth.

It will be needful and interesting to address the issue of firm-level development of the industry because from the beginning, Indian planners have been always concerned with the removal of economic backwardness of the country and to make it a developed economy. They have taken care to ensure equal development across different firms such that the weaker segments benefit from the country's economic progress. For appropriate policies towards reduction of firm-level disparities, it is significant to have an idea regarding the firms which are lagging behind. Thus, the knowledge about the growth and performance of different firms are very much needed.

Along with it, state-wise differences in the performance of pharmaceutical firms are another interesting issue. So, it is motivating to study the performance of pharmaceutical industry in various Indian states. To recognise the position of pharmaceutical industry in Indian states, different major Indian states are taken into consideration and interstate comparison is done.

To understand the position of IPI in the global economy, 15 major countries, including India, producing pharmaceutical products have been considered namely the United States, China, Germany, Japan, Ireland, Switzerland, France, Italy, India, Belgium, United Kingdom, Spain, Brazil, Canada, South Korea and the Netherlands. Data on output, export and import are analysed and compared to assess the performance of IPI.

Thus, it will be interesting to extend the literature by addressing the following important issues:

In connection with IPI at firm level:

- Analysis of TE of IPI employing firm-level data and DEA methodology. This area needs to be focused because for sustained long-run growth, an industry has to operate with higher TE. There is an immense scope to contribute in the literature considering this issue.
- Estimation and analysis of IPI's TFPG at the firm level by applying non-parametric DEA method since as far as our knowledge goes; there is a lack in the literature highlighting this area.
- It verifies the presence of structural break(s), if any, in the series of TFPG.

In connection with IPI at the state level:

- To estimate the extent of efficiency of sample states over the sample period
- To identify the factors affecting such efficiency
- To find out the TFPG of the sample states over the sample period
- To elucidate the causes of variation in TFPG
- To examine whether TFP converges in pharmaceutical industry across Indian states
- To check whether IPI is moving towards a growing industry or not
- It verifies the presence of structural break(s), if any, in the series of TFPG.

The following important issues in connection with IPI at global level are addressed:

- Position of India compared to other foreign countries in terms of production, export and import
- Inter comparison of countries and their performance in terms of the above variables
- To verify the presence of structural breaks (which may appear due to changes in economic regime over time) in the different series of production, export and import.

These are the important aspects that seek for attention in the framework of IPI.

The contribution to the literature regarding each of these problems are discussed elaborately in the specific chapter dealing with the problems.

Chapter 3

Analysis of Efficiency and Total Factor Productivity Growth of Indian Pharmaceutical Industry Using Firm-Level Data

Abstract

This chapter estimates the efficiency of the IPI using non-parametric method of data envelopment analysis (DEA) approach. For doing that it measures output-oriented technical efficiency (TE) of IPI considering each firm as a decision-making unit. Also, the factors behind the variation in TE are identified using panel regression. It also estimates total factor productivity growth (TFPG) of the IPI. For doing that it measures TFPG considering each firm as a decision-making unit using non-parametric method of DEA approach. Also, the major factors responsible for variation in TFPG of IPI are found using panel regression. This chapter then compares the efficiency and productivity of IPI. For performing that it compares TE and TFPG of IPI. This chapter also tries to identify the common factors responsible for changes in these two performance indicators, i.e. TE and TFPG. Another important contribution of this chapter is that it verifies the presence of structural breaks (which may appear due to changes in economic regime over time) in the TFPG series at the firm level by using panel structural break methodology.

Keywords: Technical efficiency; total factor productivity growth; Indian pharmaceutical industry; firm-level data; non-parametric; data envelopment analysis; output-oriented technical efficiency; panel regression; panel structural break

---

Performance Analysis of the Indian Pharmaceutical Industry: A Global Outlook, 51–88

Published under exclusive licence by Emerald Publishing Limited
doi:10.1108/978-1-83797-743-720251003

3.1. Introduction

Indian pharmaceutical industry (IPI) witnessed many structural changes in the last 50 years like patent policy reforms that have altered the industry's competitive pressures. The indigenous companies serve domestic as well as global markets having skill in reverse-engineering new processes for drugs manufacturing at little expenses. The government started encouraging Indian companies who are growing medicine manufacturing activities in the course of the early 1960s, as well as during Patent Act, 1970. IPI advanced fast following trade liberalisation. It has gone through a sequence of modifications to product patent from process one. Product Patent Act, 2005 considerably changed the business setting by establishing IPI as one noticeable front-runners in general medicines production. The situation has altered over the time period; Indian firms have developed as technically sophisticated, having reverse engineering skill as well as evolving fresh methods for medicine manufacturing (Mahajan et al., 2014).

Numerous actions were taken by the Indian Government to encourage the growth of IPI. The economy started opening foreign market for toughening rivalry among different industries' firms via trade-liberalisation. In reality, the open market competition challenged the domestic firms in respect of their survival. The presence of foreign competition in home market may compel firms which are less efficient to leave the market and rearrangement of market shares concerning exporting firms which are more efficient may increase the efficiency of the industry as a whole. Thus, to achieve growth in production and for mere survival, producing units are to function efficiently. Along with it, medicinal goods' delivery at a reasonable price is of main worry. Therefore, it is important to understand the extent of efficiency and productivity changes of IPI which may be useful for the academicians and for framing appropriate policies. At the same time, it is important to verify the presence of structural breaks if any (which may appear due to changes in economic regime over time) in the total factor productivity growth (TFPG) series.

Along with it, the Indian pharmaceutical companies are fronting huge opposition both domestically and internationally. Though there is massive rivalry, IPI appeared as one of the liveliest as well as growth-oriented Indian industries. For achieving stable growth over time, an industry requires enhancement of cost-competitiveness through promotion of Technical Efficiency (TE) and TFPG.

TE and allocative efficiency (AE) are the two categories of efficiency. Again, TE are of output or input-oriented type. This chapter is concerned with estimating TE of output-oriented type and determining factors which can explain the change in TE scores. The literature survey proposes diverse ways of calculating TE: Parametric [Stochastic Frontier Production Function Method (SFA)] or Non-parametric methodology [Data Envelopment method (DEA)]. The present chapter tries to estimate output-oriented TE by using the DEA approach considering each firm as a decision-making unit.

IPI performed differently and its performance is not at all uniform across firms as each firm is characterised by its own, encouraging its growth performance. Thus, for appropriate policies towards reduction of firm-level disparities, it is imperative to have an idea regarding the firms which are lagging behind and appropriate policies can be taken to improve the TE level of those firms. Therefore, one should properly understand and calculate the TE scores of various firms. Thus, there are worthy motives to gauze the TE of IPI using firm-level data. To realise balanced growth during the years, along with the calculation of TE, it is also necessary to describe reasons of discrepancy in TE scores.

Thus, the major aims of the current chapter are to measure output-oriented TE and TFPG employing DEA approach considering each firm as a decision-making unit and explains the possible sources of variation of such efficiency and productivity score taking into account market share, different intensities like R&D, advertisement as well as net export as possible determinants.

The rationalisation for the insertion of the above explanatory variables in case of TE are presented below:

Market Share (MS): It may be conjectured that firms having higher market share may be highly efficient due to existence of threshold production limit, economies of scale and capital market imperfection (Kumar, 2003). But after the limit, greater market power may lead firms with *X*-inefficiency (Leibenstein, 1976) thus lessening efficiency.

Research and Development Intensity (RDI): R&D produces fresh technologies as well as augments a firm's capability to utilise prevailing skills. Different studies considered R&D as the determinant of efficiency (Driffled & Kambhampti, 2003; Kumbhakar et al., 2009; Mazumder et al., 2010; among others).

Advertisement Intensity (AI): Advertisement introduces innovative produce in the market without difficulty, upsurges sales and contests with the market competition. Relations amongst AI as well as TE can be found in Carod and Blasco (2005), Goldar et al. (2004) among others.

As exports as well as imports might promote efficiency, it is motivating to discover the comparative role of exports (*X*) and imports (*M*) in raising TE. Many empirical studies are unable to isolate their effects. There are researchers who laid weightage on one and on the other hand neglect the other one. There are few studies employing total trade as an openness measure (Frank & Romer, 1999; Harision, 1996), they have assumed that export and import play an equal role in encouraging growth and also they assumed that the elasticity of import intensity due to export is zero, which is not free from limitations. But Zhang et al. (2003) used a different method, i.e. they considered net export (i.e. *X-M*) suggesting individual export and import effects.

Therefore, like Zhang et al. (2003), the present chapter employed net export, i.e. (*X-M*) and accordingly net export intensity (NXI) for evaluating the net effect of exports over imports on TE.

NXI: The role of trade-related variables in explaining variation in TE has been examined by taking NXI as a possible determinant.

The input-specific productivities like labour productivity, capital productivity among others are only partial productivity measures of industries. A comprehensive measure must link output to all the factor inputs used in production which is well-known as total factor productivity (TFP) (Tinbergen, 1942). More specifically, TFP growth measures the augmented amount in total output not achieved from the upsurge in total inputs and therefore computes change in output for the shift in the production function over time, keeping inputs constant (Abramovitz, 1956; Denison, 1962, 1967, 1985; Hayami et al., 1979).

Huge literature exists round the globe associated with the TFPG estimation of manufacturing industries for India and countries other than India allowing for diverse time periods and using various methodologies. In the perspective of IPI, studies on TFPG are very limited in number. On the other hand, there is very little efforts given in determining the part of TFPG in the performance of IPI firms and more exactly the consequence of product patents on TFPG of IPI. A study on firms' productivity will be beneficial for recognising firms whose work is not adequate and consequently appropriate measures can be in use for those lagging firms. So, there is a possibility to place into this existing literature gap by considering firm-level study.

The literature review proposes many ways of measuring TFPG: (a) Growth Accounting Approach (GAA) via constructing either Solow Index (Solow, 1957)/Kendrick Index (Kendrick, 1956, 1961, 1973)/Translog-Divisia Index (Christensen & Jorgenson, 1969, 1970; Jorgenson & Griliches, 1967; Solow, 1957)]; (b) Econometric (Parametric/semi-parametric) Methodology (estimation of production function or cost function); and (c) Non-parametric Method (using Data Envelopment Analysis (DEA).

In the perspective of IPI, studies on TFPG estimation applying contemporary developments of nonparametric methodology are very limited. Accordingly, it will be interesting to estimate the TFPG of the firms of IPI employing the DEA approach. As individual firms have distinct characteristics, their performance does not display identical depiction. As a result, to realise stable growth over the years, alongside with the measurement of TFPG, determining the factors accounting for those alterations in TFPG is very much required.

Furthermore, the literature survey revealed that not much attempt has been made to analyse the behaviour of IPI quantitatively. Mention may be made of few studies like Singh (1989), Nagarajan and Barthwal (1990), Majumder (1994), Madanmohan (1997), Chaudhuri (2005), Chaudhuri and Das (2006), Ghose and Chakraborty (2008), Mazumdar and Rajeev (2009), Mazumder et al. (2010), Saranga and Banker (2010), Chakraborty and Ghose (2010, 2011, 2013) and Ghose and Chakraborty (2012).

Singh (1989), Madanmohan (1997) in their study using firm-level data focused on different aspects of IPI like export, import and net import, technology, profitability, patterns of MNCs activity and plant exit process. Whereas Majumder (1994), Chaudhuri and Das (2006), Mazumdar and Rajeev (2009), Mazumdar et al. (2009), Saranga and Banker (2010) and Ghose and Chakraborty (2012) were concerned with the measurement of productivity or efficiency of the industry. Studies which attempted to analyse the growth performance of the industry are due to Nagarajan and Barthwal (1990), Chaudhuri (2005) and Ghose and Chakraborty (2008). Test for exogenous and endogenous structural break using modern time series approach has been carried out by Chakraborty and Ghose (2010, 2011, 2013, 2017), Chakraborty (2017) among others.

However, none of the above studies looked at or applied structural break analysis in pharmaceutical analysis except very few who studied and applied endogenous one-time structural break analysis in pharmaceutical industry analysis in the case of India. These studies are as follows:

Chakraborty and Ghose (2010) tested whether there has been a change in the level or growth of output of the IPI in the post-liberalisation period since 1991–1992 using recent advancement of structural break analysis of modern time series econometrics. The study uses the data on gross value added for the period 1973–1974 to 2007–2008 and tested for both exogenous and endogenous structural breaks in the series. In case of an exogenous structural break, the model specifying the changes only in the level happens to be trend-stationary implying the existence of a permanent and deterministic trend. There is also evidence of upward positive trend. For endogenous structural break analysis, the model specifying the changes only in the level also represents the best-fitted one with 1991–1992 as the break point. The analysis therefore suggests that there is break only in the level and at the year 1991–1992. There is also the evidence of positive and significant structural change after 1991–1992. There is evidence of a positive trend and the underlying process is TS with drift in both the cases of endogenous and exogenous structural break.

Chakraborty and Ghose (2011) identified whether there has been a change in the level or growth or both in the level as well as growth of output of 17 major states of India and in the All India level in pharmaceutical industry in the post-liberalisation period since 1991–1992 using recent advancement of structural break analysis of modern time series econometrics by using the data on gross value added for the period 1983–1984 to 2007–2008 and tested for exogenous structural break in the level, growth and both in the series of output of pharmaceutical industry in the 17 major states as well as in All India level. This paper concludes that for the states like Andhra Pradesh, Gujarat, Haryana, Maharashtra and Rajasthan the underlying process is TS for the Models A and B supporting the evidence of a deterministic trend but no statistical evidence of one-time structural break is found. In case of Karnataka, there exists onetime exogenous structural break in Model B only. For Madhya Pradesh, there exists one-time exogenous structural break in Model A only. For the states like Assam, Punjab, Tamil Nadu and West Bengal, all the three models are TS supporting the evidence of deterministic trend. In case of West Bengal only, there is evidence of one-time structural break in the level, growth and both in the level and growth of the series of output of Pharmaceutical industry after 1991–1992.

Chakraborty and Ghose (2013) applied recent development in estimation and testing of structural break in econometric time series model, using unit root test to estimate the break point of the growth of output of IPI for the period 1983–1984 to 2007–2008 by using state-level data from Annual Survey of Industries and employing endogenous structural break analysis. The distinguishing feature of this method is that the break point is not dependent on the prior belief of the researcher; rather it is endogenously determined depending on time series properties of the series. The results of estimation suggest that for most of the states the endogenously determined break point turned out to be the years after the signing of TRIPS agreement in 1995. An interstate and regional variation of the growth of output is strongly evident. The growth of output of 16 among the 17 selected states converges towards a deterministic trend, out of which seven shows positive movement. The study clearly identifies the regions and the states whose performance are satisfactory and other showing relatively poor performance and hence needs special attention. Whereas Chakraborty and Ghose (2017) identified the major determinants of growth of output of Indian Pharmaceutical using state level data. Structural break analysis of Sen (2003) is applied for measurement of growth of output. The result suggests that nine states like Assam, Gujarat, Haryana, Himachal Pradesh, Karnataka, Kerala, Maharashtra, Orissa and Punjab showed statistically significant growth rate for the entire sample period. For assessing the performance of nine states, state dummy variables for each state have been introduced taking PU, state with minimum growth rate for the entire sample period, as the benchmark. It may be mentioned that the estimated equations are found to be non-linear. It is found that large-sized firms, right composition of work-force and increase in wage rate as well as the trade-related variables like export intensity, import intensity and NXI enhances growth of output. Chakraborty (2017) tried to find out the nature of the growth process of output, employment and productivity of labour of pharmaceutical industry in the 17 major selected states, tests whether the series of the growth of output, employment and productivity of labour are converging towards a stationary process having deterministic trend and estimates the break point of these three variables for the period 1983–1984 to 2007–2008 employing endogenous structural break analysis of Sen (2003). The distinguishing feature of this method is that the break point is not dependent on the prior belief of the researcher; rather it is endogenously determined depending on time series properties of the series. The results of estimation suggest that for most of the states, the endogenously determined break point turned out to be the years after 1995, the year when the first version of product patent was implemented and The Drug and Cosmetic Act was also amended to infuse competition in this sector. Thus, important policy changes pertaining to this sector have taken place in the year 1995. An interstate and regional variation of the growth of output, employment and productivity of labour is strongly evident. The growth of output of 16 among the 17 selected states converges towards a deterministic trend, it is 14 for productivity of labour whereas for employment, all the states shows convergence towards stationary process having constant variability over time. The study clearly identifies the regions and the states whose performance are satisfactory and others showing relatively poor performance and hence needs special attention.

But none of the above studies applied panel structural break analysis in pharmaceutical industry in firm-level analysis.

Thus another important objective of this chapter is to verify the presence of structural breaks (which may appear due to changes in economic regime over time) in the TFPG series at firm level by using panel structural break methodology.

Given the scenario, this chapter attempts to assess the TFPG of the diverse sample firms over the sample period and correspondingly endeavours to discover the augmenting factors of TFPG. From the outcome of the present analysis, policies might be recommended for developing IPI. As a consequence, RDI, NXI and AI in the previous period as probable determinants of TFPG are pondered.

The justification for allowing the above explanatory variables are given below:

Research & Development intensity (RDI): R&D basically deals with the searching of numerous new paths as well as improvement of know-how which ease quicker product enlargement and henceforward productivity (Kathuria, 2001; Pal et al., 2018, etc.).

Advertisement Intensity (AI): AI assists in bringing a fresh product into the market effortlessly, upsurges sales, contests market rivalry, develops good-will with consumers and informs the consumers in so doing upsurges production and henceforth productivity (Ghose & Chakraborti, 2013; Shashikanth et al., 2018) among others.

IPI have developed itself as technically sophisticated, having skills in reverse engineering and re-exporting of the product. Victory in exports may increase productivity through decreasing technical inefficiency as well as allowing larger utilisation of economies of scale. As a result, it is fairly probable that export might develop TFPG. Trade and industry policies, following export-led growth approach, have been broadly followed based on logic that disclosure to the global market via export assists to upsurge productivity of exporters. Likewise, endogenous growth theory supporters trust that export has a vital role in increasing productivity by invention (Grossman & Helpman, 1991) as well as the transfer of technology (Barro & Sala-i-Martin, 1995). At the same time, pharmaceutical firms import a lot. There are evidences which advocates that intermediary good import is a significant track via which technological diffusion may happen (Tybout, 2000); this can favourably influence productivity. As a result, imports have an encouraging outcome on TFPG. World Bank Report (1993) spoke about foreign technology import of firms as well as its encouraging effect on productivity. Such actions allow firms to construct their internal manufacturing abilities and proficiency. These all might influence the firms' productivity. As in cooperation X and M might encourage productivity growth, it might be motivating to determine comparative role of X and M in encouraging productivity. The main limitations of several empirical research are their incapability to isolate the influence of X and M. Few emphasised on one variable and neglect the other variable. There exist few research employing export plus import as openness measure (Frank & Romer, 1999; Harision, 1996). Zhang et al. (2003) used (X-M) suggesting individual effects of X and M.

Net Export Intensity (NXI): This chapter uses (X-M) and consequently NXI to determine the net effect of exports and imports on TFPG like that of Zhang et al. (2003).

Product Patent Act, 2005 considerably transformed the IPI's business situation. As a result, it is encouraging to examine the outcome of Product Patent on TFPG. For doing that D, a dummy variable has been well-defined assigning 1 from the year 2005 forwards or else 0.

The chapter is organised as below:

Section 3.2 deliberates on methodology and data source. In Subsection 3.2.1, the procedures of estimating TE and determining factors of TE are presented. Subsection 3.2.2 is concerned with the methodology of calculating TFPG and to determine the factors affecting change in TFP. Subsection 3.2.3 presents the methodology of panel structural break. Data sources are discussed in Subsection 3.2.4. Section 3.3 presents the results of estimation of TE and TFPG elaborately. In Subsection 3.3.1, the results of TE are discussed whereas Subsections 3.3.2 and 3.3.3 discuss the results of TFPG and panel structural break. Few bottom-line comments can be found in Section 3.4.

For estimating the TFPG of the different sample firms over the sample period and also to determine the reasons underneath the difference in TFPG, annual data on IPI firms from 2000–2001 to 2019–2020 were used in this study obtained from the CMIE PROWESS database. In addition to this situation, we used Biennial Malmquist Productivity Index (MPI) of DEA and two-stage least square methodology under panel regression so as to achieve this objective. Computer programme solver in Excel and STATA 15 software were used.

3.2. Methodology and Data

In this section, the methods used are discussed for output-oriented TE estimation by employing DEA and two-stage least square methodology under panel regression for finding out determinants of TE. Along with it, the data source has been discussed. TE scores are estimated for each of the sample firms. For doing that, computer programme solver in Excel and STATA 15 software were employed.

For estimating TFPG of the different sample firms over the sample period and also to determine the reasons underneath the difference in TFPG, annual data on IPI during 2000–2001 to 2019–2020 were used in this study obtained from CMIE PROWESS database. In addition to this situation, we used Biennial MPI of DEA and two-stage least square methodology under panel regression so as to achieve this objective. Within this context, computer programme solver in Excel and STATA 15 software were used.

For verifying the presence of structural break if any in the TFPG series, the methodology of panel structural break has been employed.

3.2.1. Methodology of Estimating TE and Determining Factors of TE

The methodology can be discussed in Subsection 3.2.1.1 dealing with the measurement of efficiency and in Subsection 3.2.1.2, the methodology for panel regression is presented.

3.2.1.1. Measurement of Efficiency

TE of output-oriented type may be calculated by contrasting the actual output with frontier output. Here DEA method is used following Banker, Charnes, and Cooper (1984). The radial TE of a firm of output-oriented type using observed input-output bundle (x^0, y^0) following variable returns to scale (VRS) assumption is achieved as:

$$\zeta_y\left(x^0, y^0\right) = \frac{1}{\Phi^*} \tag{3.1}$$

where $\Phi^* = \max \varphi$

$$\text{s.t} \sum_1^N \lambda_j y^j \geq y^0;$$
$$\sum_1^N \lambda_j x^j \leq x^0;$$
$$\sum_1^N \lambda_i = 1 \text{ where } \lambda_j \geq 0;\ (j = 1, 2, \ldots N).$$

3.2.1.2. Panel Regression

As the efficiency in diverse firms of IPI do not at all times move in the similar track and there is substantial efficiency difference through the firms across the years then it can be to some extent explained. After estimating TE, a regression using two-stage least square methodology under panel regression can support for identifying reasons that augment or deter it. Thus, it turned out to be useful for academics and policy in increasing IPI efficiency. The possible factors of efficiency considered are market share, different intensities like R&D, advertisement as well as net export.

The included above-mentioned explanatory variables have already been explained which can be found in Section 3.1.

For finding out the major determinants of TE, panel data is employed and the relevant estimation method has been used. From the result of estimation, significant determinants can be obtained across all the firms. From the Hausman specification test, fixed effect model is found to be the better one compared to the random effect model.

It may happen that there may exist simultaneous relationship amongst TE and NXI as well as TE and RDI. For that reason, panel model considering the possibility of simultaneous relationship has been framed using three equations considering each of TE, NXI and RDI as dependent variables. Several substitutes of the structural equations are tried out while estimating the model and the one with superior result is reported.

The chosen model of TE considering TE, NXI and RDI as dependent variables and thus separate equations for each of these variables, TE equation (equation 3.2), NXI equation (equation 3.3) and RDI equation (equation 3.4) are presented below:

$$TE = f(RDI, NXI, AI, MS, D) \tag{3.2}$$

$$NXI = f(TE, RDI, AI, MI, MS) \tag{3.3}$$

$$RDI = f(TE, NXI, AI, MS) \tag{3.4}$$

The dummy variable, D is used to capture the outcome of product patent on efficiency.

D is defined as: $D = 1$ if time>2005 and

=0, otherwise.

The indicated equation for TE is nonlinear in AI, MS, RDI and NXI. The equation for NXI is nonlinear in TE, AI, RDI and MI and for RDI is nonlinear in TE, AI and NXI.

The relation between NXI and the explanatory variables can be explained as below:

With rise in TE, NXI may increase. Increase in TE which might be due to increase in firm production, may boost export in the manner thereby increasing net export. On the other hand, an adverse association can be obtained amongst TE and NXI might be due to upsurge in TE, output may be made more via usage of superior raw material, technology and machineries which needs additional import from the foreign market, thus importing more than export and thus NXI may decrease. An affirmative association might be existent amongst MS and NXI for the reason that the benefits for big size, improved quality inputs as well as secured market, export upsurges and consequently NXI can also increase. As well MS might have an adverse association with NXI, might be difficult due to insufficient supervision which might lead to decrease in manufacture and in that way may result in fall in net export. An optimistic association could be present in the middle of RDI and NXI might be in line for firms involved in R&D might find out better processes technology or might produce better-quality products using alike input levels (Aghion and Howitt, 1992; Grossman and Helpman, 1991) which might upsurge output and as a result net export. An optimistic association might as well be existent amongst AI and NXI. Advertisement assists to make known to a fresh product in the market place without difficulty, upsurges sales, contests market rivalry, improves good-will with consumer and informs the consumers (Mohan, 1989; Samad & Sabeerdeen, 2016; Shashikanth et al., 2018). So, extra AI might suggest additional production, export upsurges in that way increasing NXI. The association amongst Marketing intensity and NXI might be optimistic as MI function as a substitution for product differentiation due to Pal, Chakraborty and Ghose (2018), Ghose and Chakraborti (2013) among others. Consequently, additional MI suggests further product differentiation, product diversity upsurges and export might rise in so doing increases NXI.

The association amongst RDI and the above explanatory variables can be defensible as follows:

TE might move RDI positively or negatively. An optimistic association might win through amongst these two might be owing to upsurge in TE, the ability of firms through using its input efficiently might upsurge and produce additional output which may endorse RDI. As well there may be a chance of adverse association perhaps in line for numerous causes such as development in the capability of the workers, improved managing decisions, satisfactory observing efforts, etc. which might cause additional manufacture thereby creating firms more unwilling to sponsor R&D and as a result RDI may decrease. Affirmative association is likely amongst MS as well as RDI might be in line for the reason that a greater firm might be able to use scale economies which impact firms to upsurge RDI and further sustain scale economies. An optimistic association amongst NXI and RDI may exists perhaps due to the fact that with upsurge in net export, the firm might produce extra profit from foreign market and upsurge RDI. An adverse association might occur amongst AI and RDI. Advertisement assists to announce a fresh product in the market effortlessly, upsurges sales, contests with the market rivalry, develops good-will with consumer and informs the consumers (Shashikanth, Mamatha and Rao, 2018, Samad and Sabeerdeen, 2016, Mohan 1989). Consequently, additional AI points towards added expenditure on AI, as a result, firms may well spend a smaller amount for R&D in so doing decreases RDI.

Before estimating the model, one should get ensured about the three equations of the model, whether they are identified or not. The models' identification is tested with the exclusion restriction and the result suggests that the model is over identified.

Panel regression analysis is done using two-stage least square method (2SLS). After obtaining the model's reduced form, estimation is done. Getting the dependent variable's estimated value from reduced form and then plugging the dependent variable's estimated value in the structural form and at that point employing the estimation method of the panel model.

3.2.2. Methodology of Estimating TFPG and Determining Factors of TFPG

3.2.2.1. Biennial Malmquist Index (BMI) of Productivity

The present chapter implemented DEA method for calculating change in TFP. Thus, it requires the calculation of MPI which was first presented by Caves et al. (1982) which was modified by Färe, Grosskopf, Lindgren and Roos (FGLR) in 1992. The measures of productivity changes basically based on the mentioned technology for a given observed input–output data. In 1992, Färe et al. (FGLR) presented a technique of decomposing the MPI in two, i.e. technical change (TC) and technical efficiency change (TEC) on the basis of the assumption that the underlying technology follows the constant return to scale (CRS) frontier which is also considered as the benchmark technology. The FGLR assumption of CRS as a benchmark technology is not always a meaningful assumption because if one assumes VRS technology then the decomposition provided by FGLR is not applicable. In 1994, Färe, Grosskopf, Norris, and Zhang (FGNZ) re-modified FGRL decomposition by considering VRS and they also decompose the MPI into TEC, TC, and scale efficiency change (SEC). In 1997, Ray and Desli pointed out that FGNZ approach is not bias-free because FGNZ decomposition raises another problem of internal consistency because it used the assumption of CRS and VRS within the same framework. They introduced a modified decomposition by considering the VRS frontier as a benchmark technology. But the Ray and Desli's method of decomposition again is not a bias-free decomposition because when one attempts to evaluate cross-period efficiency scores (calculated by comparing firm's actual output in t^{th} period with the maximum producible output from $(t+1)^{\text{th}}$ period by using the same input set) by considering a VRS technology, then infeasibilities for some observations may arise in the linear programming problem. Pastor, Asmild and Lovell (2011) introduced a different technique of MPI which is popularly acknowledged as Biennial Malmquist

Index (BMI). In their method, Pastor et al. used the decomposition procedure as introduced by Ray and Desli but they were able to solve the infeasibility problem which was the main drawback of the Ray-Desli decomposition of the Malmquist Index. Pastor et al. estimated the TE of a DMU with the help of a biennial production possibility frontier instead of employing a contemporaneous production possibility frontier.

By considering the output-oriented TE scores with the assumption of a CRS biennial frontier, the BMI of the DMU which is producing a single output with the help of multiple inputs is calculated as follows: (Since the BMI of productivity employs the biennial CRS production possibility set, which comprises of the period *t* and *t+1* sets, one need not to compute a 'geometric mean' of two productivity indices while its measuring)

$$M_c^B\left(x_s^t,\, y_s^t;\, x_s^{t+1},\, y_s^{t+1}\right)=\frac{TE_c^B\left(x_s^{t+1},\, y_s^{t+1}\right)}{TE_c^B\left(x_s^t,\, y_s^t\right)}$$

BMI can be decomposed as:

$$M_c^B\left(x_s^t, y_s^t; x_s^{t+1}, y_s^{t+1}\right)=TEC\ X\ TC\ X\ SEC \tag{3.5}$$

Here

$$\text{TEC}=\frac{TE_v^{t+1}\left(x_s^{t+1},\, y_s^{t+1}\right)}{TE_v^t\left(x_s^t,\, y_s^t\right)}, \tag{3.6}$$

$$\text{TC}=\frac{TE_v^B\left(x_s^{t+1},\, y_s^{t+1}\right)/\,TE_v^{t+1}\left(x_s^{t+1},\, y_s^{t+1}\right)}{TE_v^B\left(x_s^t,\, y_s^t\right)/\,TE_v^t\left(x_s^t,\, y_s^t\right)},\ \text{and} \tag{3.7}$$

$$\text{SEC}=\frac{TE_c^B\left(x_s^{t+1},\, y_s^{t+1}\right)/\,TE_v^B\left(x_s^{t+1},\, y_s^{t+1}\right)}{TE_c^B\left(x_s^t,\, y_s^t\right)/\,TE_v^B\left(x_s^t,\, y_s^t\right)} \tag{3.8}$$

The suitable model of DEA for estimating TE of output-oriented type, $TE_c^B\left(x_s^t,\, y_s^t\right)$ of sth firm in period *t*, using biennial production possibility set following CRS is:

$$\varphi_s^* = \max \varphi$$

$$\text{Subject to} \sum_{k=t,\,t+1} \sum_{j=1}^{n_k} \lambda_j^k y_j^k \geq \varphi y_s^t;$$

$$\sum_{k=t,\,t+1} \sum_{j=1}^{n_k} \lambda_j^k x_j^k \leq x_s^t;$$

$$\lambda_j^k \geq 0;$$

where n_k is the number of firms observed in period k and $TE_c^B\left(x_s^t,\, y_s^t\right)=\frac{1}{\varphi_s^*}$

Output-oriented TE, $TE_v^B\left(x_s^t, y_s^t\right)$ of firm *s* in period *t,* with reference to a VRS biennial production possibility set is:

$$\varphi_s^* = \max \varphi$$

$$\text{s.t.} \quad \sum_{k=t,\,t+1} \sum_{j=1}^{n_k} \lambda_j^k y_j^k \geq \varphi y_s^t;$$

$$\sum_{k=t,\,t+1} \sum_{j=1}^{n_k} \lambda_j^k x_j^k \leq x_s^t;$$

$$\sum_{k=t,\,t+1} \sum_{j=1}^{n_k} \lambda_j^k = 1;$$

$\lambda_j^k \geq 0$; where n_k is the number of firms observed in period *k* and $TE_c^B\left(x_s^t, y_s^t\right) = \frac{1}{\varphi_s^*}$

3.2.2.2. Methodology for Determining the Factors Affecting Change in TFP

As the productivity of IPI in various firms do not all the time move in the like path and there is substantial dissimilarity in TFPG through firms over the years then it can be partially clarified. In the next stage, regression analysis of TFPG may assist to recognise reasons that improve or deter it. This suits academicians and policy makers for increasing IPI's TFPG. For determining the possible factors inducing variation in TFPG, panel data analysis employing firm-level data during the period 2000–01 to 2019–2020 has been used. The reasons which are considered as probable factors of TFPG are different intensities like R&D, net export as well as advertisement in the previous period. The variables have been in use in growth terms. The addition of the above-mentioned explanatory variables has already been explained in the introduction part.

For finding out the factors influencing TFPG, a panel estimation technique has been employed. This provides us with the factors which can be considered as important factors across all sample firms. Employing Hausman specification test, i.e. whether the fixed or random effect model is the better one, fixed effect model is found to be better compared to random effect model.

It may be the case that, there may exist a simultaneous relationship among TFPG and NXI and also TFPG and RDI. For that reason, panel model in a simultaneous set up has been framed with three equations each of TFPG, NXI and RDI as dependent variables. The anticipated model is estimated showing simultaneous relationship among different variables. Numerous substitutes of the structural equations are tried out and one with better result are reported which are represented by the following equations:

$$TFPG = f(RDI, NXI, AI, D) \tag{3.9}$$

$$NXI = f(TFPG, RDI, MI, MS) \tag{3.10}$$

$$RDI = f(TFPG, NXI, AI, MS, MI) \tag{3.11}$$

The indicated equation for TFPG is a function of RDI, NXI, AI in the previous period and *D*. The equation shows nonlinearity in NXI, RDI and AI in the previous period. The dummy variable, *D* is used to capture the outcome of product patent on TFPG ($D = 1$ if time>2005 and 0 otherwise). The indicated equation for NXI reveals nonlinearity in TFPG and RDI and the identified equation for RDI shows nonlinearity in TFPG, AI, MI, MS and NXI. The clarifications for the addition of the above variables in TFPG equation have previously been explained.

The association among NXI and the explanatory variables can be defensible as follows:

With rise in TFPG, NXI may decrease. Firms having higher TFPG may have better access to production opportunities by importing machineries and hence imports more leading to lower NXI. There can be positive relationship between RDI and NXI. This positive relationship may be due to more RDI, use of sophisticated, advanced technology will facilitate productivity growth, increasing output, export and thereby increasing NXI. Also, there can be positive relationship between MI and NXI as well as MS and NXI. The advantages of big size, secured market may lead to higher output, more export and thus higher NXI. MS is calculated as the share of sales of firms to industry sales. The relation between MI and NXI may be positive as MI serve as a proxy for product differentiation, so, more MI implies more product differentiation, product variety increases and export may increase thereby increasing NXI.

The association among RDI and the explanatory variables can be defensible as below:

TFPG might influence RDI optimistically or adversely. An optimistic association might prevail among these two might be owing to upsurge in TFPG, firms may produce more output which requires R&D and thus promotes RDI. Affirmative association is likely among MS and RDI may be owing to the cause that a greater firm might be accomplished for exploiting scale economies which effect firms to upsurge RDI and additionally maintain economies of scale. An optimistic relationship among NXI and RDI might be existent perhaps owing to the fact that with upsurge in net export the firm may make extra profit from foreign market and RDI may rise. A positive relation may exist between AI and RDI. Advertisement assists to announce a fresh product in the market effortlessly, upsurges sales, contests market rivalry, augments good-will with consumer and informs the consumers (Mohan, 1989; Samad & Sabeerdeen, 2016; Shashikanth et al., 2018). So firms may spend more on R&D thereby increasing RDI. The relation between MI and RDI may be positive as MI serve as a proxy for product differentiation, so, more MI implies more product differentiation, product variety increases and need for R&D and thus RDI increases.

The models' identification is verified under the exclusion restriction and the model is over identified. Panel regression analysis is done using two-stage least square method (2SLS). The model is estimated after getting the reduced form. After getting the estimated value of the dependent variable from the reduced form and then putting the dependent variable's predicted value in the structural form and then employing the technique of panel model analysis.

3.2.3. Methodology of Panel Structural Break

3.2.3.1. Testing the Presence of Unit Root

A major debate concerning the nature of macroeconomic data has been going on until Nelson and Plosser (1982) published their seminal work. They found that underlying process is Difference Stationary (hereafter, DSP) rather than Trend Stationary (hereafter, TSP). A TSP process implies that the effect of random shock is temporary around a trend. On the other hand, DSP process implies that this random shock has a permanent effect. Furthermore, in case of DSP process the variance or the higher order moments of Y_t is not constant. It is dependent on time. After their work a large number of studies also suggested that DSP process is the most appropriate one. For most of the macroeconomic data regression analysis using non-stationary series may lead to spurious regression. Thus, unit root testing analysis is suitable for empirical analysis.

There are so many methods which are applied for testing the unit root test. Some of the important methods for testing the unit roots are Augmented Dickey-Fuller (ADF), Phillips and Perron (1988) (PP) for testing unit root and the method suggested by the Kwiatkowski et al. (1992) (KPSS) for testing the unit root. For practical application, Kwiatkowski et al. (1992) suggested that ADF or PP test should be applied first and then the KPSS test should be used as a confirmatory test. The idea behind this reason is that if a series is stationary then the ADF or PP test should reject the non-stationarity null whereas the KPSS test should not reject its null hypothesis of that series being a stationary process.

Augmented Dickey-Fuller (ADF) Test

The test for detecting whether a series is DSP or TSP is called the unit root test, as introduced by Dickey and Fuller (1979, 1981). To understand these processes, consider the following regression equation:

$$\Delta y_t = \delta_0 + \delta_1 t + \gamma y_{t-1} + u_t \ \textit{where}\ u_t = \alpha u_{t-1} + \varepsilon_t$$

A test of null hypothesis H_0: $\lambda = 0$ is required against the alternative hypothesis H_1: $\lambda < 0$.

If the null hypothesis is failed to reject, then the underlying series is DSP. Rejection of the null hypothesis implies the underlying series is TSP. The coefficient of $Y_{t\text{-}1}$ does not follow the standard t distribution. The problem was solved by Fuller, who obtained the limiting distribution of this coefficient. These distributions were approximated empirically by Dickey (1976). MacKinnon (1990) has derived critical values from a much larger set of replications. If the underlying process is TS and the coefficient of time is statistically significant then it implies that there exists a trend in the series. And if constant term is statistically significant then there exists a drift in the model. Now if ΔY_t depends on the $\Delta Y_{t\text{-}j}$ (where $j = 1$, 2, K, $K < T$) then the above test procedure is called as Augmented Dickey–Fuller (ADF) test. The ADF test is based on estimating the following regression:

$$y_t = B'D_t + \gamma y_{t-1} + \sum_{j=1}^{p} \delta_i \Delta y_{t-j} + \varepsilon_t$$

Where *Dt* is a vector of deterministic terms (constant, trend, etc.). The *p* lagged difference terms, Δy_{t-j}, are used to approximate the ARMA structure of the errors, and the value of *p* is set so that the error ε_t is serially uncorrelated. The error term is also assumed to be homoscedastic. The specification of the deterministic terms depends on the assumed behaviour of y_t under the alternative hypothesis of trend stationarity as described in the previous section. Under the null hypothesis, y_t is $I(1)$ which implies that $\gamma = 1$.

An alternative formulation of the ADF test regression is:

$$\Delta y_t = B'D_t + \pi y_{t-1} + \sum_{j=1}^{p} \delta_i \Delta y_{t-j} + \varepsilon_t$$

The ADF unit root test checks the null hypothesis H_0: $\pi = 0$ against the alternative hypothesis H_1: $\pi = 0$; it is based on the *t*-statistic of the coefficient π from OLS estimation of the above equation. The ADF test statistic does not follow an asymptotic standard normal distribution under H_0 but it has a non-standard limiting distribution. Furthermore, this non-standard limiting distribution under the unit root null hypothesis is the same as the Dickey–Fuller distribution. So, the same critical values corresponding to the Dickey–Fuller test are applicable for the ADF test as well.

Phillips and Perron (PP) Test

Phillips and Perron (1988) developed a number of unit root tests that have become popular in the analysis of financial time series. This test is a modification of the original Dickey–Fuller test statistic using nonparametric approach. This test which should ideally be called a semi-parametric test since it considers the usual parametric regression but treats serial correlations of the error term in nonparametric way. The test regression for the PP tests is:

$$\Delta y_t = B'D_t + \pi y_{t-1} + u_t$$

where u_t is $I(0)$ and may be heteroscedastic. The PP tests correct for any serial correlation and heteroskedasticity in the errors u_t of the test regression by directly modifying the test statistics $t_{\pi=0}$ and $T\hat{\pi}$. These modified statistics, denoted Z_t and Z_π, are given by:

$$Z_t = \left(\frac{\hat{\sigma}^2}{\hat{\lambda}^2}\right)^{\frac{1}{2}} \cdot t_{\pi=0} - \frac{1}{2}\left(\frac{\hat{\lambda}^2 - \hat{\sigma}^2}{\hat{\lambda}^2}\right) \cdot \left(\frac{T.SE(\hat{\pi})}{\hat{\sigma}^2}\right)$$

$$Z_\pi = T\hat{\pi} - \frac{1}{2}\frac{T^2.SE(\hat{\pi})}{\hat{\sigma}^2}\left(\hat{\lambda}^2 - \hat{\sigma}^2\right)$$

The terms $\hat{\lambda}^2$ and $\hat{\sigma}^2$ are consistent estimates of the variance parameters

$$\sigma^2 = \lim_{T\to\infty} T^{-1}\sum_{t=1}^{T} E\left[u_t^2\right]$$

$$\lambda^2 = \lim_{T\to\infty} \sum_{t=1}^{T} E\left[T^{-1} S_T^2\right]$$

where $S_T = \sum_{t=1}^{T} u_t$.

The sample variance of the least squares residual $\hat{u}_t$ is a consistent estimate of σ^2, and the Newey-West long-run variance estimate of u_t (using $\hat{u}_t$ is a consistent estimate of λ^2). Under the null hypothesis that $\pi = 0$, the PP Z_t and Z_π statistics have the same asymptotic distributions as the ADF *t*-statistic and normalised bias statistics. One advantage of the PP tests over the ADF tests is that the PP tests are robust to general forms of heteroskedasticity in the error term u_t. Another advantage is that the user does not have to specify a lag length for the test regression.

Kwiatkowski, Phillips, Schmidt and Shin (KPSS) Test

In case of both ADF and PP tests, the null hypothesis is taken to be a unit root and the alternative hypothesis is stationary. The test proposed by Kwiatkowski et al. (1992), takes a different view of the unit root testing problem by taking stationarity as the null against an alternative of a unit root, i.e. H_0: $Y_t \sim I(0)$ against H_1: $Y_t \sim I(1)$. They derive their test by starting with the model:

$$y_t = B'D_t + \mu_t + u_t$$

$$u_t = \mu_{t-1} + \varepsilon_t \text{ Where } \varepsilon_t \sim WN(0, \sigma_\varepsilon^2)$$

where, D_t is the deterministic components (constant or constant plus time trend) and u_t is stationary and may be heteroskedastic. Notice that u_t is a pure random walk with innovation variance σ_ε^2. The null hypothesis that $y_t \sim I(0)$ is formulated as H_0: $\sigma_\varepsilon^2 = 0$, which implies that u_t is a constant. The KPSS test statistic is the Lagrange multiplier (LM) or score statistic for testing $\sigma_\varepsilon^2 = 0$ against the alternative that $\sigma_\varepsilon^2 > 0$ and is given by:

$$KPSS = \frac{\left(\frac{1}{T^2}\sum_{t=1}^{T}\widehat{S_t^2}\right)}{\widehat{\lambda^2}}$$

where $\widehat{S_t^2} = \sum_{j=1}^{t}\widehat{u}_j$, u_j is the residual of a regression of y_t on D_t and $\widehat{\lambda^2}$ is a consistent estimate of the long-run variance of u_t using $\widehat{u_t}$. Under the null that y_t is $I(0)$, Kwiatkowski, Phillips, Schmidt and Shin show that KPSS statistic converges to a function of standard Brownian motion that depends on the form of the deterministic terms D_t but not their coefficient values β. The critical values of the KPSS test statistic can be found in Kwiatkowski et al. (1992).

3.2.3.2. Methodology for Panel Unit Root Test

Commonly used unit root test namely Dicky-Fuller (DF), augmented Dicky-Fuller (ADF) and Phillips-Peron (PP) tests lack power in differentiating the unit root null from stationary alternative in the case of panel data. Using panel data unit root test as well as panel co-integration test is one way of increasing the power of unit root and co-integration tests based on single time series (Maddala & Wu, 1999). Levin and Lin (1992, 1993) and Quah (1994) being the seminal contributors.

Panel Unit Root Tests

In panel unit root test, two types of specifications are made, one with common or homogeneous unit root process (Levin, Lin, and Chu (LLC), Breitung, and also of Hadri tests) and other with individual or heterogeneous unit root process (Im, Pesaran, and Shin (IPS), and Fisher-ADF and Fisher-PP tests). This chapter uses LLC and IPS test one from each alternative specification.

LLC consider the following ADF specification:

$$\Delta Y_{i,t} = \alpha_i + \rho Y_{i,t-1} + \sum_{k=1}^{n} \varphi_k \Delta Y_{i,t-k} + \delta_i t + \theta_t + u_{it}$$

Allowing for two-way fixed effects (one coming from the α_i and the second from the θ_t, i.e. the intercept varies over states as well as time) and unit specific time trends (δ_i). In the above regression equation, α_i and θ_t are basically (i-1) states dummies and (t-1) time dummies respectively. The coefficient of lagged Y_i is restricted to be homogeneous across all units of the panel. The null (H_0) and alternative (H_1) being H_0: $\rho = 0$ and H_1: $\rho < 0$.

IPS (1997) extended the LLC test allowing heterogeneity on the coefficient of the $Y_{i,t-1}$ variable proposing a test procedure based on the average of the individual unit root test statistics and estimating the model:

$$\Delta Y_{i,t} = \alpha_i + \rho_i Y_{i,t-1} + \sum_{k=1}^{n} \phi_k \Delta Y_{i,t-k} + \delta_i t + \theta_t + u_{it}$$

With H_0: $\rho_i = 0$ for all i and H_1: $\rho_i < 0$ for at least one i. The corresponding $\bar{t}$ statistic, applicable to a balanced panel only, is defined as $\bar{t} = \frac{1}{N}\sum_{i=1}^{N} t_{\rho i}$, where $t_{\rho i}$ is individual ADF t-statistic for testing H_0: $\rho_i = 0$ for all i.

Schwarz (1978) criterion for the lag differences selection and the Newey-West 1994 method and the Bartlett Karnel for the bandwidth selection are used.

3.2.3.3. Methodology for Testing the Unit Root Under the Presence of Structural Break

It is well recognised in empirical research that structural change is a very important analysis in case of both time series and panel data. If the time span is very long then due to major changes (in policies, events, etc.) there is a high possibility to change in the likelihood and the model parameters, such as the 2007–2008 financial crisis and the 2020 COVID-19 outbreaks. So detection of the existence of breaks are therefore necessary not only for estimation purposes but also for understanding drivers of change and their effect on relationships. In time series or panel time series structural breaks (or change points) in the associations between key variables can occur. Thus, the estimations and forecasts depend on knowledge about structural breaks. Structural breaks might influence interpretations and policy recommendations. Break can be unknown or known and single and multiple breaks can occur. For examples: Financial Crisis, oil price shock, Brexit Referendum, COVID-19, etc. So, the major question for the researcher is that can we estimate when the breaks occur and test the break points?

Perron (1989) in his path breaking work showed that the standard unit root test is not consistent against TSP in the presence of structural break and has suggested a procedure for testing unit root in presence of one-time structural break in the series. The structural break is assumed to be exogenously determined from consideration of visual examination of the plots of the data.

Zivot and Andrews (1992) criticised Perron's procedure for finding out the break point, as it was based primarily on visual inspection of data and further argued that the break point should be endogenously determined (rather than exogenously determined, Perron, 1989) and can be evaluated by applying OLS considering models as follows:

$$\text{Model A: } Y_t = a^A + b^A DU_t + c^A t + d^A Y_{t-1} + \sum_{j=1}^{k} \delta_j Y_{t-j} + e_t \quad (3.12)$$

$$\text{Model B: } Y_t = a^B + g^B DT_t + c^B t + d^B Y_{t-1} + \sum_{j=1}^{k} \delta_j Y_{t-j} + e_t \quad (3.13)$$

$$\text{Model C: } Y_t = a^C + b^C DU_t + c^C t + g^C DT_t + d^C Y_{t-1} + \sum_{j=1}^{k} \delta_j Y_{t-j} + e_t \quad (3.14)$$

e_t is the error term in the model and is assumed to be independently and identically distributed random variable with zero mean and constant variance, i.e. $e_t \sim \text{iid}(0, \sigma^2)$.

Here, Model A permits an endogenous break in the level of the series, Model B allows an endogenous break in the rate of growth & Model C permits an endogenous break both in the level as well as rate of growth.

The dummy variables of the three models can be defined as under:

$$\begin{aligned} DU_t &= 1 \quad && \text{if } t > T\lambda \\ &= 0 && \text{otherwise} \\ DT_t &= t - T\lambda && \text{if } t > T\lambda \\ &= 0 && \text{otherwise} \end{aligned}$$

Here T stands for total time period and T_B is the break point.

Then, $\lambda = T_B/T$ is the break fraction and ranges from $2/T$ to $T\text{-}1/T$.

According to Zivot and Andrews (1992), out of the (T-2) regressions, that year is chosen as break year which gives the minimum value of 't' statistics corresponding to the coefficient of Y_{t-1}. In addition to it, that model is chosen as the best-fitted one which gives the minimum 't' value of the coefficient of Y_{t-1}. After finding out the best-fitted model and the break point, to test for the hypothesis d^i=1, i=A, B and C, i.e. coefficient of Y_{t-1} is equal to one and to compare it with the critical values given by Zivot and Andrews (1992) to determine the nature of the series (TSP or DSP).

Sen (2003) criticised the Zivot and Andrews (1992) conventional unit root procedure and argued that it may suffer from power distortion. Three types of characterisations are there in Zivot and Andrews (1992) namely Crash Model, Changing Growth Model and Mixed Model-of the form of break under the alternative of TSP. For all the three characterisations of the alternative, minimum

t-statistics are used to test for a unit root, when the location of break is unknown (assuming endogenous structural break). Sen (2003) argued that since the form of break is treated as unknown, the appropriate alternative should be the mixed model. When the form of break is wrongly specified, there are serious implications for the power of the minimum t-statistics. Simulation suggests that Crash Model (Changing Growth Model) minimum t-statistics fail to reject the unit root null hypothesis, provided that the break occurs according to the Changing Growth Model (Crash Model). Some loss of power is also found for Mixed Model minimum t-statistics, when the break occurs following the Crash Model or Changing Growth Model. Thus Sen (2003) applied his test on the Mixed Model which simultaneously allows for a break in the level as well as rate of growth and test for the existence of endogenous structural break (expression for Model C-equation (3.3)). The test statistic used by Sen (2003) is Sup-Wald statistic, originally put forth by Murray (1998) and Murray and Zivot (1998). It actually gives the joint null hypothesis of a unit root with no break in the intercept and the slope of the trend function. To calculate the maximum F-statistic for the null hypothesis, Sen (2003) applied the F-statistic in accordance with:

$$F_T^{Max} = Max_{T_b \in \{[\lambda_0 T],[\lambda_0 T]+1,\ldots,T-[\lambda_0 T]\}} F_T(T_b)$$

Here, T_B is the break point which is a constant fraction of the sample size T, i.e. $T_B = \lambda^C T$ with the current break fraction $\lambda^C \varepsilon (0,1)$ and the smallest integer function.

Thus Sen (2003) suggested the Mixed Model (Model C) having higher power than either Model A or Model B and also the F-statistic for testing the unit root hypothesis being more powerful than the traditional t-statistic and the power of F-statistic is more or less consistent. After getting the maximum F-statistic amongst the alternative regression equations, the estimated F-statistic $\left(F_T^{\max}\right)$ is compared with the asymptotic critical values of $F_T^{\max}$ given by Sen.[1] Finally, by analysing the nature of series, conclusion can be drawn whether the series follows TSP or DSP.

3.2.3.4. Methodology for Testing the Presence of Multiple Structural Break

Most of the studies related to structural change have considered the presence of one-time structural break only (Perron, 1989; Zivot & Andrews, 1992, etc.). However, the macroeconomic time series may contain more than one structural break. Thus it is better to consider more than one structural break for analysis. In their path breaking work, Bai and Perron (1998) provided a comprehensive analysis of several issues in the context of multiple structural change models and developed some tests that allow inference to be made about the presence of structural

[1]'On Unit-root Tests when the Alternative is a Trend-break Stationary Process', *Journal of Business and Economic Statistics*, January 2003, Vol. 21, No. 1, pp. 174-184 and corresponding table is Table 1, page 177.

change and the number of breaks. This test is helpful in the changes present and also it endogenously determines the points of break with no prior knowledge.

The method of finding out multiple structural break due to Bai-Perron consists of three steps. In the first step, one has to check whether the underlying process is stationary or not. After checking the stationarity properties of the series, in the second step one has to test whether the deterministic trend process is statistically significant or not. In the third step, after finding out the significant deterministic trend one can apply multiple structural breaks analysis suggested by Bai and Perron (1998, 2003). The details of these steps are as follows:

Step I: To find out the stationary property of the series unit root is applied. The present chapter uses three alternative tests (a) Augmented Dickey-Fuller (ADF) test, (b) Phillips and Perron (PP) test, and (c) Kwiatkowski, Phillips, Schmidt and Shin (KPSS) test available in the literature. The methodology of these three tests has already been discussed in Subsection 3.2.1.

Step II: In this step, one has to check whether there exists any deterministic trend in the series or not. For this purpose, one has to consider whether the coefficient of time arising in the above three tests is significantly different from zero or not. If the coefficient of time is significantly different from zero, then one can conclude that there exists a deterministic trend in the series.

Step III: After finding out the deterministic trend in the series, one can now apply Bai-Perron methodology for finding-out the multiple structural breaks. Now, there are two parts in the Bai-Perron methodology. In the first part, we have to identify whether there exists at all any break in the series or not. Bai-Perron mentioned this test as structural stability versus an unknown number of breaks. In the second part, if at least there exists any break then we have to test the presence of multiple structural breaks in the series. Bai-Perron called this test as sequential test.

To carry out the first part of this step III, Bai-Perron (1998) consider the following linear regression with m breaks (m+1 regimes):

$$y_t = x_t' \beta + z_t' \delta_j + \mu_t, t = T_{j-1}, \ldots\ldots, T$$

$$\left(j = 1\ldots, m+1, T_0 = 0 \text{ and } T_{m+1} = T\right)$$

where y_t is the observed dependent variable, $x_t \in \Re^p$ and $z_t \in \Re^q$ are vectors of covariates, β and δ_j are the corresponding vectors of coefficients with $\delta_i \neq \delta_{i+1}$ ($1 \leq i \leq m$) and μ_t is the error term at time t. The break dates (T_1, …, T_m) are explicitly regarded as unknown. It may be noted that this is a partial structural change model insofar as β doesn't shift and is effectively estimated over the entire sample. Then the purpose is to estimate the unknown regression coefficients and the break dates, that is to say (β, δ_1, … δm_{+1}, T_1,…,T_m), when T observations on (y_t, x_t, z_t) are available.

Bai and Perron (1998) built a method of estimation based on the least square principle. For an m-partition (T_1, …., T_m), denoted by $\{T_j\}$, the associated least square estimator of δ_i is obtained by minimising the sum of squared residuals $\sum_{i=1}^{m+1} \sum_{t=Ti-1}^{Ti} [y_t - x_t' \beta + z_t' \delta_j]^2$ under the constraint $\delta_i \neq \delta_{i+1}$ ($1 \leq i \leq m$). Let $\hat{\delta}(\{T_j\})$ be the resulting estimate. Substituting it in the objective function and denoting the resulting sum of squared residuals as $S_T(T_1, \ldots, Tm)$, the estimated break dates $(\hat{T}_1, \ldots\ldots\ldots \hat{T}_m)$ are such that

$$(\hat{T}_1, \ldots\ldots\ldots \hat{T}_m) = \arg \min_{T_1, \ldots\ldots\ldots T_m} S_T(T_1, \ldots\ldots\ldots Tm)$$

where the minimisation is taken over all partitions $(T_1, \ldots, T_m)$ such as $T_i - T_{i-1} \geq [\varepsilon T]$. The term $[\varepsilon T]$ is interpreted as the minimal number of observations in each segment. Thus the breakpoint estimators are global estimators and are global minimisers of the objective function. Finally, the regression parameter estimates are obtained using the associate least-squares estimates at the estimated m-partition, $\{\hat{T}_j\}$i.e. $\hat{\delta} = \hat{\delta}(\{T_j\})$.

A Test of Structural Stability versus an Unknown Number of Breaks

Bai and Perron (1998) considered tests of no structural change against an unknown number of breaks given some upper bound M for m. The following new class of tests is called double maximum tests and is defined for some fixed weights $\{a_1 \ldots\ldots\ldots\ldots a_m\}$ as:

$$D\max F_T(M, q, a_1, \ldots\ldots\ldots a_M) = \max a_m Sup F_T(\lambda_1, \ldots\ldots\ldots \lambda_n : q)$$
$$= \max a_m F_T(\lambda_1, \ldots\ldots\ldots \lambda_n : q)$$

The weights $\{a_1 \ldots\ldots\ldots a_m\}$ reflect the imposition of some priors on the likelihood of various numbers of structural breaks. Firstly, they set all weights equal to unity, i.e. $a_m = 1$ and label this version of the test as $UD\max F_T(M,q)$. Then they consider a set of weights that the marginal p-values are equal across values of m. The weights are then defined as $a_1 = 1$ and $a_m = c(q, \alpha, 1)/c(q, \alpha, m)$ for $m > 1$, where α is the significance level of the test and $c(q, \alpha, m)$ is the asymptotic critical value of the test $\sup F_T(\lambda_1, \ldots\ldots\ldots \lambda_n : q) \in \Lambda_\varepsilon F_T(\lambda_1, \ldots\ldots\ldots \lambda_n : q)$. This version of the test is denoted as $WD\max F_T(M, q)$.

The second part of step III is basically on sequential test.

A Sequential Test

The last test developed by Bai and Perron (1998) is a sequential test of l versus $l+1$ structural changes:

$$\sup F_T(l+1/l) = \{S_T(\hat{T}_1, \ldots\ldots\ldots \hat{T}_l) - \min\inf S_T(\hat{T}_1, \ldots\ldots\ldots, \tau, \hat{T}_{i-1}, \ldots\ldots\ldots \hat{T}_l)$$

where,

$$\Lambda_{i,n} = \{\tau; \hat{T}_{l-1} + (\hat{T}_l - \hat{T}_{l-1})\eta \leq \tau \leq \hat{T}_l + (\hat{T}_l - \hat{T}_{l-1})\eta\},$$

$S_T(\hat{T}_1, \ldots\ldots\ldots, \hat{T}_{i-1}, \tau, \hat{T}_i \ldots\ldots\ldots \hat{T}_l)$ is the sum of squared residuals resulting from the least squares estimation from each m-partition $(T_1, \ldots\ldots\ldots\ldots\ldots\ldots T_m)$ and $\hat{\sigma}^2$ is a consistent estimator of σ^2 under the null hypothesis.

The asymptotic distributions of these tests are derived in Bai and Perron (1998) and the asymptotic critical values are tabulated in Bai and Perron (1998, 2003b) for $\varepsilon = 0.05$ ($M = 9$), 0.10 ($M = 8$), 0.15 ($M = 5$), 0.20 ($M = 3$), and 0.25 ($M = 2$).

After performing the first and second part of step III, the crucial decision is the selection of major breakpoints.

The Selection Procedure

For determining the number of breaks in the underlying series first one have to look at the *UD max* $F_T(M, q)$ and *WD max* $F_T(M, q)$ statistics to check whether there exists at least one structural break or not. Then decide the number of breaks based upon an examination of the sup F_T $(l+1/l)$ statistics constructed using the break date estimates obtained from a global minimisation of the sum of squared residuals (i.e. one can select m breaks such that the tests sup F_T $(l+1/l)$ are non-significant for any $l>m$). Bai and Perron (2003) conclude that this method leads to the best results and is recommended for empirical applications.

After the determination of growth rate, it is essential to find out the major factors affecting such growth rate. The next section describes the method of finding out such determinants.

3.2.3.5. Methodology for Panel Structural Break

In empirical research, presence of structural break and handling structural breaks is an essential step. This is particularly true in panel data because its comprised of many cross-sectional units, which are all affected by major events. For example, the COVID-19 pandemic has affected all most all the sectors of the global economy. On the other hand, its impact on stock markets is still in question. Most markets look to have recovered within the time of pandemic. So it is suggesting that the relationship between stock returns and COVID-19 has been subject to structural break. It is therefore important to know if a structural break has occurred and, if it has, to infer the date of the break. The previous studies related to the testing of structural break analysis in case of the time series data only. The test of structural break analysis in case of panel data is also very important. The following methods deal with the test and estimation of structural break analysis in case of panel data.

Wachter and Tzavalis (2012) developed a break detection testing procedure for the linear panel data model with exogenous or pre-determined regressors in case of AR(p) series. They suggested that a structural break in the slope parameters as well as in the fixed effects can be accommodated in their method. They also argued that breaks in the fixed effects are not constrained by any type of cross-sectional homogeneity so they are considering that breaks are correlated with all past information. They found that Monte Carlo simulations designate that the test performs adequately even in the type of panel datasets with short time-dimension often met in practice.

Hidalgo and Schafgans (2017) delivered a new Central Limit Theorem for estimators of the slope parameters in case of a large dynamic panel data models, i.e. both n and T increase without bound, in the presence of strong cross-sectional dependence. They have provided two related tests for breaks/homogeneity in the time dimension. The first test is based on the CUSUM principle on the other hand the second test is based on a Hausman-Durbin-Wu approach. They pointed out that some of the key features of their tests are that this test has nontrivial power, i.e. when the number of individuals is a negligible fraction or when the break happens to be towards the end of the sample, this test does not suffer from the subsidiary parameter problem. They also provided a simple bootstrap algorithm to obtain (asymptotic) valid critical values for statistics. One of the important properties of the bootstrap is that there is no need to know the underlying model of the cross-sectional dependence. A Monte Carlo simulation analysis is used for the small sample behaviour of the tests and their bootstrap analogues.

Ditzen et al. (2021) introduced a new method for analysing multiple structural break in time series and panel data analysis. They argued that by their method one can detect the existence of breaks, determine their number and location, and provide break date confidence intervals. For these purposes, they introduced a new command called xtbreak, which offers researchers with a complete toolbox for analysing multiple structural breaks in time series and panel data. xtbreak also detect and date an unknown number of breaks at unknown break dates. Their test is based on asymptotically valid tests for the presence of breaks, a consistent break date estimator, and a break date confidence interval with correct asymptotic coverage. They argued that xtbreak includes three types of tests; (i) a test of no structural change against the alternative of a specific number of changes, (ii) a test of no structural change against the alternative of an unknown number of structural changes, and (iii) a test of the null of s changes against the alternative of $s + 1$ changes. They confirmed that xtbreak also includes an algorithm that employs the last test successively in order to estimate the true number of breaks. They again argued that the tested break dates can be unknown or user-defined so that as when researchers have additional information and wish to examine whether there was a break in a specific point in time. After confirming that there exists some break point in the series xtbreak analysis estimates the locations of the breaks and provides the related confidence intervals. If there exists a large number of breaks that is not at all a problem of heavy computational burden because as xtbreak apparatuses an efficient dynamic programming method described in Bai and Perron (2003), which guarantees that there are $O(T^2)$ computations, even with more than two breaks. They have also argued that xtbreak can deal with models of 'pure' or 'partial' structural change. A pure structural change model is one in which the coefficients of all explanatory variables change on the other hand in case of a partial structural change model only a subset of the coefficients changes. xtbreak is applicable used under very general conditions. In case of panel data, xtbreak can be used even if the model errors are dependent and heteroskedastic across both time and cross-sectional units. The cross-sectional dependence is expected to have an 'interactive effects', or 'common factor', structure, which means that the reliance is of the strong form. Xtbreak can allow the endogenity in the regressors to load on the same set of factors as the errors. The permissible cravings over time are also very general.

In their method there are three hypotheses. Which are as follows:

(A) H_0: no breaks versus H_1: s breaks, where the number of breaks under H_1, s, is specified by the researcher.

(B) H_0: no breaks versus H_1: $1 \leq s \leq s_{max}$ breaks, where the maximum number of breaks under H_1, s_{max}, is specified by the researcher.

(C) H_0: s breaks versus H_1: $s + 1$ breaks, where s is specified by the researcher.

To test hypotheses (A)–(C) they employed a number of test statistics. The time series versions of these tests have appeared in Bai and Perron (1998), while the panel versions have appeared in Ditzen et al. (2021).

Karavias et al. (2022) developed a new break detection toolbox that is applicable to different sized panels. They argued that their method is easy to implement and robust to general forms of unobserved heterogeneity. Their method is almost as similar as in case of the previous methods. In the first step this method includes a structural change test. After that its employed a break date estimator and in the last step they can also find out a break date confidence interval.

3.2.4. Data

Data on firm-level IPI is provided by Prowess Database of Centre for Monitoring Indian Economy during 2000–2001 to 2019–2020. The present chapter, a single-output and four-inputs technology is used. The measurement of different variables can be found in Appendix 3. Output taken is sales value and inputs are different expenses like raw material, power and fuel, salaries & wages as well as capital, obtained by Perpetual Inventory Accumulation method (PIAM) (see Appendix 4).

Panel data analysis is used to find out outcome of different factors which are RDI, NXI, market share as well as AI and time dummy for product patent on efficiency of IPI. The time dummy, D is defined as $D = 1$ if Year >2005 and zero otherwise. RDI is measured by R&D expense per unit of output. Advertising intensity (AI) is measured by advertising expense per unit of sales. The difference between export and import to sales is taken as NXI. Ratio of firms' sales to industry sales is the measure of MS. Firms are selected in such a way that all inputs and output data and factors are obtainable all the way through sample period. Based on this, 74 sample firms for IPI has been selected. All the monetary figures being adjusted by their suitable wholesale price indices.

3.3. Results of Estimation of TE, TFPG and Panel Structural Break

3.3.1. Estimated Results of TE and Determinants of TE

Estimated Results of TE

The present study has considered IPI which is formed of subordinate firms (goods) and since these subordinate goods, are of same kind, it may be supposed that these goods are sharing similar frontier functioning underneath alike technology. For each period from 2000–2001 to 2019–2020, frontier is creäted and the TE scores are obtained in case of the sample firms over the sample period, employing the computer programme solver in Excel.

TE for each of the firms over the sample period are estimated. From Table 3.1, it can be concluded that the average efficiency is 0.928 for the total sample period 2000–2001 to 2019–2020. The sample era is divided into three time periods: first period is from 2000 to 2005, second period covers 2006 to 2010 as well as period 3 runs from 2011 to 2020. Now if one considers the different periods, the average efficiencies are 0.909, 0.925 and 0.965 for period 1, 2, and 3 respectively. This average TE is maximum in period 3, then period 2 and 1 respectively. This maximum average TE in period 3 might be the outcome of product patent system in pharmaceuticals. Thus, it is found that TE is more in post-product system relative to pre-product one. In the pre-product regime, IPI produced 90% of the maximum producible output whereas in post-product regime i.e. in periods 2 and 3, the industry is found to produce 92% and 96% of the maximum producible output. The mean TE of firms are demonstrated in Fig. 3.1.

Considering all the firms during the period of study, efficiency ranges between 0.462 and 1, the mean TE being 0.928 as demonstrated by Table 3.2. Most of the firms, i.e. about 68% firms are enjoying efficiency level above the mean TE and the rest firms are having TE below the mean.

Determinants of TE: A Panel Regression

In the next step, panel regression is carried out for identifying major factors behind TE of sample firms. Indicators considered are RDI, AI, Market share and firms' NXI. As well a dummy (D) variable is considered to understand TE due to product patent relative to process patent. To take care of the simultaneity problem, in this model, there are three equations namely TE, NXI and RDI.

Nonlinear equations are found in the model and so marginal effects are calculated to realise the affirmative or destructive association. Hausman's specification

Table 3.1. Average Efficiency for Different Periods.

All Year	2000–2005	2006–2010	2011–2020
0.928823	0.909762	0.925162	0.96541

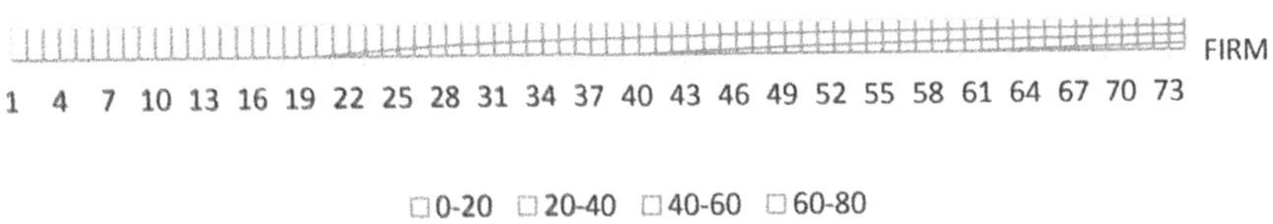

Fig. 3.1. Mean TE of Firms.

Table 3.2. Overall Picture of Efficiency.

	Range	Mean Value	% of Firm Below Mean	% of Firm Above Mean
Efficiency	0.462–1	0.928	31.08	68.02

test is done for testing random effect vis-à-vis fixed effect, for every regression which strongly discards random effect model and supports fixed effect model. Tables 3.3–3.5 demonstrates the estimated results of determinants by panel regression as well as the marginal effect for all the variables.

In case of TE equation, from the marginal effect it is evident that RDI, NXI, AI and MS has positive effect on efficiency. The relationship between AI and TE is found to be U shaped. This implies that as AI increases TE decreases but after some threshold level with rise in AI, TE also increases might be in line for firms spending further on advertisement might be extra inclined to announce a fresh product in the marketplace effortlessly, upsurges sales, combats market rivalry and consequently might be capable to upsurge production and thus TE. But MS and TE are of inverted U shaped indicating that at first TE rises with rise in MS might be the rewards of large size and protected market but afterward some threshold level TE falls with upsurge in MS. RDI and TE are also of inverted U shaped indicating that at first TE rises with rise in RDI may be R&D basically search for various new paths and develop knowledge which may ease faster product development thereby encouraging TE but after some threshold level TE falls with increase in RDI. The relationship among NXI and TE is found to be adverse, i.e. due to more import and thus more modern technology, TE may

Table 3.3. Estimated Results of Determinants by Panel Regression Taking TE as Dependent Variable.

TE	Coefficient	*z*	*P*>|*z*|	Variables	Marginal Effects
RDI	0.003657000***	4.20	0.00	RDI	0.003261
NXI	−0.0001618000***	−9.77	0.00	NXI	0.000005
AI	−0.0000716000***	−3.37	0.00	AI	0.000001
MS	2.1346540000***	4.79	0.00	MS	1.874736108
RDI^2	−0.0000000143***	−1.68	0.09		
NXI^2	−0.0000000017***	−4.59	0.00		
AI^2	0.000000195***	3.13	0.00		
MS^2	−9.6169620000***	−4.33	0.00		
TERDI	−0.0004400000***	−4.67	0.00		
TE.NXI	0.0001831000***	10.13	0.00		
RDI.NXI	0.0000000113***	3.48	0.00		
D	0.0342000000***	7.09	0		
_cons	0.9210793***	170.33	0.00		
F(73,1173) = 15.24***		Prob> *F*= 0			
Wald chi2(11) = 220566.39***		Prob>chi2 = 0			

Note: *** implies significant at 1% level of significance.

Table 3.4. Estimated Results of Determinants by Panel Regression Taking NXI as Dependent Variable.

NXI	Coefficient	*z*	*P*>|*z*|	Variables	Marginal Effects
TE	−1708.34***	−3.85	0	TE	1660.5028
RDI	4.77***	80.71	0	RDI	4.5995
AI	0.16***	4.49	0	AI	0.1356
MI	0.02	0.70	0.483	MI	0.0153
MS	−1205.50***	−2.84	0.005		
TE^2	786.6493***	2.88	0.004		
AI^2	−0.0000657***	−7.08	0		
MI^2	−8.04E−06	−1.25	0.212		
TE.RDI	−0.093949***	−75.73	0		
TE.NXI	1.051839***	275.18	0		
RDI.NXI	1.26E−06**	2.46	0.014		
_cons	918.9745***	5.22	0		
F(73,1173) = 21.2***		Prob> *F*= 0			
Wald chi2(11) = 1070000.00***		Prob> chi2 = 0			

Note: *** and ** imply significant at 1% and 5% level of significance, respectively.

Table 3.5. Estimated Results of Determinants by Panel Regression Taking RDI as Dependent Variable.

RDI	Coefficient	*z*	*P*>|*z*|	Variables	Marginal Effects
TE	494.0592***	5.8	0	TE	260.5772
NXI	0.1794789***	85.3	0	NXI	0.1618
AI	−0.0175554***	−2.88	0.004	AI	0.0175
MS	159.7055**	2.01	0.044		
TE^2	−280.2319***	−5.34	0		
AI^2	9.45E−05***	5.8	0		
TE.RDI	1.073455***	310.49	0		
TE.NXI	−0.01904419***	−85.49	0		
_cons	−216.5223***	−6.39	0		
F(73,1176)	21.9***	Prob> *F* = 0			
Wald chi2(8) = 920862.81***		Prob> chi2 = 0			

Note: *** and ** imply significant at 1% and 5% level of significance, respectively.

increase. There are interaction terms, TE.NXI and RDI.NXI which affects TE positively whereas TE.RDI affects TE negatively. Again the consequence of product patent on TE in comparison to the process patent is encouraging as well as statistically significant. It might propose that Indian pharmaceutical companies are capable to properly change their production process to manage the altered permitted situation.

In case of NXI equation, TE, RDI, AI and MI have nonlinear relationship with NXI. There are interaction terms TE.NXI and RDI.NXI which affects NXI positively whereas TE.RDI affects NXI negatively. From the marginal effect, one can conclude that TE, RDI, AI and MI have positive effect on NXI. There exist U-shaped association amongst TE and NXI. This implies that as TE increases NXI decreases but after some threshold level with rise in TE, NXI also rises. It may be initially TE rises may be with more usage of modern technology, import increases thereby reducing NXI but after the threshold limit, TE increases implying output rises, export increases and thus NXI rises.AI and MI have inverted U-shaped relationship with NXI. At first NXI rises with rise in AI might be firms' expenditure additionally on advertisement might be extra inclined to announce a fresh product in the market effortlessly, upsurges sales, contests market rivalry and as a result might upsurge production, export and thus net export but after some threshold level NXI falls with increase in AI may be more spending on advertisement may hamper production and thus export and net export. For NXI, as NXI rises with rise in MI may be because MI serve as a proxy for product differentiation so, more MI implies more product differentiation, product variety increases and export may increase thereby increasing NXI but after some threshold level NXI falls with increase in MI may be more spending on product differentiation may hamper production and thus export and net export. The affirmative relation amongst RDI and NXI might be that R&D basically search for various new paths and develop knowledge which may ease faster product development thereby encouraging production, export and thus net export. The negative relation between MS and NXI may be with rise in MS, there are advantages of big size and secured market thereby increasing production which requires fund which may thereby hamper NXI.

In case of RDI equation, the results are shown in Table 3.5, it may be concluded that TE, NXI and AI are having nonlinear association with RDI while MS is linearly and positively related. There are interaction terms TE.RDI which affects RDI positively whereas TE.NXI affects RDI negatively. The marginal effect suggests that TE, NXI and AI has incremental effect on RDI.

TE have inverted U-shaped relationship with RDI. At first RDI rises with rise in TE may be faster product development may ease and require more R&D which basically search for various new paths and develop knowledge but subsequently after some threshold level RDI decreases with rise in TE as after the limit R&D requirement is less. AI have U-shaped relationship with RDI. Then RDI falls with rise in AI may be firms spending more on advertisement have to cut spending on R&D and thus may decrease RDI but after some threshold level RDI rises with increase in AI may be more advertisement may encourage production thus generating extra profit and thereby raising R&D and thus RDI.

3.3.2. Estimated Results of TFPG and Determinants of TFPG

This chapter deals with IPI which is formed of subordinate firms (goods) and since these subordinate goods are equal, it may be presumed that they share like frontier underneath the same kind of know-how. The frontier is generated during the period 2000–2001 to 2019–2020 and the MPI measure is obtained for entire firms, employing the computer programme solver in Excel. The existing firms are then combined to produce the industry and the average of estimated MPI corresponding to their firm level complement is considered as an extent of TFPG. TFPG values of sample firms over sample period are estimated. These results are concise for producing information as regards to mean annual rate of changes of TFPG for sample firms. The outcomes are demonstrated in Table 3.6. Fig. 3.2 illustrates the mean TFPG of firms.

Table 3.6 reveals that the total mean annual rate of change of TFPG is 0.712%. The total time period is broken down into three: first period (period 1) corresponds to 2000 to 2005, period 2 ranges from 2006 to 2010 and the third period (period 3) is from 2011 to 2020. Comparing the three sub periods, the mean annual rate of change of TFPG are 0.732, 1.138 and 0.443 for periods 1, 2 and 3 respectively. This change rate of TFPG is maximum in period 2 then period 1 and then period 3. This highest change in period 2 may be the instant consequence of complete product patent system in pharmaceuticals. The mean annual rate of change of TFPG first rises in period 2 and then drops in period 3.

Decomposition of Productivity Growth

Growth in productivity embedded itself change in technology (TC), change in technical efficiency (TEC) as well as change in scale efficiency (SEC). So it can be interesting to know the movement of these three constituents. TC is linked with movement in production frontier; While TEC is movement towards the frontier whereas SEC shows the effect of production scale change on TFP.

TFPG is broken down into changes due to efficiency, scale efficiency as well as technology following equations 3.6–3.8. For IPI, the TFPG range, mean TFPG value, percentage of firms under mean TFPG, percentage of firms over mean TFPG and also TFPG change are calculated. The findings are represented in

Table 3.6. Average Annual Rates of TFP Changes.

All Year	2000–2005	2006–2010	2011–2020
0.712693	0.732243	1.1382	0.44382

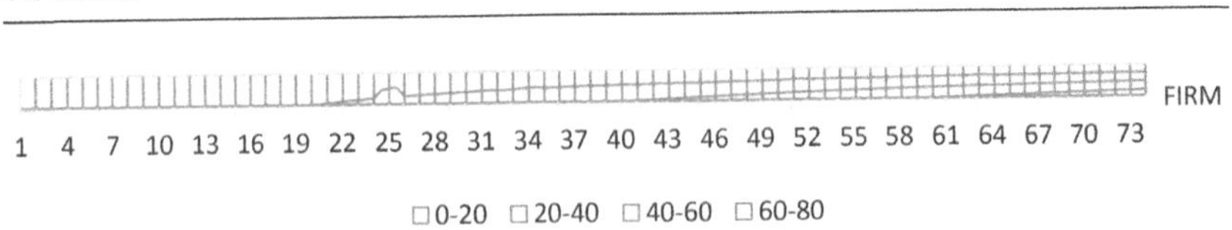

Fig. 3.2. Mean TFPG of Firms.

Table 3.7. Items in row TEC displays mean annual changes in the TE level over time for every firm, a value larger than one suggests enhancement in TE of a firm over time. Likewise, entry value bigger (smaller) than one in TC row mirrors technological progress (regress) for a firm over the period. SEC over the period for sample firms is conveyed in SEC row, with a value greater than unity once more signalling development in scale efficiency. The findings of Table 3.7 may reveal that growth in productivity is generally determined by TE change for whole period under study. Therefore, TEC is the prime source of increase in productivity.

The technological change as well as change in scale efficiency contributed equally for the productivity growth increase. Thus, it may be established that superior use of factors of production and variations in the scale as well as efficiency can gear firms to upper TFPG level over the sample period.

Table 3.7 shows that the average TFPG of the firms ranges from 0.73 to 1.68. The mean of the average BMPI or the grand mean (GRM) is 1.03. Amongst all the sample firms, 72.97% displays average BMPI lower than the GRM and the rest 27.03% of firms indicates average BMPI more than the GRM. As a result, the majority of the firms have their average BMPI less than the GRM. The study also discloses that IPI shows productivity upsurge at the rate of 3% per annum.

It is seeming from the study that in the sample period, mean technological change (TC) of the firms ranges from 0.94 to 1.71. The GRM or mean of average technological change of the firms in study period is 1.01. The estimated results of average TEC and average SEC ranges from 0.90 to 1.69 and 0.84 to 1.09 respectively. The GRMs are 1.02 and 1.01 analogous to TEC and SEC.

Determinants of TFPG: A Panel Regression

Panel regression is done to identify the major causes of TFPG of IPI. Variables considered are intensities of R&D, Advertisement in previous period as well as NXI. Furthermore, a dummy varaiable, D is included to examine the impact of product patent on TFPG.

The assessed equations are obtained as nonlinear type. Therefore, the marginal effects' sign will indicate the positive or negative association. Hausman

Table 3.7. Decomposition of TFPG.

	Range	**Mean Value**	**% of Firm Below Mean**	**% of Firm Above Mean**	**Change In TFPG**	
TFPG	0.73–1.68	1.03	72.97	27.03	3%	TEC
Technological Change (TC)	0.94–1.71	1.01	68.92	31.08		Dominates
TEC	0.90–1.69	1.02	51.35	48.65		
Scale Efficiency Change (SEC)	0.85–1.08	1.02	90.55	9.56		

specification test is done which discards the hypothesis of random effect and suggests model of fixed effect. In Tables 3.8–3.10, these results of determinants are presented.

RDI and AI in the previous period are found to be positively associated while NXI is negatively associated with TFPG. Some interaction terms like TFPG.

Table 3.8. Estimated Results of Determinants by Panel Regression Taking TFPG as Dependent Variable.

TFPG	**Coef.**	*z*	*P*>|*z*|	**Variables**	**Marginal Effects**
RDI	0.00022850***	1.77	0.08	RDI	0.000019
NXI	−0.00007610***	−4.29	0.00	NXI	−0.000004
TFPG NXI	0.00006930***	13.99	0.00	AI	0.000847
RDI.TFPG	−0.00019570***	−5.14	0.00		
AI	0.00085600***	4.70	0.00		
RDI.AI	−0.00000003	−0.65	0.52		
D	−0.0872357***	−3.79	0.00		
_cons	1.11857100***	29.23	0.00		
	$F(73,956) = 18.635$***	Prob> $F = 0$			
	Wald chi2(6) = 3174.84***	Prob>chi2 = 0			

Note: *** implies significant at 1% level of significance.

Table 3.9. Estimated Results of Determinants by Panel Regression Taking NXI as Dependent Variable.

NXI	**Coef.**	*z*	*P*>|*z*|	**Variables**	**Marginal Effects**
TFPG	−129.4328***	−3.51	0	TFPG	−65.0489
RDI	3.722104***	19.93	0	RDI	2.908494
MI	1.130407***	7.82	0		
MS	26297.36***	7.85	0		
RDI^2	−0.0000662***	−2.73	0.006		
RDI.TFPG	−0.7445733***	−13.87	0		
TFPG.NXI	0.155209***	14.75	0		
_cons	78.48907	1.1	0.271		
	$F(73,955) = 8.04$***	Prob> $F = 0$			
	Wald chi2(7) = 10530.33***	Prob>chi2 = 0			

Note: *** implies significant at 1% level of significance.

Table 3.10. Estimated Results of Determinants by Panel Regression Taking RDI as Dependent Variable.

RDI	Coef.	z	$P>\|z\|$	Variables	55.591 pt
TFPG	22.000730***	3.33	0.001	TFPG	29.10111
NXI	0.098146***	14.15	0	NXI	0.090732
AI	0.158907**	2.22	0.027	AI	0.179593
MI	0.262126***	4.3	0	MI	0.088449
MS	1509.770000	1.62	0.106	MS	365.9738
AI^2	−0.000174***	−6.43	0		
MI^2	−0.000114***	−6.62	0		
NXI^2	−0.000002***	−7.73	0		
RDI.TFPG	0.023676***	6.37	0		
MS.MI	−7.939041***	−9.3	0		
AI.MS	6.302940***	7.17	0		
_cons	59.036020***	3.5	0		
$F(73,951) = 14.37$***		Prob>$F = 0$			
Wald chi2(11) = 8979.67***		Prob>chi2 = 0			

Note: *** and ** imply significant at 1% and 5% level of significance, respectively.

NXI, RDI.AI and RDI.TFPG are also considered which are found to be statistically significant; the first term affects TFPG positively but the end two terms impacts TFPG negatively. Marginal effect values are presented in Tables 3.8–3.10. The marginal effects of RDI on TFPG and AI in the previous period on TFPG are positive which signifies that the total outcome of RDI and advertising intensity in the previous period are positive. But the NXI's marginal effect is obtained as negative.

The affirmative association among RDI and TFPG might be owing to the fact that R&D basically includes the search for numerous new paths as well as know-how progress which ease product expansion and make it sooner in so doing boosting TFPG. The affirmative association among advertising intensity of previous period and TFPG perhaps may be owing to firms expenditure more on advertisement in the previous period might be more prone to bring in a fresh market product in the current period without difficulty, upsurges sales and as a consequence may amplify productivity. But there occurs an adverse relationship amongst NXI and TFPG which signifies that import have additional encouraging impact over export to endorse TFPG. The cause might be with more import firms can have access to machineries which may progress its production method thereby shifting the frontier and thus TFPG.

All over again the outcome of product patent on TFPG compared to the process patent happened to be pessimistic but statistically significant. It might put forward that IPI are incapable of suitably modifying to cope up with the changed legal environment.

In the case of NXI, the marginal effect suggests that RDI has an encouraging influence on NXI and TFPG has adverse consequences on NXI. The positive relation between RDI and NXI may be due to R&D basically search for various new paths and develop knowledge which may ease faster product development thereby encouraging production, export and thus NXI. As well the association among RDI and NXI is of an inverted U shaped. However, there happens to be undesirable relationship among NXI and TFPG indicating that TFPG has extra positive impact on import over export. The cause may be with additional TFPG firms can have right to use machineries which might progress its production method thereby shifting the frontier and this may be done by import. Some interaction terms namely RDI.TFPG and TFPG.NXI are statistically significant of which the first term affects TFPG negatively but the end term affects TFPG positively.

In case of RDI equation, the marginal effects show that TFPG, NXI, MS, MI and AI has incremental effect on RDI. The relationship between RDI and AI, RDI and MI as well as RDI and NXI are nonlinear and of inverted U shaped. There are interaction terms TFPG.RDI, MS.MI and AI.MS of which the first and third terms affect RDI positively whereas the second term affect RDI negatively.

The encouraging association among TFPG and RDI might be owing to higher TFPG firms' may have several new paths as well as develop skill which may help quicker product development thereby encouraging RDI.

Association among RDI and NXI is found to be affirmative might be owing to higher export and thus more NXI, there is more and more requirement of R&D for various new paths and knowledge development which may ease faster product development thereby encouraging RDI.

The positive relation between MS and RDI may be with rise in MS, there are advantages of big size and secured market thereby increasing production which may encourage RDI.

Also as MI serve as a proxy for product differentiation more MI implies more product differentiation, product variety increases and there is need of increasing RDI.

Along with it, RDI rises with increase in AI may be more AI implies more advertisement which may encourage production, may generate extra profit and thereby may raise R&D and thus RDI.

3.3.3. Results of Panel Structural Break Analysis

There exist no such structural changes in the series of TFPG in firm-level analysis across the years as suggested by Table 3.11.

Comparison of Efficiency and TFPG of IPI using Firm-Level Data

TE and TFPG can be considered as the indicator for assessing performance of any industry. So for understanding the performance of IPI, a detailed analysis

Table 3.11. Results of Panel Structural Break Analysis in TFPG at Firm Level.

Sequential test for multiple breaks at unknown breakpoints (Ditzen, Karavias & Westerlund. 2021)				
		Bai & Perron Critical Values		
	Test Statistic	**1% Critical Value**	**5% Critical Value**	**10% Critical Value**
F(1|0)	1.77	12.29	8.58	7.04
F(2|1)	0.03	13.89	10.13	8.51
F(3|2)	0.13	14.80	11.14	9.41
F(4|3)	0.62	15.28	11.83	10.04
F(5|4)	1.88	15.76	12.25	10.58
Detected number of breaks:		.	.	.
Maximum number of breaks reached with null always rejected.				
No breaks found, cannot estimate breakpoints.				

regarding TE and TFPG of IPI using firm-level data has been made in this chapter. The present chapter is thus also involved in looking at the comparison of the firms in IPI based on TE as well as TFPG values. At the same time the common factors affecting TE and TFPG is a matter of much concern.

Results of TE and TFPG of IPI

In case of TE, the average value is found to be 0.928 for the overall sample period 2000–2001 to 2019–2020. After breaking the sample period into three subphases, phase 1 corresponds to 2000–2005, phase 2 covers the period 2006–2010 and phase 3 covers 2011–2020, the average efficiency turned out to be 0.909, 0.925 and 0.965 for periods 1, 2 and 3 respectively. The average TE is highest in period 3 followed by period 2 and then 1. This maximum average TE in period 3 may be the effect of product patent regime in pharmaceuticals. Thus it is found that TE is more in product patent regime, i.e. after 2005 as relative to the period prior to the product patent regime, i.e. before 2005. In the pre-product regime, IPI produced 90% of the maximum producible output whereas in post-product regime, i.e. in periods 2 and 3, the industry is found to produce more, i.e. 92% and 95% of the maximum producible output. Considering all the firms over the sample period, efficiency ranges between 0.462 and 1, the mean TE being 0.928. Most of the firms, i.e. about 68% are enjoying efficiency level above the mean TE and the rest firms are having TE below the mean.

For TFPG, overall average annual rate of change of TFPG is found to 0.712% for the overall period 2000–2020. The overall period is broken down into three sub phases, phase 1 corresponds to 2000–2005, phase 2 covers the period 2006–2010 and phase 3 is 2011–2020. Now if one considers the different periods, the average annual rate of change of TFPG are 0.732, 1.138 and 0.443 for periods 1, 2 and 3 respectively. This rate of changes of TFPG is highest in period 2 followed by period 1 and then 3. This maximum change in period 2 may be the immediate effect of complete product patent system in pharmaceuticals. The average annual rate of change of TFPG first increases in period 2 and then falls in period 3. Fig. 3.3 illustrates the mean TE and mean TFPG of the firms.

Results of Determinants of TE and TFPG of IPI

For TE, it is evident that RDI, NXI, AI and MS are the enhancing factors of efficiency. The relationship between AI and TE is found to be U shaped. But MS and TE as well as RDI and TE are of inverted U shaped. Whereas there exists a negative relationship amongst NXI and TE. Again, the effect of product patent on TE compared to the process patent is encouraging.

For TFPG, RDI and AI in the previous period are the enhancing factors of TFPG whereas NXI is the retarding factor of TFPG of IPI. Again the effect of product patent on TFPG compared to the process patent is adverse.

The determining factors of TE and TFPG as well as the common factors affecting TE and TFPG can be seen in Table 3.12.

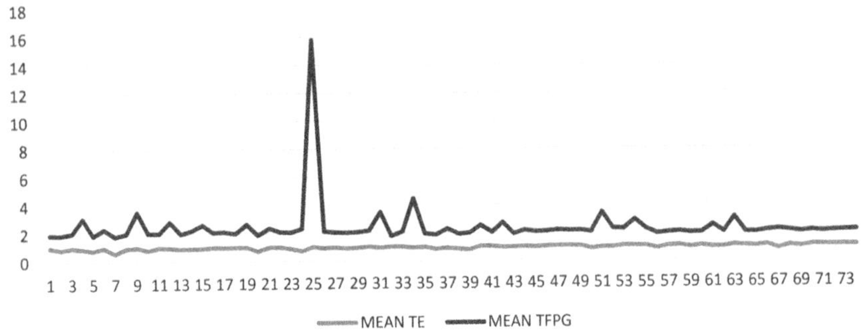

Fig. 3.3. Mean TE and TFPG of Firms.

Table 3.12. Determinants of TE and TFPG of Pharmaceutical Firms in India.

Determinants of TE	Determinants of TFPG	Common Determinants of TE and TFPG
Positive Relation: RDI, NXI, AI and MS Negative Relation: NXI	Positive Relation: RDI and AI in the previous period Negative Relation: NXI	RDI and AI

3.4. Conclusion

The present chapter used the data envelopment method for evaluating the IPI efficiency employing firm-level data. Furthermore, this chapter attempts to estimate TFPG of the sample firms over the sample period and also tries to identify the encouraging factors of TE and TFPG.

For IPI, the efficiency scores have indicated that about 68% firms are enjoying above average TE. The consequences are also revealing the situation that altered Indian patent laws are not harmful for performance of Indian pharmaceutical companies as it is found that TE is more in post-product system relative to pre-product one.

> Panel regression is employed for identifying major causes behind TE suggesting that there happens to be a nonlinear association amongst TE and the possible determinants. The relationship between AI and TE is found to be U shaped. But MS and TE as well as RDI and TE are of inverted U shaped. The variables RDI, NXI, AI and MS are found to be efficiency enhancing factors. In the post product regime, IPI became more efficient relative to pre product period. Indian pharmaceutical companies are capable of suitably modify their production process to manage with transformed permitted atmosphere.

For calculating productivity growth, BMI approach of DEA is employed to recognise the performance of IPI. There is 3% change in TFPG found on the whole sample period. It can be inferred that total mean annual rate of change of TFPG is 0.712693% during the period 2000–2001 to 2019–2020. The total period is divided into three sub-periods, first period is from 2000 to 2005, second period is from 2006 to 2010 and the period 3 is from 2011 to 2020. This rate of TFPG changes is maximum in period 2, then by period 1 and followed by period 3. The highest change in period 2 might be the direct result of complete product patent in pharmaceuticals. The mean annual rate of change of TFPG first improved in period 2 and then reduced in the 3rd period.

Assessed TFPG is broken down into changes due to efficiency, scale efficiency as well as technology. The result shows that TEC is the major source of productivity boost.

Accordingly, it encouraged us to determine the causes which can promote productivity growth in IPI. In this situation, regression in a panel set up is done for identifying the major factors of IPI. From the result of this analysis, it can be said that there is existence of nonlinear association among TFPG and all the explanatory variables. Raising RDI and AI in the previous period leads to higher productivity growth in IPI. These are the factors that can improve TFPG. In contrast, enhancing export relative to import may be harmful for productivity growth in IPI. Yet again the result of product patent on TFPG compared to the process patent turned out to be depressing and statistically significant.

There is wide variation in TE and TFPG for the sample firms. The average TE is highest in period 3 followed by period 2 and then 1. This maximum average TE in period 3 may be the effect of product patent regime in pharmaceuticals. Thus TE is more in product patent system, i.e. after 2005 as relative to the period prior to the product patent system, i.e. before 2005.

Whereas rate of change of TFPG is highest in period 2 followed by period 1 and then 3. This maximum change in period 2 may be the immediate effect of full-fledged product patent regime in pharmaceuticals. The average annual rate of change of TFPG first increases in period 2 and then falls in period 3. It turns out that in period 3, TE is maximum whereas TFPG is minimum.

The common determinants that are found to enhance TE and TFPG turned out to be RDI and AI.

There exist no such structural changes in the series of TFPG in firm-level analysis across the years.

Chapter 4

Analysis of Efficiency and Total Factor Productivity Growth of Indian Pharmaceutical Industry Using State-Level Data

Abstract

This chapter investigates the performance of the Indian Pharmaceutical Industry (IPI) using state-level data. It looks at the performance of pharmaceutical industries in major Indian states. For doing that it estimates technical efficiency and total factor productivity growth (TFPG) of Indian states. This chapter helps to compare the Indian states as well as to identify the position of the states in the IPI. This chapter attempts to find out the factors affecting TE and TFPG of IPI employing data on 17 major selected states of India. Another important contribution of this chapter is that it verifies the presence of structural breaks (which may appear due to changes in economic regime over time) in the TFPG series at the state level by using panel structural break methodology.

Keywords: Efficiency; total factor productivity growth; Indian pharmaceutical industry; state-level data; performance; Indian states; panel structural break

4.1. Introduction

Industry plays a crucial role in the economic development of any country. Ensuring stable industrial growth may be helpful and keep going continued economic development. One of the engines of industrial growth is the manufacturing sector. It fuels growth, productivity and efficiency and also strengthens agriculture and service sectors.

Performance Analysis of the Indian Pharmaceutical Industry: A Global Outlook, 89–108

Published under exclusive licence by Emerald Publishing Limited
doi:10.1108/978-1-83797-743-720251004

Among the different manufacturing industries in India, the Indian pharmaceutical industry (IPI) has emerged nowadays as one of the most vibrant segments and deserves special attention.

Owing to the criticality of the pharmaceutical products for the health protection of the population, pharmaceuticals have been a much-loved sector for policy makers in both the developed and many developing countries, and India is not an exception.

It will be interesting to address the issue of state-level development of IPI because from the beginning Indian planners have been always concerned with the removal of economic backwardness of the country and to make it a developed economy. They have taken care to make sure equal development across various states and also diverse regions such that the weaker sections of the population gain from the economic advancement of the country.

Since India consists of different states and union-territories, each state has its individual particular features that influence the growth and performance of pharmaceutical industry in several counts. In addition, the spread of industry in various states varies. For this reason, the growth and performance of pharmaceutical industry in diverse states do not at all times progress in the same path. For appropriate policies towards the reduction of disparities at the state level, it is important to have an idea regarding the states which are lagging behind and also the relative position of the states with respect to good-performing states. Thus, the knowledge about the growth performance of different states is very much needed. At the same time, it is important to verify the presence of structural breaks if any (which may appear due to changes in economic regime over time) in the total factor productivity growth (TFPG) series.

Furthermore, the literature survey revealed that not much attempt has been made to analyse the behaviour of IPI quantitatively. Mention may be made of few studies like Singh (1989), Nagarajan and Barthwal (1990), Majumder (1994), Madanmohan (1997), Chaudhuri (2005), Chaudhuri and Das (2006), Ghose and Chakraborty (2008), Mazumdar and Rajeev (2009), Mazumder et al. (2010), Saranga and Banker (2010), Chakraborty and Ghose (2010, 2011, 2013) and Ghose and Chakraborty (2012) among others.

Singh (1989), Madanmohan (1997) in their study using firm-level data focused on different aspects of IPI like export, import and net import, technology, profitability, patterns of MNCs activity and plant exit process. Whereas Majumder (1994), Chaudhuri and Das (2006), Mazumdar and Rajeev (2009), Majumdar et al. (2009), Saranga and Banker (2010) and Ghose and Chakraborty (2012) were concerned with the measurement of productivity or efficiency of the industry. Studies which attempted to analyse the growth performance of the industry are due to Nagarajan and Barthwal (1990), Chaudhuri (2005) and Ghose and Chakraborty (2008). Test for exogenous and endogenous structural break using the modern time series approach has been carried out by Chakraborty and Ghose (2010, 2011, 2013, 2017), Chakraborty (2017) among others.

However, none of the above studies looked at or applied structural break analysis in pharmaceutical analysis except very few who studied and applied endogenous one-time structural break analysis in pharmaceutical industry analysis in the case of India. For a detailed survey, please refer to Chapter 3.

The objectives of the present chapter stem from the above observations regarding the movement of pharmaceutical industries in the major selected states of India from the period 1983–1984 to 2019–2020.

Thus, the major aim of the current chapter is to investigate the performance of the IPI using state-level data. It looks at the performance of pharmaceutical industries in major Indian states. For doing that it estimates the technical efficiency (TE) and TFPG of Indian states. This chapter helps to compare the Indian states as well as to identify the position of the states in the IPI. Another important objective of this chapter is to verify the presence of structural breaks (which may appear due to changes in economic regime over time) in the TFPG series at the state level by using panel structural break methodology.

Thus, the major objectives that the present chapter undertakes may be listed below:

To estimate the extent of efficiency of sample states over the sample period
To identify the factors affecting such efficiency
To find out the TFPG of the Indian states
To elucidate the causes of variation in TFPG
To verify the presence of structural breaks (which may appear due to changes in economic regime over time) in the TFPG at the state level by using panel structural break methodology.

This chapter is organised as below.

Section 4.2 presents the methodology and data. Subsection 4.2.1 is concerned with procedures of state-level analysis of IPI and data sources are discussed in 4.2.2. Section 4.3 presents the results of the estimation elaborately. This part discusses the result of state-level analysis of IPI. Few bottom-line comments can be found in Section 4.4.

4.2. Data and Methodology

This section discusses the methodology and data source of the present chapter. Subsection 4.2.1 is concerned with empirical procedures of state-level analysis of IPI and data sources are discussed in Subsection 4.2.2.

4.2.1. Methodology

This section is concerned with the methodology of the present chapter. Subsection 4.2.1A is concerned with empirical procedures of state-level analysis of efficiency and determinants of TE. The methodology for state-level analysis of TFPG of the pharmaceutical industry and determinants of TFPG is discussed in Subsection 4.2.1B. The methodology for the panel structural break can be found in Chapter 3 (See Subsection 3.2.3).

4.2.1.A. Analysis of Efficiency of the IPI Using State-Level Data

The output-oriented TE is measured by applying the Data Envelopment Analysis (DEA) approach using state-level data of 17 major selected states considering each state as a producing unit. The empirical procedure of measuring TE and two-stage least square methodology under panel regression for finding out determinants of TE are discussed by employing a computer programme solver in Excel and STATA 15 software.

Measurement of Efficiency

TE of output-oriented type may be calculated by contrasting the actual output with frontier output. Here, Banker et al. (1984) of the DEA method is used. The radial TE of a firm of output-oriented type using observed input–output bundle (x^0, y^0) following variable returns to scale (VRS) assumption is achieved as:

$$\zeta_y(x^0, y^0) = \frac{1}{\Phi^*} \tag{4.1}$$

where $\Phi^* = \max \varphi$

$$\text{s.t} \sum\nolimits_1^N \lambda_j y^j \geq y^0;$$
$$\sum\nolimits_1^N \lambda_j x^j \leq x^0;$$
$$\sum\nolimits_1^N \lambda_j = 1 \text{ where} \lambda_j \geq 0; (j = 1, 2, \ldots N)$$

Determinants of TE: A Simultaneous Panel Regression

TE is expressed as a function of firm size (MF), degree of mechanisation (K/L), employee per production worker (E/L) and relative wage rate (W). The arguments for the inclusion of these factors in explaining TE are the following:

The degree of mechanisation (K/L) is captured by the ratio of capital to labour input, i.e. K/L. By incorporating advanced and sophisticated technology into the production process, the higher degree of mechanisation can help to enhance the TE of an industry. But it can also hinder TE owing to improper management of more capitalistic and sophisticated technology (Jeanneney & Hua, 2003). As a result, the producer may choose labour-intensive production methods, i.e. decrease in K/L might lead to more TE scores.

Employee per production worker (E/L) is incorporated to find out the composition of workforce. A higher number of employees per production worker generally can indicate a superior degree of bureaucratic control inside the firm ensuing in inefficiency in the production unit. Such a line of reasoning postulated a depressing association between E/L and TE. A positive association can be obtained among E/L and TE if the blend of workforce is just exact to run the production procedure efficiently.

Firm size (MF) can be another determinant of TE. It is interesting to observe whether bigger firms are better in acting to smaller firms or vice-versa, i.e. whether big firms have any size effect on TE of IPI. There exists an argument involving firm size and efficiency of the firm in the existing studies. Some of the studies found a positive relation between firm size and efficiency while some of the studies postulated a negative relation. Here mention may be made of the studies like Bhandari and Roy (2011), Truett and Truett (2009), Bhandari and Maity (2007), Cheng and Lo (2004), Ramaswamy (1994), etc. Also, in the literature, different measures of firm size are available due to Mukherjee (1963), Ahluwalia (1991), Majumder (1997), Lundvall and Battese (2000), Urata and Kawai (2002), Biesebroeck (2005), Palangkaraya et al. (2005), Castany et al. (2007), among others. In tune with Lundvall and Battese (2000), the present chapter uses intermediate inputs (sum of materials consumed and fuels consumed) (MF) as a measure of firm size.

It is motivating to check whether the efficiency wage hypothesis holds in case of IPI or not. As relative wage rate, W (defined as the ratio of real wage rate in the Pharmaceutical industry at state level to real wage rate in overall Indian manufacturing) rises, through the participation of skilled workers in the production procedure, TE can increase.

To understand whether TE of IPI is affected by trade-related variables, net export intensity (X-M)/Y is incorporated as a possible determinant of TE along with other determinants mentioned before.

Panel data set usage allows us to control for unobserved cross-section heterogeneity. From this analysis, significant determinants across all the states can be found. Furthermore, this chapter allows the possibility of contemporaneous correlation among the units by forming a seemingly unrelated regression (SUR) framework. Besides the problem of cross-section heteroscedasticity has been taken into account by using White Cross-Section. The SUR structure and adjustment for heteroscedasticity (White Cross-Section) are described in Appendix 1. Hausman test is carried out for getting better model, i.e. fixed or random and the fixed effect model is found to be the improved one. The model is found to be identified using exclusion restriction.

A quite familiar problem may be that there may be two-way causality between TE and (X-M)/Y. For that reason, the panel model in a simultaneous set-up has been framed with two equations: technical efficiency (equation 4.2) and net export intensity (equation 4.3). Equations (4.2) and (4.3) are shown below:

$$\begin{aligned} TE = f(&MF, \frac{K}{L}, \frac{E}{L}, W, \frac{(X-M)}{Y}, (MF)^2, \left(\frac{K}{L}\right)^2, \left(\frac{E}{L}\right)^2, \\ &W^2, \left(\frac{(X-M)}{Y}\right)^2, MF*\frac{K}{L}, \frac{K}{L}*\frac{E}{L}, \frac{E}{L}*\frac{(X-M)}{Y}, \\ &MF*\frac{E}{L}, MF*\frac{(X-M)}{Y}, \frac{K}{L}*\frac{(X-M)}{Y}, \\ &MF*W, \frac{K}{L}*W, \frac{E}{L}*W, \frac{(X-M)}{Y}*W) \end{aligned} \tag{4.2}$$

$$\frac{(X-M)}{Y} = f\left(TE, MF, \frac{K}{L}, \frac{E}{L}, REER, (MF)^2, \left(\frac{K}{L}\right)^2, \left(\frac{E}{L}\right)^2, REER^2\right) \tag{4.3}$$

TE is expressed as a function of MF, K/L, E/L, W and (X-M)/Y. All the explanatory variables are nonlinearly related to TE. The relation between net export intensity and the explanatory variables can be explained as below:

If TE rises it implies that net export intensity increases may be due to more efficient use of inputs thereby raising production and thus net export intensity. With rise in MF and E/L, net export intensity can improve. This might be owing to the fact that with rise in firm size and right composition of work force, production may rise leading to rise in export and thus net export intensity. Also, with higher degree of mechanisation, due to adoption of better technology, production will rise, raising net export intensity. As REER rises, export increase and import falls leading to rise in net export intensity.

4.2.1.B. Analysis of TFPG of IPI Using State-Level Data and Determinants of TFPG

For estimating the TFPG of the different sample states over the sample period, the Biennial Malmquist Productivity Index (MPI) of the DEA approach is employed using state-level data of 17 major selected states considering each state as a producing unit. The empirical procedure of measuring TFPG and two-stage least square methodology under panel regression for finding out determinants of TE are discussed using a computer programme solver in Excel and STATA 15 software was used.

Biennial Malmquist Index (BMI) of Productivity

The present chapter implemented DEA method for calculating change in total factor productivity. Thus, it requires calculation of MPI which was first developed by Caves, Christensen, and Diewert (1982) which was modified by Färe, Grosskopf, Lindgren and Roos (FGLR) in 1992. The measures of productivity changes basically based on the mention technology for a given observed input–output data. In 1992, Färe et al. (FGLR) introduced a technique of decomposing the MPI into TC and TEC basis of the assumption that the underlying technology follows the constant return to scale (CRS) frontier which is also considered as the benchmark technology. The FGLR assumption of CRS as a benchmark technology is not always a meaningful assumption because if one assumes VRS technology then the decomposition provided by FGLR is not applicable. In 1994, Färe, Grosskopf, Norris, and Zhang (FGNZ) re-modified FGRL decomposition by assuming VRS and also decomposed MPI into TEC, TC and SEC. In 1997, Ray and Desli pointed out that FGNZ technique is not bias free for the reason that FGNZ decomposition raises another problem of internal consistency because it used the assumption of CRS and VRS within the same framework. Ray and Desli introduced a different decomposition by considering the VRS frontier as a benchmark technology. But the Ray and Desli's method of decomposition again is not a bias free decomposition because when one tries to approximate cross-period efficiency scores (calculated by comparing firm's actual output in period *t* with the maximum producible output from period t+1 by using the same input set) by considering a VRS technology, then infeasibilities for some observations may arise in the linear programming problem. Pastor et al. (2011) introduced a novel method of MPI which is generally acknowledged as the BMI. In their method, Pastor et al. used the decomposition procedure as introduced by Ray and Desli but they were able to solve the infeasibility problem which was the main drawback of the Ray-Desli decomposition of the Malmquist Index. Pastor et al. estimated the TE of a Decision-Making units (DMU) with the help of a biennial production possibility frontier instead of employing a contemporaneous production possibility frontier.

By considering the output-oriented TE scores with the assumption of a CRS biennial frontier, the BMI of the DMU which is producing a single output with the help of multiple inputs is calculated as follows: (Since the BMI of productivity uses the biennial CRS production possibility set, which takes into account the period t and t+1 sets, one need not to compute a 'geometric mean' of two productivity indexes while calculating it)

$$M_c^B\left(x_s^t,\, y_s^t;\, x_s^{t+1},\, y_s^{t+1}\right) = \frac{TE_c^B\left(x_s^{t+1},\, y_s^{t+1}\right)}{TE_c^B\left(x_s^t,\, y_s^t\right)} \tag{4.4}$$

BMI can be decomposed as

$$M_c^B\left(x_s^t,\, y_s^t;\, x_s^{t+1},\, y_s^{t+1}\right) = TEC\ X\ TC\ X\ SEC \tag{4.5}$$

Here

$$\text{TEC} = \frac{TE_v^{t+1}\left(x_s^{t+1},\, y_s^{t+1}\right)}{TE_v^t\left(x_s^t,\, y_s^t\right)}, \tag{4.6}$$

$$\text{TC} = \frac{TE_v^B\left(x_s^{t+1},\, y_s^{t+1}\right) / TE_v^{t+1}\left(x_s^{t+1},\, y_s^{t+1}\right)}{TE_v^B\left(x_s^t,\, y_s^t\right) / TE_v^t\left(x_s^t,\, y_s^t\right)}, \text{ and} \tag{4.7}$$

$$\text{SEC} = \frac{TE_c^B\left(x_s^{t+1},\, y_s^{t+1}\right) / TE_v^B\left(x_s^{t+1},\, y_s^{t+1}\right)}{TE_c^B\left(x_s^t,\, y_s^t\right) / TE_v^B\left(x_s^t,\, y_s^t\right)} \tag{4.8}$$

The suitable model of DEA for estimating TE of output-oriented type, $TE_c^B\left(x_s^t,\, y_s^t\right)$ of sth firm in period t, using biennial production possibility set following CRS is

$$\varphi_s^* = \max \varphi$$

Subject to $\sum_{k=t,\,t+1} \sum_{j=1}^{n_k} \lambda_j^k y_j^k \geq \varphi y_s^t;$

$$\sum_{k=t,\,t+1} \sum_{j=1}^{n_k} \lambda_j^k x_j^k \leq x_s^t;$$
$$\lambda_j^k \geq 0;$$

n_k is the number of observed firm in time k and $TE_c^B\left(x_s^t,\, y_s^t\right) = \frac{1}{\varphi_s^*}$

Output-oriented TE, $TE_v^B\left(x_s^t,\, y_s^t\right)$ of firm s in period t, with reference to a VRS biennial production possibility set is

$$\varphi_s^* = \max \varphi$$

$$\text{s. t.} \sum_{k=t,\,t+1} \sum_{j=1}^{n_k} \lambda_j^k y_j^k \geq \varphi y_s^t;$$
$$\sum_{k=t,\,t+1} \sum_{j=1}^{n_k} \lambda_j^k x_j^k \leq x_s^t;$$
$$\sum_{k=t,\,t+1} \sum_{j=1}^{n_k} \lambda_j^k = 1;$$

$\lambda_j^k \geq 0$; n_k is the number of observed firms in time k and $TE_c^B\left(x_s^t,\, y_s^t\right) = \frac{1}{\varphi_s^*}$

Determinants of TFPG: A Simultaneous Panel Regression

As the productivity act of IPI in diverse states does not at all times shift in the same lane and there is a significant disparity in TFPG across states over the years then it can be partially justified. After calculating TFPG, a regression analysis on TFPG values can help to identify factors that augment or deter it. This, in turn, becomes useful for academicians and policy makers for augmenting the TFPG of IPI. For determining the possible factors affecting difference in TFPG, an estimation method in a panel set up using state-level data over the period 1983–1984 to 2019–2020 has been used.

The variables considered as probable determinants of TFPG are firm size (MF), degree of mechanisation (K/L), composition of work force (E/L), market share (MS) and relative wage rate (W). The addition of the above-mentioned variables can be justified as below.

For firm size, one may think that larger firms may have better access to production opportunities and can be capable to exploit scale economies compared to smaller ones and hence can generate higher TFPG relative to smaller firms. So, it is checked here if the phenomenon is true for TFPG of firms in IPI, i.e. large sized firms are more productive than smaller size firms or not. On the other hand, as size is associated with market power (Shepherd, 1986) and market power encourages to improve X-inefficiencies, it can lead to relatively inferior performance (Leibenstein, 1966). As a result, theory does not offer any bias for bigger firm/smaller firm to boost up TFPG. The empirical literature survey on this issue recommend that the researches differ both with respect to choice of the variables describing firm size and the inference arrived at regarding the optimistic, pessimistic or zero effect of firm size on TFPG. The present chapter uses amount of intermediate inputs (I) measured by material and fuel consumed as measure of firm size in tune with Lundvall and Battese (2000). K/L acts as a technological variable and usually, affirmative association among K/L and TFPG is common (Ray (1997)) with the logic that capital-intensive technology or advanced technology will augment productivity growth by encouraging learning by doing. Whereas negative association between these two variables (Ahluwalia, 1991) is based on the argument that the industries with higher K/L were the heavy industries under the public sector which places barriers on the operation of these industries with its negative effect on productivity. E/L, also a technological variable, captures the composition of work force. A larger E/L generally signify more bureaucratic control inside the firm that can hinder productivity. There are economists who are the believers of over manning which resulted in fall in productivity like Ray (1997). In the background, non-production employees' recruitment is quite commonly a response to the political pressure to provide employment. These (political) employees are more probable to discourage productivity. This line of reasoning recommends a pessimistic association among E/L and TFPG. Whereas an optimistic association among E/L and TFPG signifies that the combination of work force is correct to operate efficiently and to enhance TFPG. It is quite interesting to check whether wage productivity relation holds in case of IPI or not. If relative wage rate is quite high for any industry then skilled workers want to enter that industry and considering skill as an encouraging factor of TFPG, it can be said that as W rises, through the skilled workers' involvement in the production technique, TFPG can rise. It can be further said that more the MS less is the rivalry. MS represents the effect of market structure on TFPG. A pessimistic relation among MS and TFPG may occur due to fall in MS, market rivalry rise can create cost-consciousness and drive for technological improvement. Other researchers can comment on the facility of large size, safe market and suggest an optimistic linkage among MS and TFPG. The inference from the empirical literature survey also differs and does not give us an unique answer (Katz, 1969; Kendrick, 1973).

Under a SUR structure, each regression is adjusted for both contemporaneous correlation and heteroscedasticity and regression is done in a panel set up.

A quite familiar problem may be that TFPG and MS might be reliant on each other, i.e. higher TFPG might be owing to higher MS and vice-versa. Thus, there is possibility of presence of simultaneity. The specified equation for MS is a function of relative wage rate, degree of mechanisation in the previous period and TFPG. The equation shows nonlinearity in TFPG and W.

Similarly, one may argue that with rise in W, more skilled workers can be employed in the production process, thereby increasing growth of output and hence MS. High K/L in the previous period may have some positive impact on degree of mechanisation in the current period leading to high MS. Increase in TFPG results in high MS may be by producing more with same inputs. The model is identified under the exclusion restriction.

An associated query may be that whether TFPG of IPI is influenced by trade variables. Thus ((X-M)/Y) is incorporated as a probable factor of TFPG along with other determinants mentioned before.

It is quite possible that TFPG and (X-M)/Y might be reliant on each other, i.e. more TFPG might be caused owing to more (X-M)/Y or the other way round.

For that reason, a panel model in a simultaneous set up has been formed with three equations: TFPG, MS along with net export intensity which are shown below in equations (4.9), (4.10) and (4.11), respectively.

$$TFPG = f\begin{bmatrix} MF,\ \frac{K}{L},\ \frac{E}{L},\ MS,\ W,\ \frac{(X-M)}{Y}, \\ (MF)^2,\ \left(\frac{K}{L}\right)^2,\ \left(\frac{E}{L}\right)^2,\ (MS)^2,\ W^2,\ \left(\frac{X-M}{Y}\right)^2 \end{bmatrix} \tag{4.9}$$

$$MS = f\begin{bmatrix} W,\ \left(\frac{K}{L}\right)_{t-1},\ TFPG,\ \frac{(X-M)}{Y},\ TFPG^2, \\ TFPG{*}W,\ TFPG{*}W^2,\ TFPG^2{*}\frac{(X-M)}{Y} \end{bmatrix} \tag{4.10}$$

$$\frac{(X-M)}{Y} = f\begin{pmatrix} TFPG,\ REER,\ REER_{t-1},\ MS,\ REER^2,\ TFPG{*}MS, \\ TFPG^2{*}MS,\ TFPG{*}REER,\ TFPG{*}REER^2 \end{pmatrix} \tag{4.11}$$

For the methodology for Panel Structural Break see Chapter 3, Subsection 3.2.3.

4.2.2. Data

The secondary data employed in this study are gross value of output (Y), number of workers (L), capital, materials consumed, fuels consumed, employees other than workers and Wage of 17 major selected states [Andhra Pradesh (AP), Assam (AS), Bihar (BI), Gujarat (GU), Haryana (HA), Himachal Pradesh (HP), Jammu & Kashmir (JK), Karnataka (KA), Kerala (KE), Maharashtra (MH), Madhya Pradesh (MP), Orissa (OR), Punjab (PU), Rajasthan (RA), Tamil Nadu (TN),Uttar Pradesh (UP) and West Bengal (WB)] of India over the period 1983–1984 to 2019–2020. Relevant figures are deflated by appropriate price indexes. Also, data on number of workers and wage of all India manufacturing industry has been used to construct relative wage rate. Data are obtained from Annual Survey of Industries (ASI), Summary Results for Factory Sector. Data on export of drugs, pharmaceuticals and fine chemicals and Import of Medicinal & pharmaceutical products at All India level are collected from Foreign Trade Statistics of India. Data on price indices are obtained from the Index Number of Wholesale Prices in India. Unit value index of medicinal & pharmaceutical products are provided by Directorate General of Commercial Intelligence and Statistics. Real effective exchange rate data has been collected from Handbook of Statistics on Indian Economy, RBI. The period of analysis is from 1983–1984 to 2019–2020. Computation of state-level data on export and import is discussed in Appendix 2.

4.3. Result of Estimation

This chapter assesses the performance of IPI for 17 major selected states of India considering the period 1983–1984 to 2019–2020. The chapter explores two different aspects, i.e. TE and TFPG of pharmaceutical industries of India using state-level data. The findings of the present chapter can be discussed under two heads: in Section 4.3.1, the results of TE of Indian states are discussed and Subsection 4.3.2 presents the results of TFPG of Indian states.

4.3.1. Results of TE of Indian States

The output-oriented TE using state-level data are estimated using DEA approach considering each state as a decision-making unit. Then the factors influencing such TE are determined. TE is estimated by using BCC model of DEA employing computer programme solver in Excel. Two-stage least square methodology under panel regression are employed to identify factors that enhance or hinder TE. For that STATA 15 program was used.

The possible sources of variation of efficiency score are found out taking into account the simultaneity problem and considering MF, K/L, E/L, W and (X-M)/Y as possible determinants.

The major findings related to TE, could be listed as follows:

First, the average TE of all states taken together is found to be 0.72, implying efficiency level is moderate, on average the industry produces 72% of the maximum producible output.

Secondly, mean TE values of all the 17 major selected states reveal that there is ample difference in TE score amongst the states, the highest being achieved by Maharashtra and the lowest is for Bihar.

The results can be found in Table 4.1. The mean TE of all the states taken together as well the mean TE values of all the 17 major selected states are demonstrated in Fig. 4.1.

Finally, the results of determinants of TE show that all the factors considered such as MF, K/L, E/L and W are found to be statistically significant. All the variables MF, K/L, E/L and W are positively related except the degree of mechanisation (K/L) which is negatively related. TE increases with large sized firms who are

Table 4.1. Estimated values of TE.

State	Mean TE	State	Mean TE
AP	0.72743	MH	0.84171
AS	0.69396	MP	0.7424
BI	0.3503	OR	0.67956
GU	0.78374	PU	0.74283
HA	0.77797	RA	0.68313
HP	0.79737	TN	0.7308
JK	0.52875	UP	0.78089
KA	0.8382	WB	0.76236
KE	0.82353	AVERAGE	0.722645

technically efficient, may be owing to easier right to use to better quality inputs and gain from economic advantages to manufacture larger value of output. A rise in K/L encourages a smaller efficiency might be owing to limitations in the management of more capitalistic and sophisticated technology. It might also be likely that Indian pharmaceuticals have installed fresh plant and machinery in recent times. Such investment might have been done keeping future opportunities in mind and at present these capitals are not fully utilised (Mazumder et al., 2010). The appropriate combination of workforce will promote the industry to operate efficiently. An increase in W fosters TE, since with high W, trained workers are occupied in the production method thus serving to realise high TE. Added to that net export intensity will have a favourable impact on TE. An increase in net export intensity may lead to an increase in TE due to economies of scale, knowledge spill-over from international contacts and spill-over effects from technology diffusion. The results of the determinant analysis can be found in Tables 4.2 and 4.3.

4.3.2 Results of TFPG of Indian States

TFPG is estimated using state-level data using DEA approach considering each state as a decision-making unit. Then the factors influencing such TFPG are determined. TFPG is estimated by using BMI of DEA employing a computer programme solver in Excel. Two-stage least square methodology under panel regression is employed to identify factors that enhance or hinder TFPG using STATA 15 software.

The factors that are considered as possible causes of TFPG are firm size (MF), degree of mechanisation (K/L), composition of workforce (E/L), MS, relative wage rate (W) and net export intensity (X-M)/Y taking into account the simultaneity problem as before. The variables considered are in growth terms.

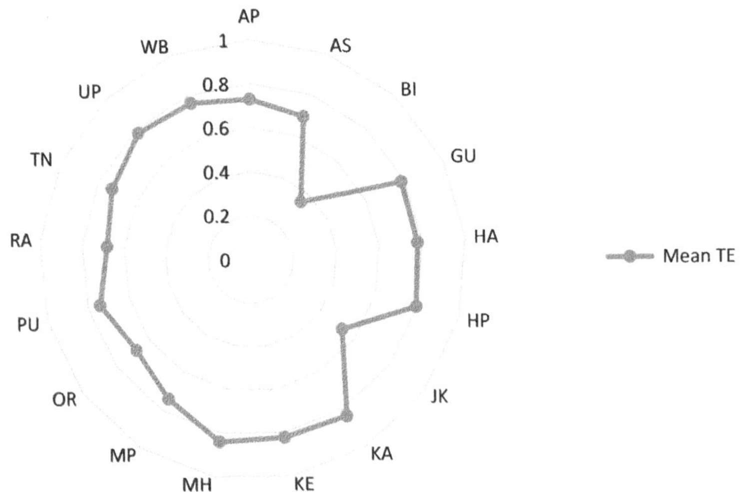

Fig. 4.1. Mean Efficiency Statewise.

Table 4.2. Estimated Results of Simultaneous Equation Model: The Case of TE Equation.

Variable	Coefficient	*t* ratio	Variables	Marginal Effects
Constant	−3.2974***	−7.834792	MF	0.00092
LnMF	0.09818***	15.698982	K/L	−0.1188
LnK/L	−0.03189***	−7.031877	E/L	0.21316
LnE/L	0.008638***	4.008645	W	0.02446
LnW	0.413555***	5.413123	(X−M)/Y	0.00966
Ln(X−M)/Y	0.000559***	4.000560		
(LnMF)2	−0.000018***	−16.13006		
(LnK/L)2	−0.1399 ***	−10.46692		
(LnE/L)2	−0.24305***	−7.403782		
(LnW)2	−0.000886	−0.000886		
(Ln(X−M)/Y)2	−0.000032***	−3.131530		
LnMFLnK/L	0.760284***	11.291999		
LnK/L LnE/L	0.206201***	4.307128		
LnE/LLn(X−M)/Y	−0.9872***	−6.667701		
LnMFLnE/L	−0.013633	−0.276120		
LnMFLn(X−M)/Y	0.000882***	3.000882		
LnK/LLn(X−M)/Y	−0.042254	−0.042253		
LnMFLnW	−0.000058**	−2.000058		
LnK/LLnW	−0.255495	−0.255393		
LnE/LLnW	−0.00036***	−9.000360		
Ln(X-M)/YLnW	−0.179365	−0.270221		
Adjusted *R*-squared	0.9266			

Note: *** and ** imply significant at 1% and 5% level of significance, respectively.

Regarding productivity issues, the results may be summed up as below:

First, the mean TFPG of all the states altogether is found to be 0.13.

Secondly, mean TFPG values of all the 17 major selected states reveal that there is wide variation in TE score among the states, ranging from 0.0001 to 0.78.

The results can be found in Table 4.4.

Results of Determinant Analysis of TFPG

Finally, the results of determinants of TFPG show that MF, K/L, E/L, MS and W have favourable effects on TFPG. Also, the variables are statistically significant. Large sized units may become more productive compared to smaller ones, having better access to production opportunities, due to usage of new technologies and also can utilise economies of scale. Enhancement of K/L induces higher growth in productivity by encouraging learning by doing. The relation between E/L and TFPG is positive which shows that the right combination of work force can operate production efficiently and thus boost up TFPG.

Table 4.3. Estimated Results of Simultaneous Equation Model: The Case of Net Export Intensity Equation.

Variable	Coefficient	t–Statistic	VARIABLES	MARGINAL EFFECTS
C	−0.244037 ***	−2.9368	M_{TE}	0.3267
TE	0.2949697 ***	9.246393	M_{REER}	0.2787
MF	0.281615***	53.91305	M_{MF}	0.00289
$\frac{K}{L}$	0.5068772 ***	9.998985	$M_{K/L}$	0.01489
$\frac{E}{L}$	0.1566349 ***	5.472021	$M_{E/L}$	1.2722
REER	0.072342***	5.73748		
MF^2	−0.000515 ***	−43.4904		
$(K/L)^2$	−0.446784 ***	−6.88991		
$(E/L)^2$	−0.845347 ***	−5.13895		
$REER^2$	−0.00033***	−6.93547		
Adjusted R-squared	0.971766			

Note: *** implies significant at 1% level of significance.

Table 4.4. Results of Estimated values of TFPG.

State	Mean TFPG	State	Mean TFPG
AP	0.2629	MH	0.1867
AS	0.1724	MP	0.0249
BI	0.2208	OR	0.0001
GU	0.0172	PU	0.0618
HA	0.0093	RA	0.1099
HP	0.0380	TN	0.0153
JK	0.7892	UP	0.0220
KA	0.3283	WB	0.0588
KE	0.0044		

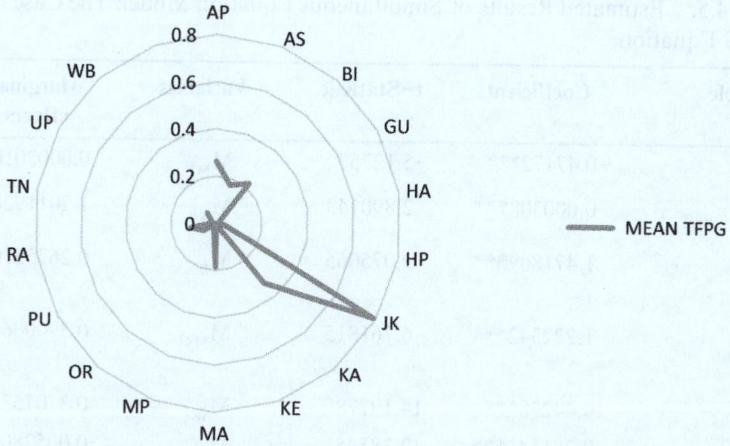

Fig. 4.2. Mean TFPG Statewise

Producing units having high MS experience a bigger and secured market and also face lesser competition. As a result, productivity may rise. A higher number of skilled workers in the production process can be involved by raising W leading to higher TFPG. In addition to it, variable (X-M/Y) also boosts up TFPG. With increase in (X-M)/Y, TFPG increases might be owing to the change in the frontier for the reason that of knowledge spill-over from the international contacts and spill-overs from technology diffusion.

The results of the determinant analysis can be found in Tables 4.5–4.7.

Results of Panel Structural Break Analysis

In case of export, there exists one-time structural break in the series as is evident from Table 4.8. The break point is 2004 in case of TFPG at state level. If we test the first hypothesis, i.e., H_0: no breaks versus H_1: s breaks then from the results one can conclude that existence of one-time break is very much supported by the results. Now if we run the second hypothesis, i.e. H_0: no breaks versus H_1: $1 \leq s \leq s_{max}$ breaks then from the results one can conclude that maximum number of breaks is one. Finally, for the third hypothesis, i.e. H_0: s breaks versus H_1: $s + 1$ breaks from the results one can conclude that null hypothesis is fail to accept against alternative hypothesis, i.e. there exists one-time breaks in the series of TFPG at state level. One of the possible reason for this break may be that IPI has experienced a massive transformation – from 'process patents regime' in the seventies to a modern and World Trade Organization (WTO) compatible regime under the TRIPS Agreement in 2005. The rank of IPI is 3rd in volume and 14th in value in the global pharmaceutical market (Kalani, 2011). Since 2005, India has started full-fledged product patent regime in pharmaceuticals and are to develop new drugs themselves or to collaborate with the MNCs as manufacturing or marketing partners for the new drugs developed by the MNCs (Chaudhuri, 2005).

Table 4.5. Estimated Results of Simultaneous Equation Model: The Case of TFPG Equation.

Variable	Coefficient	t−Statistic	Variables	Marginal effects
C	−0.47172***	−5.12757	M_{MF}	0.00030100
MF	0.000308***	2.890143	$M_{K/L}$	1.20119200
$\frac{K}{L}$	1.471809***	9.075065	$M_{E/L}$	0.26755100
$\frac{E}{L}$	1.222342***	6.761815	M_{MS}	0.39000600
MS	0.44238***	14.19778	M_W	0.37075300
W	0.381143***	12.38545	$M_{(X-M)/Y}$	0.00528000
$\frac{(X-M)}{Y}$	0.005739***	6.327378		
MF^2	−3.12E−08	−0.90097		
$(K/L)^2$	−1.59023***	−8.73598		
$(E/L)^2$	−0.74976***	−6.40796		
MS^2	−0.30935***	−12.7675		
W^2	−0.00509***	−4.96239		
$((X-M))/Y^2$	−9.81E−06***	−2.73153		
Adjusted R-squared	0.968748			

Note: *** implies significant at 1% of significance.

Table 4.6. Estimated Results of Simultaneous Equation Model: The Case of Market Share Equation.

Variable	Coefficient	t−Statistic	Variables	Marginal effects
C	−0.00566	−0.65646	M_W	0.0318770
W	0.019823***	3.513325	M_{TFPG}	0.0402000
$\left(\frac{K}{L}\right)t-1$	0.02759***	4.979795	$M_{(X-M)/Y}$	0.0029900
$TFPG$	0.105198***	9.571205		

Table 4.6. (*Continued*)

Variable	Coefficient	*t*−Statistic	Variables	Marginal effects
$\frac{(X-M)}{Y}$	0.002985***	32.58295		
$TFPG^2$	−0.00562	−0.68471		
$TFPG * W$	−0.05524***	−6.60689		
$TFPG * W^2$	−0.00985***	−5.08071		
$TFPG^2 * \frac{(X-M)}{Y}$	1.45E−05	0.35045		
Adjusted *R*-squared	0.983346			

Note: ***implies significant at 1% level of significance.

Table 4.7. Estimated Results of Simultaneous Equation Model: The Case of Net Export Intensity Equation.

Variable	Coefficient	*t*-Statistic	Variables	Marginal Effects
C	58.61867***	2.849979	M_{TFPG}	0.2308
TFPG	126.2681***	2.480669	M_{REER}	1.12772
REER	−1.51961***	−4.04262	M_{MS}	0.6381
$REER_{t-1}$	0.800135***	3.373135		
MS	247.5058***	22.7001		
$REER^2$	0.07588***	4.954225		
$TFPG * MS$	−188.331***	−5.07999		
$TFPG^2 * MS$	−156.323***	−6.48732		
$TFPG * REER$	−2.00723***	−2.41746		
$TFPG * REER^2$	0.02657*	1.905969		
Adjusted *R*-squared	0.96825			

Note: ***and * imply significant at 1% and 10% level of significance, respectively.

Table 4.8. Results of Panel Structural Break in TFPG at State Level.

Sequential test for multiple breaks at unknown breakpoints
(Ditzen, Karavias & Westerlund. 2021)

Bai & Perron Critical Values

	Test Statistic	1% Critical Value	5% Critical Value	10% Critical Value
$F(1\|0)$	19.88	12.29	8.58	7.04
$F(2\|1)$	1.29	13.89	10.13	8.51
$F(3\|2)$	0.21	14.80	11.14	9.41
$F(4\|3)$	0.02	15.28	11.83	10.04
$F(5\|4)$	0.02	15.76	12.25	10.58
Detected number of breaks:		1	1	1

Maximum number of breaks reached with null always rejected.

Estimation of break points

$N = 17$
$T = 25$
$SSR = 37.64$
Trimming = 0.15

#	Index	Date	[95% Conf. Interval]	
1	**22**	**2004**	**2001**	**2007**

Test for multiple breaks at known breakdates
(Karavias, Narayan & Westerlund. 2021)
$H0$: no break(s) vs. $H1$: 1 break(s)

Bai & Perron Critical Values

	Test Statistic	1% Critical Value	5% Critical Value	10% Critical Value
supW(tau)	19.88	12.29	8.58	7.04

Estimated break points: 2004
Trimming: 0.15

Test for multiple breaks at known breakdates
(Karavias, Narayan & Westerlund. 2021)
$H0$: no break(s) vs. $H1$: $1 <= s <= 1$ break(s)

Bai & Perron Critical Values				
	Test Statistic	**1% Critical Value**	**5% Critical Value**	**10% Critical Value**
UDmax(tau)	19.88	12.37	8.88	7.46

* evaluated at a level of 0.95.
Trimming: 0.15

Test for multiple breaks at unknown breakpoints
(Ditzen, Karavias & Westerlund. 2021)
*H*0: 0 vs. *H*1: 1 break(s)

Bai & Perron Critical Values				
	Test Statistic	**1% Critical Value**	**5% Critical Value**	**10% Critical Value**
F(s+1|s)*	19.88	12.29	8.58	7.04

* $s = 0$
Trimming: 0.15

4.4. Conclusion

The present chapter investigates the performance of IPI employing data on major states of India. This chapter helps to compare the Indian states as well as to identify the position of states in the context of IPI.

The major findings of the present chapter on TE are that, the average TE of all the states altogether found to be 0.72, implying efficiency level is moderate, on average the industry produces 72% of the maximum producible output. The mean TE value shows that there is large difference in TE score among the 17 major selected states. The results of determinants of TE shows that all the factors considered such as MF, K/L, E/L and W are found to be statistically significant and positive except degree of mechanisation (K/L) which is negatively related. The positive or negative relation between the explanatory variable and the dependent variable is evident from the sign of the average elasticity of TE with respect to the determinants. TE increases with large sized firms who are technically efficient, might be owing to easier right to use to better quality inputs and gain from economic advantages to produce higher value of output. A rise in K/L induces a smaller efficiency might be owing to limitations in the supervision of added capitalistic and sophisticated technology. Appropriate combination of work force will promote the industry to operate efficiently. Increase in W fosters TE, as with high W, skilled workers are occupied into the production procedure thus serving to attain high TE. Added to that net export intensity have a favourable impact on TE. As a consequence, the study reveals that in order to encourage TE, any policy changes that will direct to enlarge in firm size, right composition of work force, increase in relative wage rate and increase in net export intensity should be emphasised.

The major findings of the present chapter on TFPG are that first, there is wide variation in TFPG values among the states. Large sized units may become more productive compared to smaller ones, having better access to production opportunities, due to usage of new technologies and also can utilise economies of scale. Enhancement of K/L induces higher growth in productivity by encouraging learning by doing. The relation between E/L and TFPG is positive which shows that the right combination of workforce can operate production efficiently and thus boost up TFPG. Producing units having high MS experience a bigger and secured market and also face lesser competition. As a result, productivity may rise. A higher number of skilled workers in the production process can be involved by raising W leading to higher TFPG. (X-M/Y) also found to boost up TFPG. With increase in (X-M/Y), TFPG may rise might be owing to the shift in the frontier for the reason that of knowledge spill over from the international contacts and spill-overs from technology diffusion.

Thus, the analysis reveals that for fostering TFPG, any policy changes that will direct to enhance in MF, K/L, E/L, increase in relative wage rate, high MS and increase in net export intensity should be emphasised.

The break point is 2004 in case of TFPG at the state level. One of the possible reasons for this break may be that IPI has experienced a massive transformation – from 'process patents regime' in the seventies to a modern and WTO-compatible regime under the TRIPS Agreement in 2005. The ranking of IPI is 3rd in volume and 14th in value in the global pharmaceutical market (Kalani, 2011). Since 2005, India has started a full-fledged product patent regime in pharmaceuticals and is to develop new drugs themselves or to collaborate with the MNCs as manufacturing or marketing partners for the new drugs developed by the MNCs (Chaudhuri, 2005).

Chapter 5

Total Factor Productivity Convergence in Pharmaceutical Industry Across Indian States

Abstract

The present chapter tries to understand whether the total factor productivity (TFP) of the pharmaceutical industry across the 17 major states of India converges or not in terms of sigma and beta convergence over the period 1983–1984 to 2019–2020 by employing the conventional sigma convergence as well as the modern panel data approach of beta convergence. The novelty of the present chapter is that TFP is found by estimating production function by a semi-parametric approach which addresses the endogeneity problem. Then it is checked whether the series of TFP of Pharmaceutical Industries across the major selected states of India converges or not employing the sigma convergence and beta convergence hypothesis having a balanced panel with 476 observations. The empirical result suggests sigma divergence but beta convergence based on all the available panel unit root tests. Beta convergence is also confirmed by the tests based on dynamic panel models of the first differenced generalised method of moments (GMM) and system GMM.

Keywords: Total factor productivity; Indian pharmaceutical industry; semi-parametric; endogeneity; sigma convergence; beta convergence; panel unit root tests; dynamic panel; generalised method of moments

Performance Analysis of the Indian Pharmaceutical Industry: A Global Outlook, 109–118

doi:10.1108/978-1-83797-743-720251005

5.1. Introduction

To achieve steady growth over the years, any industry needs to improve cost-competitiveness by encouraging total factor productivity (TFP). TFP measures the amount of increase in total output which is not accounted for the increase in total inputs and thus measures the shift in output due to the shift in the production function over time, holding all inputs constant (Abramovitz, 1956; Denison, 1962, 1967, 1985; Hayami et al., 1979).

In the case of Indian industries, the evidence suggests that Indian Government policies mainly after 1994 became less friendly to less productive firms. Thus for growth or even for mere survival, improved performance of the industrial firms and increase in productivity is required. Along with it, for the Indian Pharmaceutical Industry (IPI), the provision of pharmaceutical goods at an affordable price is a major concern. Naturally, the measurement of productivity changes in IPI is of great interest, both academically as well as for policy outlook.

The literature suggests different ways of estimating TFP growth: (i) Growth Accounting Approach (GAA) [i.e. by constructing either Solow Index (Solow, 1957), or Kendrick Index (Kendrick, 1956, 1961, 1973) or Translog-Divisia Index (Christensen & Jorgenson, 1969, 1970; Jorgenson & Griliches, 1967; Solow, 1957)]. (ii) Econometric (Parametric) Approach i.e. by estimating production function or cost function. An example of parametric method can be found in Kumbhakar et al. (1999, 2000), Kumbhakar and Lovell (2000), among others. (iii) Non-parametric Approach (i.e. through Data Envelopment Analysis [DEA]) (Ray, 2004 among others) and (iv) Semi-parametric Approach, i.e. by estimating production function with correction for endogeneity – Levinsohn Petrin (LP, 2003).

A huge amount of literature exists around the globe dealing with the estimation of TFP growth of manufacturing industries for India as well as for other countries considering different time periods and using different methodologies.[1] In the context of IPI, studies on TFP growth are very few in number and they mostly commented on productivity changes at the firm level or All India level. Some worth mentioning studies on the productivity of IPI are due to Saranga and Banker (2010), Pannu et al. (2010), Kamiike et al. (2012), Ghose and Chakraborty (2012) among others. These studies have mostly used non-parametric method for estimation of TFPG except Kamiike et al. (2012) and Ghose and Chakraborty (2012) who have employed parametric techniques to find out the TFPG of IPI.

There is dearth in the literature studying TFP of IPI using semi-parametric approach by addressing the issue of endogeneity problem while estimating production function for calculating TFP using state-level data.

---

[1]Siggel (1992), Kumbhakar et al. (1999), Kumbhakar et al. (2000), Felipe and McCombie (2001), Mahadevan (2002), Kumbhakar (2003), Kruger (2003), Sun (2007), Oh et al. (2008), etc. Studies on TFPG relating to India can be found in Hashim and Dadi (1973), Banerjee (1975), Ahluwalia (1991), Madheswaran et al. (2007), Ghose and Roy Biswas (2012) among others.

The present chapter adds to the literature in this direction by estimating the TFP of pharmaceutical industries in the major selected states using semi-parametric estimation technique which addresses the endogeneity problem.

A related problem is the issue of convergence in terms of productivity growth in the selected states, i.e. whether a poor state tends to catch up to rich ones in terms of TFP ensuring steady growth of the pharmaceutical industry over the years at the state level.

Since each state have individual characteristics, their performance does not show a uniform picture. This makes it evident that one should not hope to discover much homogeneity among the Indian states. Keeping this in mind, we proceed to investigate the convergence question in pharmaceutical industries across the major selected states of India.

Since the seminal works of Barro & Sala-i-Martin (1992) and Mankiw et al. (1992), the empirical literature on the convergence hypothesis of neoclassical growth of income and consumption has developed substantially. There are two basic concepts of convergence viz. 'sigma convergence' and 'beta convergence'. The 'sigma convergence' occurs if the dispersion of per capita economic levels (in logarithmic values) represented by income, consumption, or output across a group of economies or regions declines over time. Whereas the 'beta convergence' is satisfied when a poor economy/region tends to grow faster than the rich one, and this convergence is obtained if the regression of average (over a period of time) income/output growth on initial income/output level has a significant negative slope coefficient.

It may be remarkable to note that evidence for convergence of economic growth in terms of these two concepts is not necessarily identical in case of many countries for which such studies have been undertaken. For example, for the USA, many studies such as those by Evans and Karras (1996a, 1996b), Sala-i-Martin (1996), and Evans (1997a, 1997b) found beta convergence in per capita log income among the states of the USA whereas Tsionas (2000) found that sigma convergence does not hold for the US states over different periods. It is also essential to note that the classical approach to convergence based on cross-country regression came under criticism by Quah (1993), Quah (1996), and Bernard and Durlauf (1996). Quah (1993) pointed out that the convergence hypothesis must incorporate the time series properties of the cross-country variances. Quah (1994) and Evans and Karras (1996) developed a formal panel unit root test for evaluating the convergence hypothesis.

The survey of literature suggests that there is large heterogeneity in convergence across industries; resulting in some industries managing to converge while the others do not.[2] Several studies on the OECD countries have shown stronger convergence patterns across service sectors but not in manufacturing industries (Bernard & Jones, 1996), while more recent industry-level studies on wider countries coverage, including developing nations, found that manufacturing industries, but not services, exhibit strong unconditional convergence (Rodrik, 2011).

---

[2]Bernard and Jones (1996), Madden and Savage (1999), Sorensen (2001), Calabrese et al. (2010), Rodrik (2011), Moshi (2013) among others.

There is dearth in the literature regarding studies on convergence using pharmaceutical industry data and also employing the modern panel data approach for convergence hypothesis especially the dynamic panel approach.

The novelty of the present chapter is that after finding the TFP of IPI by estimating production function by a semi-parametric approach which addresses the endogeneity problem, the major objective is to understand the convergence of TFP across states of India employing the sigma convergence hypothesis as well as beta convergence hypothesis using the balanced panel.

The format of the present chapter is as follows: Section 5.2 presents the methodology and data sources. Section 5.3 presents the result of analysis. Section 5.4 summarises the conclusion of this study.

5.2. Methodology and Data Source

5.2.1. Methodology

This section is discussed under two heads; in Subsection 5.2.1.1, the methodology for estimation of TFP using data on Indian states is discussed. Subsection 5.2.1.2 presents the different approaches used to study convergence in terms of TFP of pharmaceutical industries across the major Indian states.

5.2.1.1. Methodology for Estimation of TFP

TFP is estimated for the sample states, considering each state as a producing unit, by estimating production function considering three inputs – labour (*L*), capital (*K*), and material & fuel consumed (*MF*).

The TFP of a producing unit is defined as:

$$\mathrm{TFP}_{it} = \frac{Y_{it}}{X_{1it}^{\widehat{\beta_1}} X_{2it}^{\widehat{\beta_2}}} \tag{5.1}$$

where X_1 and X_2 are the inputs.

The following Cobb–Douglas specification has been estimated:

$$\ln Y = a_0 + a_L \ln L + a_K \ln K + a_{MF} \ln MF + u \tag{5.2}$$

For estimating the production function, semi-parametric estimation technique proposed by Levinsohn and Petrin (2003) which addresses the endogeneity problem has been employed.

5.2.1.2. Methodology for Studying Convergence of TFPG

The different approaches used to study the convergence of TFP of pharmaceutical industries across the states of India can be discussed under the following heads:

5.2.1.2.1. Tests for Absolute Convergence (Sigma Convergence). The well-known concept in case of absolute convergence is sigma convergence.

This convergence (divergence) in terms of TFP is said to exist if the dispersion of logarithmic values of TFP across the states follows a downward (upward) trend. Usually, standard deviation (SD) and coefficient of variation (COV) are used as measures of dispersion.

The econometric models considered for testing sigma convergence are the following:

$$SD_t = a_0 + a_1 t + e_{1t} \tag{5.3}$$

$$COV_t = b_0 + b_1 t + e_{2t} \tag{5.4}$$

Here the error terms, e_{1t} and e_{2t} are assumed to be white noise with zero mean and constant variances. In models (5.3) and (5.4), the null hypothesis (H_0) of no sigma convergence suggests a_1=0 and b_1=0 respectively, while statistically significant negative (positive) values of the coefficients of time denote absolute convergence (divergence) for the respective models under the alternative hypothesis.

However, one major drawback of sigma convergence is that it does not include any dynamic consideration.

5.2.1.2.2. Tests for Beta Convergence. The existing literature suggests different approaches for testing beta convergence such as (a) Convergence hypothesis using panel unit root tests, (b) Convergence hypothesis using Arellano-Bond dynamic panel data estimation and (c) Convergence hypothesis using System dynamic panel data estimation.

(a) Convergence hypothesis using panel unit root tests

The beta convergence is the main focus in the literature on empirical growth. Panel unit root tests have been used in several recent studies for understanding beta convergence instead of cross-section methodology as the latter compromises on the time series properties of the cross-section variances (Das & Bhattacharya, 2008; Evans & Karras, 1996; Quah, 1994).

Let $\widetilde{y_{it}} = y_{it} - \overline{y_t}$ is the deviation from cross-state average of log of TFPG in the ith state for the tth period, where $\overline{y_t} = \frac{1}{n}\sum y_{it}$, the convergence hypothesis implies the following (Evans and Karras (1996)):

$$\lim_{j \to \infty} E_t\left(\widetilde{y_{i,t+j}}\right) = \mu_t$$

Here μ_t is the state-specific parameter determining the level of ith state's parallel growth path. The above condition holds if and only if $\left\{\widetilde{y_i}\right\}$ is stationary. Now, in case μ_t is zero, the convergence will be stated to be absolute.

Though Quah (1994) first developed the panel unit root test for convergence but this test could not be used in case both individual and time specific effects are included (see Maddala & Kim, 1998). Therefore, the exhaustive panel unit root test as suggested by Levin et al. (2002), i.e. LLC test have been considered in the present chapter. LLC consider the following ADF specification:

$$\Delta Y_{it} = \alpha_i + \rho Y_{it-1} + \Sigma \varnothing_k \Delta Y_{it-k} + \delta_i t + \theta_i + u_{it} \tag{5.5}$$

It allows for two-way fixed effects (one coming from α_i and the second from the θ_t, i.e. the intercept varies over states as well as time) and unit-specific time trends (δ_i). In the regression equation (5.5), α_i and θ_t are basically (i-1) states dummies and (t-1) time dummies respectively. The coefficient of lagged Y_i is restricted to be homogeneous across all units of the panel. The null (H_0) and alternative (H_1) being $H_0 : \rho = 0$ and $H_1 : \rho < 0$.

IPS (2003) extended the LLC test allowing heterogeneity on the coefficient of the $Y_{i,t-1}$ variable proposing a test procedure based on the average of the individual unit-root test statistics and estimated the following model:

$$\Delta Y_{it} = \alpha_i + \rho Y_{it-1} + \Sigma \varnothing_k \Delta Y_{it-k} + \delta_i t + \theta_i + u_{it} \tag{5.6}$$

With $H_0 : \rho_i = 0$ for all i and $H_1 : \rho_i < 0$ for at least one i. The corresponding $\bar{t}$ statistic, applicable to a balanced panel only, is defined as $\bar{t} = \frac{1}{N}\sum_{i=1}^{N} t_{\rho i}$, where $t_{\rho i}$ is individual ADF t-statistic for testing $H_0 : \rho_i = 0$ for all i. Schwarz (1978) criterion for the lag differences selection and the Newey-West 1994 method and the Bartlett Karnel for the bandwidth selection are used.

Another test has been proposed by Maddala and Wu (1999) which is originally due to Fisher. Maddala and Wu (1999) compared the power of the LLC, IPS and the Fisher test and suggested that in a wide number of situations, the Fisher test is more powerful than the IPS or LLC tests.

The growing literature suggests that the conventional assumption of cross-sectional independence of disturbances for the panel unit root tests may not be appropriate (Pesaran, 2004, Baltagi, 2005, Breitung & Das, 2005), Levin et al. (2002) argued that the demeaned series satisfies this cross-sectional independence. In view of that the present chapter has also considered the demeaned series of panel unit root tests.

(b) Convergence hypothesis using Arellano-Bond dynamic panel data estimation

Arellano and Bond (1991) derived consistent estimators for the dynamic panel model based on generalised method of moments (GMM) of the first differenced values.

The model is as below:

$$\begin{aligned} &\ln Y_{it} - \ln Y_{it-1} = \mu_t + \beta \ln Y_{it-1} + v_{it} \\ &\text{Or } \ln Y_{it} = \mu_t + \beta^* \ln Y_{it-1} + v_{it} \end{aligned} \tag{5.7}$$

where $\beta^* = 1 + \beta$

The GMM first differenced takes the following form:

$$\Delta \ln Y_{it} = \beta^* \ln Y_{it-1} + v_{it} \tag{5.8}$$

The beta convergence hypothesis holds when $\beta^*<1$.

(c) Convergence hypothesis using System dynamic panel data estimation

As the GMM estimator based on the first difference suffers from the problem of weak correlations between the growth rate of the variable (Y) and the lagged (log) Y, the system GMM estimator has been subsequently developed by Bond and Blundell (1998), which represents a significant improvement over the former.

Equation (5.8) along with equation (5.7) constitutes the system GMM.

It is assumed that $E(v_{it}, v_{is}) = 0$, for $i = 1, 2, 3, \ldots, n$; $t \neq s$ and $E(y_{it}, v_{is})=0$ for $T=3,4,\ldots,T$; $s \geq 2$

The beta convergence hypothesis holds when $\beta^*<1$.

5.2.2. The Data

The secondary data employed in this study are obtained from the Annual Survey of Industries (ASI), Summary Results for the Factory Sector published by the Central Statistics Office, Government of India. The variables used are gross value of output; number of workers; fixed capital; materials consumed and fuels consumed covering the period 1983–1984 to 2019–2020. Relevant figures are deflated by appropriate price indices. The 17 sample states are Andhra Pradesh, Assam, Bihar, Gujarat, Haryana, Himachal Pradesh, Jammu and Kashmir, Karnataka, Kerala, Madhya Pradesh, Maharashtra, Orissa, Punjab, Rajasthan, Tamil Nadu, Uttar Pradesh and West Bengal.

5.3. Empirical Findings

5.3.1. Results of Estimation of TFP

For estimating the Cobb–Douglas production function, a semi-parametric estimation technique proposed by Levinsohn and Petrin (2003) which takes care of the endogeneity problem has been employed. The production function is estimated considering three inputs – labour, capital and material & fuel consumed. It is found that all the three estimated coefficients are positive and statistically significant at 1% level of significance. The sum of the coefficients as obtained is slightly higher than unity. The Wald test fails to reject the null hypothesis of constant returns to scale. Thus econometric estimation of Cobb–Douglas production function has been done satisfactorily. Hence for calculating TFP, the values of the estimated coefficients of the three inputs, labour, capital and material & fuel consumed, are employed.

5.3.2. Results on Tests of Convergence

5.3.2.1. Findings on Sigma Convergence

The estimated equations show that the coefficients of trend of both the SD and COV in equations (5.5) and (5.6) are positive and statistically significant. The result is presented in Tables 5.1 and 5.2 respectively.

The observation, therefore, is that the TFP show significant sigma divergence across the Indian states.

5.3.2.2. Findings on Beta Convergence

5.3.2.2.1. Results of Panel Unit Root Tests. The results of panel unit root tests proposed by LLC, IPS, ADF-Fisher and PP-Fisher are presented in Table 5.3. In case of LLC test, the coefficient of the lagged dependent variable is found to be negative in sign and statistically significant; it implies beta convergence for the series of (logarithm) of TFP of all the major Indian states to the all-India average. Exactly the same conclusion on the stationarity of the demeaned series has been obtained by the other tests such as IPS, ADF-Fisher and PP-Fisher, i.e. the coefficient of the lagged dependent variable is negative and statistically significant.

Table 5.1. Result of Trend Equation of SD.

Variable	Coefficient	*t* Statistic	Prob.
C	−4.7069	−6.45735	0
Ln $Y_{\text{it}-1}$	0.34537	7.68928	0

Table 5.2. Result of Trend Equation of COV.

Variable	Coefficient	*t* Statistic	Prob.
C	−8.5348	−5.9845	0.0022
Ln Y_{it-1}	0.36247	7.94899	0

Table 5.3. Results of Panel Unit Root Test.

Test	Statistic Value	*p*-Value
LLC	−2.98263*	0.0014
IPS	−2.49478**	0.0154
ADF-Fisher Chi-Square	40.689**	0.0383
PP-Fisher Chi-Square	61.8589*	0.0002

Note: **and * imply significant at 5% and 10% level of significance, respectively.

Table 5.4. Results of Arellano-Bond Dynamic Panel Data Estimation.

Variable	Coefficient	Test Statistics	Prob.
C	0.0158767	0.78	0.529
Ln Y_{it-1}	0.5457281	7.69	0

Table 5.5. Results of System Dynamic Panel-Data Estimation.

Variable	Coefficient	Test Statistics	Prob.
C	0.0385262	0.58	0.588
Ln Y_{it-1}	0.345822	8.05	0

Taking all these test results of LLC, IPS, ADF-Fisher and PP-Fisher, therefore, it can be concluded that the assumption of stationarity of the demeaned series holds for this panel data. Hence, the hypothesis of beta convergence holds for TFP across the 17 major Indian states over the period 1983–1984 to 2010–2011.

5.3.2.2.2. Results of Dynamic Panel Model Estimation. The dynamic panel results presented in Table 5.4 as revealed from the first-differenced GMM-based results following the Arellano and Bond estimation procedure show that the coefficient of the lagged dependent variable is statistically significant and is positive. The estimated coefficient is 0.446 and is less than 1 implying the prevalence of convergence in TFP of the pharmaceutical industry across Indian states over the period 1983–1984 to 2019–2020.

5.3.2.2.3. Results of System Dynamic Panel Data Estimation. The GMM system-based results presented in Table 5.5 also show positive and statistically significant coefficient, i.e. 0.326. The coefficient estimate is also less than 1 in this case. Thus one may conclude that the time series of TFP of the pharmaceutical industry across the 17 Indian states has achieved beta convergence over the period 1983–1984 to 2019–2020.

5.4. Conclusion

The present chapter attempts to understand convergence in terms of both sigma and beta convergence of TFP of pharmaceutical industry across the major states of India over the period 1983–1984 to 2019–2020 by applying the modern panel data-based methodologies available for convergence hypotheses such as panel unit root tests and dynamic panel models. Also, the conventional testing of sigma convergence using the time trend of SD and COV as measures of dispersion has been followed here.

TFP of the sample states has been estimated using a semi-parametric approach proposed by Levinsohn and Petrin (2003) which takes care of the endogeneity problem.

The findings on the basis of the conventional approach of sigma convergence clearly indicate that sigma convergence has not been achieved in levels of (log) of TFP of pharmaceutical industries across the major Indian states during the period 1983–1984 to 2019–2020. Whereas methods based on the panel data clearly suggests significant presence of convergence in the TFP of pharmaceutical industries. This perhaps implies that each sample state has converged to its own steady-state level.

All the standard panel unit root tests, clearly demonstrates beta convergence in the series of (log) of TFP of pharmaceutical industries across the states considered. Beta convergence is also found in the dynamic panel framework through the first different GMM and system GMM methods.

Therefore, based on a number of modern as well as conventional statistical tests, beta convergence in TFP of pharmaceutical industries across the Indian states from 1983–1984 to 2019–2020 is an established empirical finding. In view of the fact that all these tests are based on statistically very sound methodologies as opposed to the conventional sigma convergence, conclusion can be made very strongly about the convergence in terms of TFP of pharmaceutical industries across the major states of India.

Chapter 6

Moving Towards a Growing Indian Pharmaceutical Industry

Abstract

Indian pharmaceutical industry (IPI) is one of the few industries which has been affected in a major way due to TRIPS agreement as from 2005 the existing process patent regime gave way to the product patent regime although the process started since 1995. In such an environment, it will be interesting to examine whether there has been any improvement in the performance of IPI after 1995, i.e. after the period of first version of the product patent regime. For this, an econometric analysis has been carried out for some selected variables like output, employment, productivity of labour, productivity of capital, capital labour ratio, export intensity, export price, import intensity and price by applying a recent development using unit root test to estimate the break point of these major variables using All India level data from the period 1983–1984 to 2007–2008. The distinguishing feature of this method is that the break point is not dependent on prior belief of the researchers; rather it is endogenously determined depending on time series properties of variables. The results of estimation suggest that seven out of nine variables considered converges towards a deterministic trend. Among these seven variables, for four the break point turned out to be years after 1995. Variation in the growth performance among the variables is strongly evident. There is an improvement in the performance of output, employment and price after 1995. The study clearly identifies the variables whose performance is satisfactory and other showing relatively poor performance and hence needs special attention.

Keywords: Indian pharmaceutical industry; unit root; jobless growth; structural break; TRIPS agreement; product patent regime; deterministic trend

Performance Analysis of the Indian Pharmaceutical Industry: A Global Outlook, 119–129

doi:10.1108/978-1-83797-743-720251006

6.1. Introduction

Indian pharmaceutical industry (IPI) has expanded drastically in the last few decades. It has come a long way since the time of independence when the industry was dominated by the multi nationals. The growth of the industry can broadly be classified into different phases.

During the phase corresponding to the period 1970–1990, Patent Act of 1911 was amended, which came into force in 1972. This change brought a renaissance to the IPI. After the changes in the patent law, large-scale production of bulk drugs was started by the indigenous sector in the late 1970s, particularly in the 1980s, as a result of which first, imports were replaced and secondly, consumption increased significantly leading to the unprecedented growth in formulation activity. Exports started increasing steadily. Till 1987–1988, imports were larger than exports except for a few years, but with steady increase in exports the country has become a net exporter since 1988–1989. The net result of this is that MNCs lost their market domination. The favourable environment attracted the entry of a number of new firms.

The period after 1990s saw significant changes in this sector with introduction of trade liberalisation measures. In 1994, Government of India signed The Trade-Related Intellectual Property Rights System (TRIPS) agreement which came into existence with World Trade Organisation (WTO) established on 1 January 1995 replacing The General Agreement on Tariff and Trade (GATT). There was sharp and steady increase in production and also of bulk drug production. As a result, net exports as a percentage of exports have increased (Chaudhuri, 2005). The industry, in addition to meeting the domestic demand, is in a position to export a significant volume of pharmaceutical products to various destinations, including the developed markets of USA, EU and Japan. Thus, IPI has emerged as a global player in the pharmaceutical industry.

IPI is one of the few industries which have been affected in a major way due to TRIPS agreement as from the year 2005 the existing process patent regime gave way to the Product Patent regime.

TRIPS agreement is an effort of the international community to move towards a global economy. Before the TRIPS agreement, many developing countries were not aware of the pharmaceutical patents and other intellectual property rights on drugs and patents were not available for pharmaceutical inventions. The scenario had changed after the TRIPS agreement, as all WTO Members have to make patents available for only new drugs or new indications, formulations or processes invented after 1995 for at least 20 years from the filing date. The transition periods were provided to developing and least-developed countries for giving enough time to implement the various TRIPS standards. However, developing and least-developed countries, having transitional periods and not granting drug patents before 2000, 2005 or 2006, a special provision in the TRIPS agreement called 'mail-box' system preserves the novelty of drugs that may be invented between 1995 and the end of the transitional periods, to store patent applications as from 1995 until the transitional period expires. During this period, the patent applications will be examined according to the TRIPS standards and, if the patent term is granted starting from the filing date, it will last for what remains of the 20 years.

IPI enjoyed a longer transition period and introduced product patents from 1 January 2005, although from 1995 onwards began the process of establishing a new patent regime.

Thus, the year 1995 is important for IPI because the first version of the product patent was implemented. The Drug and Cosmetic Act was also amended in 1995 to infuse competition in this sector. In other words, important policy changes pertaining to this sector have taken place this year (Mazumder et al., 2010). One of the very important reforms pertaining to the pharmaceutical sector, namely, the abolishment of licencing came into effect from year 1994 onwards, while the implications of TRIPS agreement were felt for the first time in the year 1995 (Saranga & Banker, 2010).

In such a vibrant environment it would be interesting to examine whether there has been any improvement in the performance of IPI after 1995 which has led to improvement in the performance of some major selected variables of IPI like output (Y), employment (L), productivity of labour (Y/L), productivity of capital (Y/K), capital labour ratio (K/L), export intensity (X/Y), export price (P_X), import intensity (M/Y) and price (P).

For this, an econometric analysis has been carried out to bring out

- Whether there is any improvement in the growth performance of the above major selected variables?

The answer to this question is basically contingent upon whether the series of major selected variables are converging towards a stationary process having a deterministic trend because if the series follows DS type, it basically indicates the existence of a stochastic trend and no definite conclusion can be made about the extent of the growth of the series. Thus, the study requires the answer of the following question:

- Does the major selected variables considered are converging towards a stationary process having deterministic trend?

The literature survey revealed that not much attempt has been made to analyse the behaviour of IPI quantitatively. Mention may be made of few studies like Singh (1989), Nagarajan and Barthwal (1990), Majumder (1994), Madanmohan (1997), Chaudhuri (2005), Chaudhuri and Das (2006), Ghose and Chakraborty (2008), Mazumdar and Rajeev (2009), Majumdar et al. (2009), Saranga and Banker (2010), Chakraborty and Ghose (2010, 2011, 2013) and Ghose and Chakraborty (2012).

Singh (1989), Madanmohan (1997) in their study using firm-level data focused on different aspects of IPI like export, import and net import, technology, profitability, patterns of MNCs activity and plant exit process. Whereas Majumder (1994), Chaudhuri and Das (2006), Mazumdar and Rajeev (2009), Majumdar et al. (2009), Saranga and Banker (2010) and Ghose and Chakraborty (2012) were concerned with the measurement of productivity or efficiency of the industry. Studies which attempted to analyse the growth performance of the industry are due to Nagarajan and Barthwal (1990), Chaudhuri (2005) and Ghose and Chakraborty (2008). Test for exogenous and endogenous structural break using modern time series approach has been carried out by Chakraborty and Ghose (2010, 2011, 2013).

However, none of the above studies looked at the variation in the growth of the major selected variables of IPI as considered in the present chapter using structural break unit root test of modern time series approach.

The contribution of the present chapter is that it might be the first attempt to employ endogenous structural break analysis based on unit root test by using Sen (2003) approach taking All India data from the period 1983–1984 to 2019–2020 to find out the nature of growth process of nine major selected variables of IPI. Here, we basically want to test whether there is an improvement in the performance of IPI after 1995, the year when first version of the product patent started.

The format of the present study is as follows: Section 6.2 gives the methodology and data sources. Section 6.3 presents the result of analysis. Section 6.4 summarises the conclusion of this study.

6.2. Methodology and Data Source

6.2.1. Methodology

Regarding the nature of macroeconomic data, a major debate has been going on until Nelson and Plosser (1982) published in their seminal work, that the underlying process is Difference Stationary (DS) rather than Trend Stationary (TS). For a TS process, the effect of random shock is temporary around a trend whereas for a DS process this random shock has a permanent effect. Moreover, in case of DS process, the variance of the series depends on time.

The unit root test due to Dickey and Fuller (1979, 1981) can detect whether a series is DS or TS. To understand this process, the following regression equation is considered:

$$\Delta Y_t = \delta_0 + \delta_1 t + \gamma Y_{t-1} + U_t \text{ where } U_t = \alpha U_{t-1} + \varepsilon_t$$

The test procedure is as under:

The null hypothesis is H_0: $\gamma = 0$. Rejection of the null hypothesis implies that the underlying series is TS and failure of the rejection implies that the underlying series is DS. But the coefficient of Y_{t-1} does not follow the standard t distribution which was solved by Fuller by getting limiting distribution of this coefficient and finally these distributions were approximated empirically by Dicky (1976). From a much larger set of replications, McKinnon (1990) has derived critical values.

A TS process and statistically significant coefficient of time imply that there exists a trend in the series. Statistically significant constant term suggest there exists a drift in the series.

If ΔY_t depends on ΔY_{t-j} (where $j = 1, 2, K, K < T$) then the above test procedure is called Augmented Dickey-Fuller test.

Perron (1989) in his path breaking work has shown that the standard unit root test is not consistent against trend stationarity in the presence of structural break and has suggested a procedure which is appropriate for testing unit root in the presence of one-time structural break in the series which is assumed to be exogenously determined from consideration of visual examination of the plots of the data.

But Zivot and Andrews (1992) argued that Perron's procedure for finding out the break point is not an appropriate method, because Perron's method was based primarily on visual inspection of data. He argued that the break point should be endogenously determined and can be evaluated considering the three models as follows:

$$\text{Model A: } Y_t = a_1 + b_1 \text{ DU}_t + c_1 t + d_1 \ Y_{t-1} + e_1 \sum \Delta Y_{t-1} + e_t$$
$$\text{Model B: } Y_t = a_2 + g_2 \text{ DT}_t + c_2 t + d_2 \ Y_{t-1} + e_2 \sum \Delta Y_{t-1} + e_t$$
$$\text{Model C: } Y_t = a_3 + b_3 \text{ DU}_t + c_3 t + g_3 \text{ DT}_t + d_3 \ Y_{t-1} + e_3 \sum \Delta Y_{t-1} + e_t$$

where

The above three regressions can be estimated by the OLS method and with the break fraction γ ranging from 2/T to T-1/T.

$$\begin{aligned} \text{DU}_t &= 1 \text{ if } t > T\gamma \\ &= 0 \text{ otherwise} \\ \text{DT}_t &= t - T\gamma \text{ if } t > T\gamma \\ &= 0 \text{ otherwise} \end{aligned}$$

Model A allows an endogenous break in the level of the series, Model B permits an endogenous break in the rate of growth and Model C admits both changes in the level as well as growth.

If DT_t is positive (negative) and significant, then it can be concluded that there has been an acceleration (deceleration) in the growth after break. If DU_t is statistically significant then we can conclude that there exists a significant change in the level at the break point. Such conclusions are meaningful only if the underlying process is of TS type. T stands for total time period and γ stands for time break, i.e. $\gamma = T_B/T$. The parameters of the ith regression are denoted by a_i, b_i, c_i, d_i, e_i, g_i and T_B is the break point.

Regarding the choice of the lag value, Perron has suggested the following procedure: One should start with a reasonably high value of k, and choose that particular k, say k*, such that the value of the statistic for k* is greater than 1.64 in absolute value and for all other is less than 1.64.

However, the present chapter does not follow Perron's procedure in case of the choice of lag as this procedure is sensitive to a particular value of 't' statistic around 10% level of significance. Rather the chapter uses visual descriptions of the series and in particular the figures of the correlogram. It suggests that the series is AR (1) type with the autocorrelations dying out and only the first partial correlation coefficient is significant.

From the estimated regression, the value of the '*t*' statistics for testing the null hypothesis $d_i = 1$ can be obtained.

Zivot and Andrews (1992) proved that among the overall *T*-2 regressions one can choose that year as break point year which gives us the minimum value of the '*t*' statistics corresponding to the coefficient of Y_{t-1}. Choose that model as the best fitted model which gives us the minimum '*t*' value of the coefficient of Y_{t-1}. The estimated results are compared with the critical values given by the Zivot and Andrews to determine the nature of the series.

Sen (2003) argued that Zivot and Andrews (1992) procedure can be improved by considering the maximum '*F*' statistic instead of taking the minimum '*t*' statistic and also argued that Model C has a higher power than either Model A or Model B. So Sen (2003) considered Model C and suggested the test based on the maximum *F* statistic, having the following form:

$$F^{Max} = Max_{T_b \in \{[\lambda_0 T],[\lambda_0 T]+1,\ldots,T-[\lambda_0 T]\}} F_b(T_b)$$

The test procedure is as below:

- Among the overall *T*-2 regressions choose that year as break point year which gives us the maximum value of the '*F*' statistics.
- After finding out the break point one can compare the results with the critical values provided by Sen (2003) to determine the nature of the series.

6.2.2. Data Source

The present chapter uses the variables like output (*Y*) measured by gross value added (GVA) at constant price, employment (*L*) measured by number of workers, productivity (*Y*/*L*) measured by the ratio of real GVA to number of workers, productivity of capital (*Y*/*K*) measured by the ratio of real GVA to capital stock (*K*), capital labour ratio (*K*/*L*) measured by the ratio of *K* to *L*, export intensity (*X*/*Y*) measured by the ratio of real export to real GVA, export price (P_X) measured by the unit value index of exports, import intensity (*M*/*Y*) measured by the ratio of real import to real GVA and price (*P*) measured by wholesale price index of drugs and medicines. The data on *Y*, *L*, fixed capital and *L* at All India level from the period 1983–1984 to 2019–2020 has been provided by 'Annual Survey of Industries, Summary results for the Factory Sector' published by Central Statistical Organisation (CSO), Government of India.

The data on capital stock (*K*) have been obtained by the Perpetual Inventory Accumulation Method. Data on *X* and *M* are collected from Foreign Trade Statistics of India, published by the Directorate General of Commercial Intelligence and Statistics. Data on the unit value index of exports (P_X) have been collected from the Handbook of Statistics on Indian Economy, Reserve Bank of India. Value of exports and imports has been deflated by the unit value index of exports and imports to arrive at the data on real value of exports and imports.

6.3. Results of Analysis

The results of the present chapter as shown in Table 6.1 can be summarised as follows:

- For all the variables considered in the present study except Y/L and $K/$L, i.e. for the seven variables like Y, L, Y/K, X/Y, P_X, M/Y and P the underlying series is of Trend Stationary (TS) type implying convergence towards a stationary process. So, for all the seven variables the variability of the series remains constant over time.
- The underlying process is DS for Y/L and K/L suggesting the existence of a stochastic trend in the series of productivity of labour and capital-labour ratio and the variability of these series is not constant, rather it depends on time. Hence, no definite conclusion can be drawn about the trend of Y/L and K/L or about the break point of these series. Thus, the performance of Y/L and K/L is very poor because first the growth process for these two variables follows a stochastic trend suggesting that no definite conclusion can be made on the extent of growth for these variables and secondly the series does not possess constant variability over time. Moreover, the coefficient of time is negative but not statistically significant in case of K/L showing one cannot infer about the change in the variability of the K/L series but in case of Y/L the coefficient is negative and significant suggesting that the variability has decreased over time, however being of DS type it is not convergent.
- The break points for Y, L, Y/K and P correspond to the period after 1995 as the break point is 1997–1998 for Y and Y/K and 2000–2001 for L and P.

But in case of X/Y and M/Y the break point is 1992–1993, the period after Dunkel Draft submission (1991). Whereas for P_X, the break point is 1989–1990, the period just after India became a net exporter (since 1988–1989).

Since the series of Y/L and K/L are of DS type, the rest of the analysis will be discussed excluding these two series.

- The coefficient of DU_T is positive and significant only in case of P_X showing that the level increases at the break point. For the rest of the series, it is negative and significant implying that the level decreases at the break point.

Regarding the coefficient of time, it is found to be positive and significant in case of L implying that there exists an increasing trend for the entire study period but in case of P_X it is negative and significant suggesting that there exists a negative trend for the entire period of analysis. For the rest of the series, the coefficient of time is insignificant and no conclusion can be made regarding the trend for the entire period of analysis.

Table 6.1. Endogenous Structural Break Analysis in All India for Different Variables of IPI.

Variable	Constant	DU_t	T	DT_t	Y_{t-1}	ΔY_{t-1}	*F*-Value	Break Point	Nature of Series
Y	0.589	−0.194***	0.0163	0.014*	−0.089	0.501***	13.056***	1997–1998	TS
	(0.789)	(3.658)	(0.798)	(1.689)	(0.596)	(4.932)			
L	2.671	−0.169***	0.014*	0.043***	−0.274	0.447***	9.489*	2000–2001	TS
	(1.039)	(3.489)	(1.787)	(3.879)	(1.254)	(3.461)			
Y/L	2.789	0.243	−0.038	0.001	0.528	0.607	7.980	2000–2001	DS
	(1.092)	(1.432)	(2.878)	(0.174)	(1.875)	(4.571)			
Y/K	−0.439	−0.197***	0.0171	0.007	−0.145	0.578***	13.252***	1997–1998	TS
	(0.671)	(3.840)	(0.798)	(0.729)	(0.715)	(4.279)			
K/L	−0.512	0.178	−0.014	−0.034	−0.301	0.398	6.873	2000–2001	DS
	(1.104)	(3.289)	(1.679)	(3.124)	(1.647)	(3.421)			
X/Y	−0.724*	−0.591***	0.041	−0.069**	−1.988	0.521***	18.233***	1992–1993	TS
	(1.789)	(3.675)	(0.824)	(1.996)	(0.841)	(6.863)			
P_X	1.245***	0.591***	−0.071**	0.064**	−0.304**	0.387***	34.927***	1989–1990	TS
	(3.754)	(6.517)	(2.398)	(2.247)	(2.06)	(5.781)			
M/Y	−1.251***	−0.794***	−0.045	0.017	0.572**	0.743***	15.827***	1992–1993	TS
	(2.974)	(5.140)	(1.065)	(0.804)	(2.792)	(6.921)			
P	−0.069	−0.142***	0.005	−0.004	0.014	0.497***	15.912***	2000–2001	TS
	(0.124)	(4.974)	(1.143)	(0.894)	(0.167)	(5.387)			

Note: ***, ** and * represents significant at 1%, 5% and 10% level of significance, respectively.

The coefficient of D_T is found to be positive and significant in case of *Y*, *L* and P_X implying that the rate of growth increases after the break whereas the rate of growth has fallen in case of *X*/*Y* after the break as the coefficient of D_T is negative and significant. For the rest of the series, the coefficient of D_T is insignificant and nothing can be concluded about the rate of growth after the break for these series.

- On the basis of the above results one can divide the seven variables under the following groups:

Group A: This group consists of only one variable employment, *L* where the growth increases for the entire period of study as well as after the break point. However, there is a fall in the level at the break point. Thus, on the whole more or less the performance of *L* is satisfactory in the entire sample period as well as after the break point.

Group B: The variable P_X falls under this group. Here trend is negative for the entire period of study but the rate of growth increases after the break point 1989–1990. Also, there is a rise in the level at the break point. Hence, the performance of P_X is moderate as it performed very well after the break point but not for the entire sample period.

As for P_X there is a fall in the growth rate for the entire period. So it can be said that India is exporting pharmaceuticals at a lesser price (Report of the Task Force, Ministry of Commerce & Industry, 12 December 2008).

Also, after the break point, 1989–90 the increase in the rate of growth of P_X can be explained *as:* Till 1987–1988, imports were larger than exports except for a few years but with steady increase in exports the country has become a net exporter since 1988–1989 (Chaudhuri, 2005).

Group C: It consists of only variable output, *Y* where the trend is insignificant for the entire period of study. Also, there occurs a fall in the level of output at the time of break but the rate of growth increases after the break 1997–98. So for the entire sample period, the performance of this variable is inconclusive but after the break point it acted moderately.

Group D: The variables *M*/*Y*, *Y*/*K* and *P* forms this group. Here one cannot surely conclude about their trend for the entire period of analysis and also about the growth of the series after the break point. But there is a fall in the level at the break point. It implies that at their respective break points, 1992–1993, 1997–1998 and 2000–2001 there is a fall in level of *M*/*Y*, *Y*/*K* and *P*.

The fall in *M*/*Y* in the year 1992–1993 may be due to the fact that the period during the 1970s to the end of 1990s corresponds to the period of rapid progress of import substitution and then strengthening of export orientation in the IPI (Kamiike & Sato, 2011).

Decline in *Y*/*K* at the break 1997–1998 may be due to the fact that for capital, cheaper and easier access in the post-reforms period facilitated its larger use than earlier, but output did not increase proportionately (Virmani & Hashim, 2009). Also, Uchikawa (2001, 2002) has pointed out that there was an investment boom in Indian industry in the mid-1990s and this boom raised production capacities substantially but demand did not rise which led to capacity under-utilisation.

At the time of the break (2000–2001) there is a significant decline in the prices of drugs/medicines. This may be due to the fact that in India, given that pharmaceutical industry was protected only by process patents and not product patents till 2005, the scope for competition was immense and it was this lack of intellectual property rights that brought down the prices of drugs, which were patented elsewhere in the world (Jha, 2010). The consumers have not suffered much because of the new patent regime as drugs/medicines are much more accessible to the consumers (Revised Report Submitted to the UNCTAD, August, 2010).

Group E: Only one variable X/Y forms this group. Nothing can be said about the trend for the entire sample period as there occurs a positive but insignificant trend for the entire sample period. But there is a fall in the growth after the break 1992–1993 and there is a fall in the level of the series. Hence, the performance of X/Y for the entire sample period is inconclusive and bad after the break. For X/Y, there is a significant fall in the growth rate after the break 1992–1993. Our result is in conformity with Chaudhuri (1993). According to Chaudhuri (1993) one of the implications of Dunkel Draft will be lesser exports.

- The break points of different variables reveal that the lowest break point year is 1989–1990 for P_X and the highest break point year is 2000–2001 for L and P. Break point year is 1997–1998 for Y and Y/K. So, it is clear that out of the seven variables showing TS process, break point years are after 1995 for four variables Y, L, Y/K and P.

6.4. Conclusion

This chapter attempts to test the growth performance of nine major selected variables of IPI by applying a recent development in estimation and testing of structural break in the econometric time series model from the period 1983–1984 to 2019–2020. The distinguishing feature of this method is that it is not dependent on the prior belief of the researchers regarding the occurrence of the break point. Rather the study tested for endogenous structural break in the series using Sen (2003) approach and finds out the break point of the series of different variables at All India level. It then examines whether all the variables considered in the present study converges towards a stationary series having deterministic trend.

The following conclusions emerge from the analysis:

- All the variables considered in the present study except Y/L and K/L show convergence towards stationary process having constant variability over time.
- The result of the study shows that only for the variables like Y, L, Y/K and P, the break point occurred after 1995. But in case of X/Y and M/Y the break point year occurred at 1992–1993, i.e. the period when policies of liberalisation were introduced in the Indian economy and Dunkel Draft was submitted (1991). For P_X, it is 1989–1990.

- The variables like Y, L and P_X performed well after the break. Thus, one can say there is an improvement in the performance of employment, output and export price after the break.

In the Indian literature, there is a considerable evidence of jobless growth for Indian manufacturing. According to Alessandrini (2009), there is a discrepancy between the rate of growth of the economy and the rate of growth of employment. He pointed out that the capability of the Indian economy to generate employment seems to be limited. According to Virmani and Hashim (2009), the manufacturing sector in India performed unsatisfactorily in creating employment. They further pointed out that special policy attention is to be taken for the creation of employment in manufacturing as high growth in output may not guarantee sufficient employment. According to Papola and Sahu (2012), the long-term trend of a decline in the rate of employment growth is a fact that cannot be ignored. Bhalotra (1998) concluded that employment declined in Indian factories in the 1980s.

However that does not imply all the sectors under manufacturing have experienced a decline in employment. For example, Mehrotra et al. (2013) pointed out that there are certain sectors of manufacturing like textiles; wearing apparel and leather products; paper and paper products, and publishing and reprinting of recorded media; basic metals; motor vehicles and other transport equipment; furniture; and medical and optical instruments, watches and clocks which has experienced reasonable increase in total employment. Our results also show that there is a significant improvement in employment in IPI and hence this result does not support the case of jobless growth for all the sectors of the economy simultaneously.

- At the time of the break (2000–2001) it is found that there is a significant decline in P prices of drugs/medicines. So, P performed well at the break point.

The study of the growth of selected major variables of IPI at All India level by using modern time series technique clearly identifies the variables whose performance are satisfactory and other variables showing relatively poor performance and hence needs special attention. However, it is to be noted that the growth of seven among the nine selected major variables converges towards a deterministic trend. Out of seven, for four variables like Y, L, Y/K and P the break point corresponds to the period after 1995. Among them three variables Y, L and P performed well. For the entire sample period the performance of Y is inconclusive but after the break point it acted moderately and the performance of L is satisfactory in the entire sample period as well as after the break point. For P, at the time of the break (2000–2001) there is a significant decline.

Chapter 7

Position of Indian Pharmaceutical Industry in the Global Economy

Abstract

This chapter examines the performance of the Indian pharmaceutical industry and pharmaceutical industries of leading countries namely the United States, China, Germany, Japan, Ireland, Switzerland, France, Italy, Belgium, United Kingdom, Spain, Brazil, Canada, South Korea and the Netherlands. This chapter looks at the trends of three lead variables namely output, export and import of the IPI and pharmaceutical industries of leading countries and tries to compare the IPI with the other countries in terms of the above three variables and thus helps to identify the position of IPI in the global context. Also, this chapter verifies the presence of structural breaks (which may appear due to changes in economic regime over time) in the different series of production, export and import using panel structural break methodology.

Keywords: Indian pharmaceutical industry; global economy; export; import; structural break; panel data

7.1. Introduction

Among the different manufacturing industries in India, the Indian pharmaceutical industry (IPI) has emerged as one of the most vibrant segments and deserves special attention. The economic reforms of 1991 further propelled the IPI onto the global platform by removing licencing restrictions. IPI holds a significant place in the global economy. It may provide a position of leadership to continue excelling and thriving through the help of a talent pool. This is possible through cultivating and promoting quality in pharmaceutical learning for formulation research within the country. The nation is the largest provider of generic medicines in the

Performance Analysis of the Indian Pharmaceutical Industry: A Global Outlook, 131–145

doi:10.1108/978-1-83797-743-720251007

world and supplies medicines to many countries. The success of the pharmaceutical industry in India has allowed the country to not only meet these needs but also to export its expertise and knowledge to other countries, helping to improve global health and well-being. The top medicine-producing countries in the world among others are the United States, China, Germany, Japan, Ireland, Switzerland, France, Italy, India, Belgium, United Kingdom, Spain, Brazil, Canada, South Korea and the Netherlands.

Thus, the major aim of the current chapter is to investigate the performance of the IPI and pharmaceutical industries of leading countries namely the United States of America, China, Germany, Japan, Ireland, Switzerland, France, Italy, Belgium, United Kingdom, Spain, Brazil, Canada, South Korea and the Netherlands. This chapter looks at the trends of three lead variables namely output, export and import of the IPI and pharmaceutical industries of leading countries and tries to compare IPI with the other countries in terms of the above three variables and thus helps to identify the position of IPI in the global context.

Further for measuring the growth, the literature survey revealed that not much attempt has been made to analyse the behaviour of IPI quantitatively. Mention may be made of few studies like Singh (1989), Nagarajan and Barthwal (1990), Majumder (1994), Madanmohan (1997), Chaudhuri (2005), Chaudhuri and Das (2006), Ghose and Chakraborty (2008), Mazumdar and Rajeev (2009), Mazumdar et al. (2009), Saranga and Banker (2010), Chakraborty and Ghose (2010, 2011, 2013) and Ghose and Chakraborty (2012).

Singh (1989), Madanmohan (1997) in their study using firm-level data focused on different aspects of IPI like export, import and net import, technology, profitability, patterns of MNCs activity and plant exit process. Whereas Majumder (1994), Chaudhuri and Das (2006), Mazumdar and Rajeev (2009), Majumdar et al. (2009), Saranga and Banker (2010) and Ghose and Chakraborty (2012) were concerned with the measurement of productivity or efficiency of the industry. Studies which attempted to analyse the growth performance of the industry are due to Nagarajan and Barthwal (1990), Chaudhuri (2005) and Ghose and Chakraborty (2008). Test for exogenous and endogenous structural break using modern time series approach has been carried out by Chakraborty and Ghose (2010, 2011, 2013, 2017), Chakraborty (2017) among others.

Chakraborty and Ghose (2010) tested whether there has been a change in the level or growth of output of IPI in the post-liberalisation period since 1991–1992 using recent advancement of structural break analysis of modern time series econometrics. The study uses the data on gross value added for the period 1973–1974 to 2007–2008 and tested for both exogenous and endogenous structural break in the series. In case of exogenous structural break, the model specifying the changes only in the level happens to be trend-stationary implying the existence of permanent and deterministic trend. There is also evidence of upward positive trend. For endogenous structural break analysis, model specifying the changes only in the level also represents the best fitted one with 1991–1992 as the break point. The analysis therefore suggests that there is break only in the level and at the year 1991–1992. There is also the evidence of positive and significant structural change after 1991–1992. There is evidence of positive trend and the underlying process is TS with drift in both the cases of endogenous and exogenous structural break.

Chakraborty and Ghose (2011) identified whether there has been a change in the level or growth or both in the level as well as the growth of output of 17 major states of India and in the All India level in the pharmaceutical industry in the post-liberalisation period since 1991–1992 using recent advancement of structural break analysis of modern time series econometrics by using the data on gross value added for the period 1983–1984 to 2007–2008 and tested for an exogenous structural break in the level, growth and both in the series of output of pharmaceutical industry in the 17 major states as well as in All India level. This paper concludes that for the states like Andhra Pradesh, Gujarat, Haryana, Maharashtra and Rajasthan the underlying process is TS for the Model A and Model B supporting the evidence of a deterministic trend but no statistical evidence of one-time structural break is found. In case of Karnataka, there exists onetime exogenous structural break in Model B only. For Madhya Pradesh, there exists one-time exogenous structural break in Model A only. For the states like Assam, Punjab, Tamil Nadu and West Bengal, all the three models are TS supporting the evidence of deterministic trend. In case of West Bengal only, there is statistical evidence of structural change after 1991–1992 and also the evidence of one-time structural break in the level, growth and both in the level and growth of the series of output of pharmaceutical industry.

Chakraborty and Ghose (2013) applied recent development in estimation and testing of structural break in econometric time series model, using unit root test to estimate the break point of the growth of output of Indian pharmaceutical industry for the period 1983–1984 to 2007–2008 by using state-level data from Annual Survey of Industries and employing endogenous structural break analysis. The distinguishing feature of this method is that the break point is not dependent on the prior belief of the researcher; rather it is endogenously determined depending on time series properties of the series. The results of estimation suggest that for most of the states the endogenously determined break point turned out to be the years after the signing of TRIPS agreement in 1995. An interstate and regional variation of the growth of output is strongly evident. The growth of output of 16 among the 17 selected states converges towards a deterministic trend, out of which seven shows positive movement. The study clearly identifies the regions and the states whose performance are satisfactory and other showing relatively poor performance and hence needs special attention. Whereas Chakraborty and Ghose (2017) identified the major determinants of growth of output of Indian pharmaceutical using state-level data. Structural break analysis of Sen (2003) is applied for measurement of growth of output. The result suggests that nine states like Assam, Gujarat, Haryana, Himachal Pradesh, Karnataka, Kerala, Maharashtra, Orissa and Punjab showed statistically significant growth rate for the entire sample period. For assessing the performance of nine states, state dummy variables for each state have been introduced taking Punjab (PU), state with minimum growth rate for the entire sample period, as the benchmark. It may be mentioned that the estimated equations are found to be non-linear. It is found that large sized firms, right composition of work-force and increase in wage rate as well as the trade related variables like export intensity, import intensity and net export intensity enhances growth of output. Chakraborty (2017) tried to find out the nature of the growth process of output, employment and productivity of labour of pharmaceutical industry in the 17 major selected states, tests whether the series of the growth of output, employment and productivity of labour are converging towards a stationary process having deterministic trend and estimates the break point of these three variables for the period 1983–1984 to 2007–2008 employing endogenous structural break analysis of Sen (2003). The distinguishing feature of this method is that the break point is not dependent on the prior belief of the researcher; rather it is endogenously determined depending on time series properties of the series. The results of estimation suggest that for most of the states, the endogenously determined break point turned out to be the years after 1995, the year when the first version of product patent was implemented and The Drug and Cosmetic Act was also amended to infuse competition in this sector. Thus, important policy changes pertaining to this sector have taken place in the year 1995. An interstate and regional variation of the growth of output, employment and productivity of labour is strongly evident. The growth of output of 16 among the 17 selected states converges towards a deterministic trend, it is 14 for productivity of labour whereas for employment, all the states shows convergence towards stationary process having constant variability over time. The study clearly identifies the regions and the states whose performance are satisfactory and others showing relatively poor performance and hence needs special attention.

However, none of the above studies applied panel structural break analysis in pharmaceutical industry analysis.

One of the important characteristics of IPI is that they re-engineer the imported technology and then re-export the product. Export plays a very important role for the growth in the pharmaceutical sector. [Theoretical and empirical literature supporting the positive role of exports (Sun et al. (1999), Driffield and Kambhampati (2003), Goldar et al. (2004), Ray (2006)]. The findings of Indian studies are mixed and industry-specific even during post-reform period. The pharmaceutical firms also have to do a lot of imports. Evidence suggests that the imported intermediary good is an important channel through which technological diffusion takes place (Tybout 2000); theories of import-led growth due to Grossman and Helpman (1991).

Thus one may be also interested in knowing the extent of growth of exports and imports of IPI.

Thus, the major objectives that the present chapter undertakes may be listed as below:

- To assess the position of India compared to other foreign countries in terms of production, export and import of pharmaceuticals.
- To compare the countries in terms of the above three lead variables namely output, export and import of pharmaceuticals.
- To verify the presence of structural breaks in the different series of production, export and import using panel structural break methodology.

The chapter is organised as below:

Section 7.2 discusses methodology and data. Subsection 7.2.1 is concerned with procedures of country-level analysis of the pharmaceutical industry and data sources are discussed in Subsection 7.2.2. Section 7.3 presents the results of estimation elaborately. A few bottom-line comments can be found in Section 7.4.

7.2. Methodology and Data

This section discusses the methodology and data source of the present chapter. Subsection 7.2.1 discusses the methodology for country-level analysis of the pharmaceutical industry and data sources are discussed in Subsection 7.2.2.

7.2.1. Empirical Procedures of Country-Level Analysis of Pharmaceutical Industry

This section is concerned with the methodology for country-level analysis of pharmaceutical industry. This part is concerned with the investigation of the performance of Indian pharmaceutical industry and pharmaceutical industries of leading countries namely the United States, China, Germany, Japan, Ireland, Switzerland, France, Italy, India, Belgium, United Kingdom, Spain, Brazil, Canada, South Korea and Netherlands. It looks at the trends of three lead variables namely output, export and import of Indian pharmaceutical industry and pharmaceutical industries of leading countries and tries to compare IPI with the other countries in terms of the above three variables. This chapter helps to identify the position of Indian pharmaceutical industry in the global context.

For measuring the growth performance of each of these variables, the specification of average annual growth rate (AAGR) have been used.

Year-to-year growth rate (YOY) is measured by the formula as given in relation (7.1)

$$\text{Growth rate of variable (say } Y\text{) in a period } t = A / B \qquad (7.1)$$

where A = difference in the magnitude of the variable in period t and t-1
B = magnitude of the variable in period t-1.

$$\text{AAGR} = \text{Average of YOY} \qquad (7.2)$$

The empirical literature on growth suggests some limitations.

The majority of the growth analysis relied upon the assumption of deterministic trend (assuming means and variances are well-defined constants and independent of time) and hence they are devoid of testing for difference or trend stationarity using unit root of modern time series approach (with some exceptions such as Mukhopadhyay & Sarkar 2001; Ghose & Pal, 2007; Sengupta et al., 2009; Roy Biswas & Ghose, 2012 among others). But those assumptions are not always valid as the series may be non-stationary in nature as pointed out by researchers over the last three decades or so. Thus, for getting a valid result, the stationary properties of the series are to be checked.

But in the presence of structural break, the standard unit root test is inconsistent against Trend Stationary Process[1] (TSP) (Perron, 1989). Perron (1989), in presence of one-time exogenous structural break in the series, suggested a method appropriate for testing unit root. Zivot and Andrews (1992) pointed out that Perron's procedure is not an appropriate one and argued that the break point should be endogenously determined (rather than exogenously determined Perron, 1989). However, according to Sen (2003), the power of Zivot and Andrews (1992) test statistic is low and recommended some methods to improve the power of the test.

Thus it will be motivating to observe the true nature of the time series data of pharmaceutical industries in the leading countries and accordingly test whether the growth process converges to a path having trend-preserving properties, to verify the presence of structural breaks (which may appear due to changes in economic regime over time) in the different series and its persistence level.

Methodology for Panel Structural Break:

In empirical research, the presence of structural break and handling structural breaks is an essential step. This is particularly true in panel data because it comprised of many cross-sectional units, which are all affected by major events. For example, the COVID-19 pandemic has affected almost all the sectors of the global economy. On the other hand, its impact on stock markets is still in question. Most markets look to have recovered within the time of pandemic. So, it is suggesting that the relationship between stock returns and COVID-19 has been subject to structural break. It is therefore important to know if a structural break has occurred and, if it has, to infer the date of the break. The previous studies related to the testing of structural break analysis in case of the time series data only. The test of structural break analysis in case of panel data is also very important. For detailed methodology please refer to Chapter 3.

7.2.2. Data

The secondary data employed in this study are exports, imports and production of pharmaceutical products in different countries covering the period 1995 to 2021. The leading countries considered are the United States of America, China, Germany, Japan, Ireland, Switzerland, France, Italy, India, Belgium, United Kingdom, Spain, Brazil, Canada, South Korea and the Netherlands based on the availability of the data. The data is obtained from WITS, World Integrated Trade Solution, Trade Statistics by Product (HS 6-digit), various websites like https://oec.world/en/profile/hs/pharmaceutical-products; https://www.efpia.eu; https://microdata.gov.in/nada43/index.php/catalog/ASI.

---

[1]A TSP implies that the effect of random shock is temporary around a stable trend.

7.3. Results of Estimation

To understand the position of the Indian pharmaceutical industry in the global economy, India along with 15 major countries producing pharmaceutical products have been considered namely the United States, China, Germany, Japan, Ireland, Switzerland, France, Italy, India, Belgium, United Kingdom, Spain, Brazil, Canada, South Korea and the Netherlands. Data on output, export and import are analysed and compared to assess the position of India compared to other foreign countries in terms of production, export and import and also inter-comparison of countries and their performance in terms of the above three variables are made.

7.3.1. Results of Growth

The results show positive growth rates of output for all the countries except the Netherlands and France. The grand mean i.e. the average of all countries taken together is 0.034. For six countries namely Ireland, Italy, India, Belgium, Spain,

Table 7.1. Growth of Export, Import and Output of Different Countries.

Export		**Import**		**Output**	
Countries	**Growth Rate**	**Countries**	**Growth Rate**	**Countries**	**Growth Rate**
Belgium	0.1489	**Belgium**	0.1457	**Italy**	0.083886956
Brazil	0.1041	**Brazil**	0.1314	**Belgium**	0.067528215
Canada	0.1212	**Canada**	0.1037	**Ireland**	0.056876995
China	0.2037	**China**	0.1844	**Spain**	0.051887968
France	0.0806	**France**	0.0943	**India**	0.049552835
Germany	0.1148	**Germany**	0.1219	**Switzerland**	0.042688134
India	0.1589	**India**	0.1442	**United Kingdom**	0.014961253
Ireland	0.2050	**Ireland**	0.1288	**Germany**	0.003839547
Italy	0.1164	**Italy**	0.1007	**Netherlands**	−0.00841105
Japan	0.1021	**Japan**	0.0934	**France**	−0.015378493
Netherlands	0.1081	**Netherlands**	0.1128	**Grand Mean**	0.034743236
South Korea	0.1964	**South Korea**	0.1394		
Spain	0.1458	**Spain**	0.1146		
Switzerland	0.1118	**Switzerland**	0.1180		
United Kingdom	0.0545	**United Kingdom**	0.0863		
United States	0.1145	**United States**	0.1521		
Grand Mean	0.1304	**Grand Mean**	0.1210		

Table 7.2. Position of Different Countries in terms of Export, Import and Production.

Export		Import		Output	
Countries Growth Rate Greater Than Grand Mean	**Countries Growth Rate Less Than Grand Mean**	**Countries Growth Rate Greater Than Grand Mean**	**Countries Growth Rate Less Than Grand Mean**	**Countries Growth Rate Greater Than Grand Mean**	**Countries Growth Rate Less Than Grand Mean**
Ireland	Canada	China	Switzerland	Italy	United Kingdom
China	Italy	United States	Spain	Belgium	Germany
South Korea	Germany	Belgium	Netherlands	Ireland	Netherlands
India	United States	India	Canada	Spain	France
Belgium	Switzerland	South Korea	Italy	India	
Spain	Netherlands	Brazil	France	Switzerland	
	Brazil	Ireland	Japan		
	Japan	Germany	United Kingdom		
	France				

and Switzerland, the growth rate is above the grand mean indicating good performance whereas for the remaining four countries such as the United Kingdom, Germany, Netherlands and France, the growth rate is below the grand mean. The result suggests that India stands in the fifth position in the global economy in terms of production of pharmaceuticals. The results can be found in Tables 7.1 and 7.2.

All the countries' growth rates for exports and imports are found to be positive. It seems a positive trend for all the sample countries in case of export and import during the sample period. Inter-comparison of countries reveals that the growth of export is maximum for Ireland and minimum for United Kingdom whereas it is maximum for China and minimum for United Kingdom in the case of import.

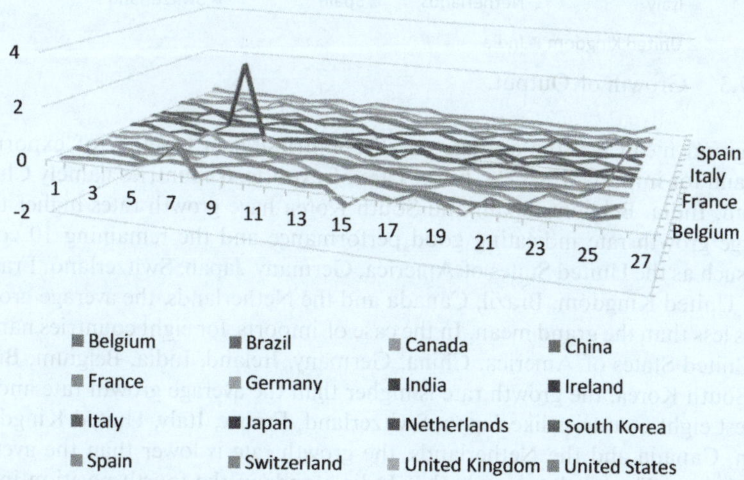

Fig. 7.1. Growth of Export.

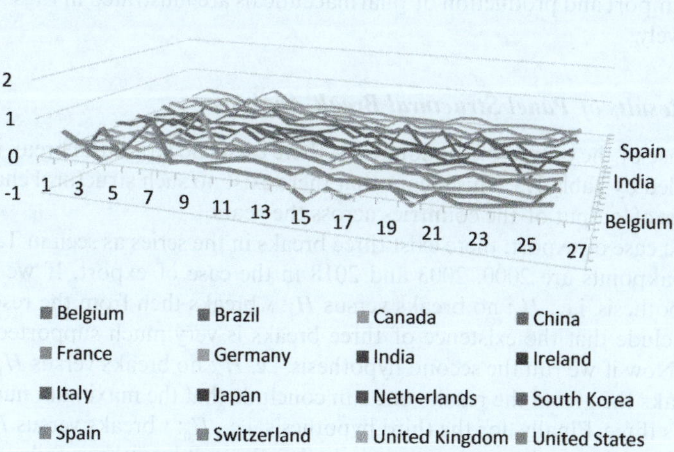

Fig. 7.2. Growth of Import.

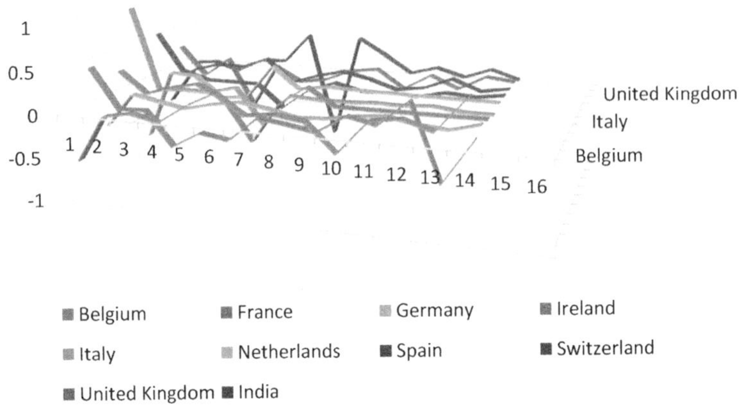

Fig. 7.3. Growth of Output.

The grand mean, i.e. the average of all countries/taken together of exports is 13% and for imports it is 12%. In the case of exports, 6 countries namely China, Ireland, India, Belgium, Spain and South Korea have growth rates higher than average growth rate indicating good performance and the remaining 10 countries such as the United States of America, Germany, Japan, Switzerland, France, Italy, United Kingdom, Brazil, Canada and the Netherlands, the average growth rate is less than the grand mean. In the case of imports, for eight countries namely the United States of America, China, Germany, Ireland, India, Belgium, Brazil and South Korea, the growth rate is higher than the average growth rate and for the rest eight countries like Japan, Switzerland, France, Italy, United Kingdom, Spain, Canada and the Netherlands, the growth rate is lower than the average growth rate. The result suggests that India stands in the fourth position in the global economy for both the export and import of pharmaceuticals. The trend of export, import and production of pharmaceuticals are illustrated in Figs. 7.1–7.3, respectively.

7.3.2. Results of Panel Structural Break Analysis

In the case of the output of the countries, there exists no structural break in series as revealed by Table 7.3. This means that there exist no such structural changes in the series of output of the countries across the years.

In the case of export, there exist three breaks in the series as seen in Table 7.4. The breakpoints are 2000, 2003 and 2018 in the case of export. If we test the first hypothesis, i.e., H_0: no breaks versus H_1: s breaks then from the results one can conclude that the existence of three breaks is very much supported by the results. Now if we run the second hypothesis, i.e. H_0: no breaks versus H_1: $1 \leq s \leq s_{max}$ breaks then from the results one can conclude that the maximum number of breaks is three. Finally, for the third hypothesis, i.e., H_0: s breaks versus H_1: $s + 1$ breaks from the results one can conclude that the null hypothesis fails to accept against the alternative hypothesis, i.e., there exists three breaks in the series of exports.

In the case of import, there exist four breaks in the series as is evident from Table 7.5. The breakpoints are 2000, 2003, 2015, and 2018. As in the case of exports if we test the first hypothesis, i.e., H_0: no breaks versus H_1: s breaks then from the results it is obvious that the existence of four breaks is very much

Table 7.3. Panel Structural Break Analysis Results in Case of Output.

No additional breaks found for 5 breaks.

Sequential test for multiple breaks at unknown breakpoints (Ditzen, Karavias & Westerlund. 2021)

		Bai & Perron Critical Values		
	Test Statistic	**1% Critical Value**	**5% Critical Value**	**10% Critical Value**
F(1|0)	0.57	12.29	8.58	7.04
F(2|1)	0.05	13.89	10.13	8.51
F(3|2)	0.59	14.80	11.14	9.41
F(4|3)	0.10	15.28	11.83	10.04
Detected number of breaks:		.		.

Maximum number of breaks reached with null always rejected.

Table 7.4. Panel Structural Break Analysis Results in Case of Export.

Sequential test for multiple breaks at unknown breakpoints (Ditzen, Karavias & Westerlund. 2021)

		Bai & Perron Critical Values		
	Test Statistic	**1% Critical Value**	**5% Critical Value**	**10% Critical Value**
F(1|0)	8.29	12.29	8.58	7.04
F(2|1)	3.93	13.89	10.13	8.51
F(3|2)	12.34	14.80	11.14	9.41
F(4|3)	0.31	15.28	11.83	10.04
F(5|4)	7.08	15.76	12.25	10.58
Detected number of breaks: (min)		.	3	1
(max)		.	3	3

(Continued)

Table 7.4. (*Continued*)

Null hypothesis rejected more than once after non-rejection. The detected number of breaks indicates the minimum and maximum number of breaks for which the null hypothesis is rejected.

Estimation of break points

			N = 16 T = 26 SSR = 12.65 *Trimming* = 0.15

#	Index	Date	[95% Conf. Interval]	
1	5	2000	1999	2001
2	8	2003	2002	2004
3	23	2018	2012	2024

Test for multiple breaks at unknown breakdates (Ditzen, Karavias & Westerlund. 2021)
*H*0: no break(s) vs. *H*1: 3 break(s)

	Bai & Perron Critical Values			
	Test Statistic	**1% Critical Value**	**5% Critical Value**	**10% Critical Value**
supW(tau)	7.39	7.60	5.96	5.21

Estimated break points: 2000 2003 2018
Trimming: 0.15

Test for multiple breaks at unknown breakdates (Ditzen, Karavias & Westerlund. 2021)
*H*0: no break(s) vs. *H*1: 1 <= *s* <= 3 break(s)

	Bai & Perron Critical Values			
	Test Statistic	**1% Critical Value**	**5% Critical Value**	**10% Critical Value**
UDmax(tau)	8.29	12.37	8.88	7.46

* evaluated at a level of 0.95.
Trimming: 0.15

Test for multiple breaks at unknown breakpoints (Ditzen, Karavias & Westerlund. 2021)
*H*0: 2 vs. *H*1: 3 break(s)

	Bai & Perron Critical Values			
	Test Statistic	**1% Critical Value**	**5% Critical Value**	**10% Critical Value**
F(s+1|s)*	12.34	14.80	11.14	9.41

* *s* = 2
Trimming: 0.15

Table 7.5. Panel Structural Break Analysis Results in Case of Import.

Sequential test for multiple breaks at unknown breakpoints (Ditzen, Karavias & Westerlund. 2021)

		Bai & Perron Critical Values		
	Test Statistic	**1% Critical Value**	**5% Critical Value**	**10% Critical Value**
F(1|0)	24.82	12.29	8.58	7.04
F(2|1)	18.48	13.89	10.13	8.51
F(3|2)	20.86	14.80	11.14	9.41
F(4|3)	17.79	15.28	11.83	10.04
F(5|4)	1.09	15.76	12.25	10.58
Detected number of breaks:		4	4	4

The detected number of breaks indicates the highest number of breaks for which the null hypothesis is rejected.

Estimation of break points

N = 16
T = 26
SSR = 6.17
$Trimming$ = 0.15

#	Index	Date	[95% Conf. Interval]	
1	5	2000	1999	2001
2	8	2003	2002	2004
3	20	2015	2008	2022
4	23	2018	1996	2040

Test for multiple breaks at unknown breakdates (Ditzen, Karavias & Westerlund. 2021) $H0$: no break(s) vs. $H1$: 4 break(s)

		Bai & Perron Critical Values		
	Test Statistic	**1% Critical Value**	**5% Critical Value**	**10% Critical Value**
supW(tau)	7.81	6.19	4.99	4.41

Estimated break points: 2000 2003 2015 2018
Trimming: 0.15

(Continued)

Table 7.5. (*Continued*)

Test for multiple breaks at unknown breakdates (Ditzen, Karavias & Westerlund. 2021)
*H*0: no break(s) vs. *H*1: 1 <= *s* <= 4 break(s)

		Bai & Perron Critical Values		
	Test Statistic	**1% Critical Value**	**5% Critical Value**	**10% Critical Value**
UDmax(tau)	24.82	12.37	8.88	7.46

* evaluated at a level of 0.95. Trimming: 0.15

Test for multiple breaks at unknown breakpoints (Ditzen, Karavias & Westerlund. 2021)
*H*0: 3 vs. *H*1: 4 break(s)

		Bai & Perron Critical Values		
	Test Statistic	**1% Critical Value**	**5% Critical Value**	**10% Critical Value**
F(s+1|s)*	17.79	15.28	11.83	10.04

* $s = 3$
Trimming: 0.15

supported by the results. In the case of the second hypothesis, i.e., H_0: no breaks versus H_1: $1 \leq s \leq s_{max}$ breaks it is found that the maximum number of breaks is four. Finally, for the third hypothesis, i.e., H_0: s breaks versus H_1: $s + 1$ breaks from the results it can be concluded that there exist four breaks in the series of import.

Now comparing the results of exports and imports one interesting result is that common break points for these two series are 2000, 2003 and 2018.

7.4. Conclusion

This chapter investigates the performance of the Indian pharmaceutical industry and pharmaceutical industries of leading countries namely the United States, China, Germany, Japan, Ireland, Switzerland, France, Italy, India, Belgium, United Kingdom, Spain, Brazil, Canada, South Korea and Netherlands. This chapter looks at the trends of three lead variables namely output, export and import of the Indian pharmaceutical industry and pharmaceutical industries of leading countries and tries to compare IPI with the other countries in terms of the above three variables. This chapter helps to identify the position of the Indian pharmaceutical industry in the global context. Also, this chapter verifies the presence of structural breaks in the different series of production, export and import using panel structural break methodology.

The major findings of this chapter are listed below:

Firstly, there is a positive growth rate of output for all the countries except the Netherlands and France.

Secondly, the inter-comparison of countries reveals that the growth of output is maximum for Italy and minimum and negative for France.

Thirdly, the grand mean of output is 0.034. For six countries namely Ireland, Italy, India, Belgium, Spain, and Switzerland, the growth rate is above average growth rate indicating good performance whereas for the remaining countries such as the United Kingdom, Germany, Netherlands and France, the growth rate is below the grand mean.

Fourthly, India stands in the fifth position for the production of pharmaceuticals in the global economy.

Fifthly, all the countries' growth rates for exports and imports are found to be positive. It seems a positive trend for both exports and imports for most of the sample period.

Sixthly, the inter-comparison of countries reveals that the growth of exports is maximum for Ireland and minimum for the United Kingdom whereas it is maximum for China and minimum for United Kingdom in the case of imports.

Seventhly, the grand mean for exports is 13% and for imports it is 12%. Most of the countries, i.e. six have growth rates higher than average. Whereas for eight countries the growth rate is higher than average in case of import.

Eighthly, India stands in the fourth position for both export and import of pharmaceuticals.

Finally, the results of the panel structural break analysis show that there exist no such structural changes in the series of output of the countries across the years. In the case of export, there exist three breaks in the series. The break points are 2000, 2003 and 2018 in the case of export. If we test the first hypothesis, then from the results one can conclude that the existence of three breaks is very much supported by the results. Now if we run the second hypothesis, then from the results one can conclude that the maximum number of breaks is three. Finally, for the third hypothesis, from the results one can conclude that the null hypothesis fails to accept against alternative hypothesis, i.e. there exists three breaks in the series of exports. In the case of import, there exist four breaks in the series. The break points are 2000, 2003, 2015 and 2018. As in the case of exports if we test the first hypothesis, then from the results it is obvious that the existence of four breaks is very much supported by the results. In the case of the second hypothesis, it is found that a maximum number of breaks is four. Finally, for the third hypothesis, from the results, it can be concluded that there exist four breaks in the series of imports. Comparing the results of exports and imports one interesting result found is that common break points for these two series are 2000, 2003 and 2018.

Chapter 8

Summary and Overall Conclusion

Abstract

This chapter summarises the whole study and makes the concluding observations on each of the seven chapters and recommends some policies for the betterment of the pharmaceutical industries in different Indian states and for the Indian pharmaceutical industry as a whole.

Keywords: Technical efficiency; total factor productivity growth; firm-level data; state-level data; export; import; structural break; panel data; conclusion; policy suggestions

8.1. Introduction

The Indian pharmaceutical industry (IPI) has emerged as one of the most vibrant segments among the different manufacturing industries in India and deserves special attention.

The economic reforms of 1991 further propelled the IPI onto the global platform by removing licencing restrictions. IPI holds a significant place in the global economy. The country through the pharma sector is considered to be one of the most valuable nations. As of 2021, India is the largest country for the production of low-cost generic drugs which is advantageous for exporting medicines to other countries. Therefore, the share of medicines global pharmaceutical export is 20% in terms of the generic pharma sector. The nation is the largest provider of generic medicines in the world and supplies medicines to many countries.

Thus, the principal objective of the book is to investigate the performance of pharmaceutical industries in some countries as well as states of India. In order to present the contents, the book develops seven major chapters. This chapter makes the concluding observations on each of the seven chapters and recommends some policies for the betterment of the Indian states as well as the IPI.

Performance Analysis of the Indian Pharmaceutical Industry: A Global Outlook, 147–160

Published under exclusive licence by Emerald Publishing Limited
doi:10.1108/978-1-83797-743-720251008

Chapter 1 sketches an introduction to the IPI and pharmaceutical industry in different countries. This chapter then finds the major objectives of the book and the relevant research questions for exploring the objectives. It then presents the structure of the present study, i.e. the chapterisation of the book is presented briefly.

This chapter introduces the development of the IPI in different phases such as till the 1970s, with the modification of the Indian Patent Act 1970, i.e. after the 1970s, with the trade liberalisation and the signing of the TRIPS agreement, and in the product patent regime, i.e. since 2005. This chapter also discusses the position of IPI in the global economy along with the top medicine-producing countries in the world. The objectives of the present study are presented separately with the firm-level data, state-level data as well as All India and global-level data. All the research questions are also presented in this chapter related to the firm-level data, state-level data as well as All India and global-level data. Then the relevance of the present study in the existing literature is discussed considering each of the book chapters separately through outlining the structure of the present study.

Chapter 2 discusses a survey of literature on the pharmaceutical industry related to efficiency, productivity and other issues in India and across the globe. It discusses the existing study highlighting the gaps and presents the connection of the present study with the existing literature.

This chapter discusses a survey of literature on the pharmaceutical industry related to efficiency, productivity and other issues in India and across the globe. Econometric theoretical literature on technical efficiency as well as econometric theoretical literature on total factor productivity growth (TFPG) are discussed in separate sections. Individual sections discuss studies on the performance of the pharmaceutical industries in the Indian context, studies on the performance of the pharmaceutical industries in the international context, studies on efficiency in Indian pharmaceutical industry, studies on TFPG in the IPI, other studies on IPI and also studies on the performance of the pharmaceutical industries in the international context (other than India). This chapter discusses the existing study highlighting the gaps and presents the connection of the present study with the existing literature in the conclusion section.

Chapter 3 estimates the efficiency of the IPI using non-parametric method of data envelopment analysis (DEA) approach. To doing that it measures output-oriented technical efficiency of the IPI considering each firm as a decision-making unit. Also, the factors behind the variation in technical efficiency are identified using panel regression. It also estimates the productivity growth of the IPI. For that, it measures TFPG considering each firm as a decision-making unit using non-parametric method of the DEA approach. Also, the major factors responsible for variation in TFPG of the IPI are found using panel regression. Also, this chapter compares efficiency and productivity of the IPI. It compares technical efficiency and TFPG of the IPI. This chapter also tries to identify the common factors responsible for changes in these two performance indicators. Another important contribution of this chapter is that it verifies the presence of structural breaks in the TFPG series at the firm level by using panel structural break methodology.

The present chapter assesses the performance of IPI by considering 74 sample firms from 2000–2001 to 2019–2020. For estimating Technical efficiency (TE), the present book uses 1-output and 4-inputs technology. The output is sales value and inputs are expenses of raw material, power and fuel, salaries & wages as well as capital. All the monetary figures are adjusted by means of suitable price indices.

TE is estimated by using the Banker–Charnes–Cooper (BCC) model of DEA employing a computer programme solver in Excel. Two-stage least square methodology under panel regression is employed to identify factors that enhance or hinder TE. For that, STATA 15 program were used. To take care of the simultaneity problem, the panel model in a simultaneous framework has been framed with three equations considering TE, net export intensity (NXI) and Research and Development Intensity (RDI) as dependent variables. The proposed model is estimated in a panel set-up showing simultaneous relationships among different variables.

The major findings of Chapter 3 related to technical efficiency, could be listed as follows:

First of all, it is found that TE is more in post-product system relative to pre-product one. The sample period is broken down into three: first period is from 2000 to 2005, second period covers 2006 to 2010 as well as period 3 runs from 2011 to 2020. Now if one considers the different periods, the average efficiencies are 0.909, 0.925 and 0.965 for periods 1, 2 and 3 respectively. This average TE is highest in period 3 followed by period 2 and then 1. This maximum average TE in period 3 may be the effect of product patent regime in pharmaceuticals. Thus, it is found that TE is more in post-product system relative to pre-product one. In the pre-product regime, IPI produced 90% of the maximum producible output whereas in post-product regime i.e. in periods 2 and 3, the industry is found to produce 92% and 96% of the maximum producible output. Secondly, considering all the firms over the sample period, efficiency ranges between 0.462 and 1, the mean TE being 0.928. Most of the firms, i.e. about 68% firms are enjoying efficiency level above the mean TE and the rest firms are having TE below the mean. Finally, it is determined that RDI, NXI, Advertisement intensity (AI) and Market share (MS) are the encouraging factors of efficiency. The relationship between AI and TE is found to be U shaped. This implies that as AI increases TE decreases but after some threshold level with rise in AI, TE also rises may be due to firms spending more on advertisement may be more prone to introduce a new product in the market easily, increases sales, fights market competition and thus may increase production and thus TE. But MS and TE are of inverted U shaped indicating that at first TE rises with rise in MS may be the benefits of large size as well as protected market. But after some threshold level TE falls with increase in MS. RDI and TE are also of inverted U shaped indicating that at first TE rises with rise in RDI may be research and development basically search for various new paths and develop knowledge which may ease faster product development thereby encouraging TE but after some threshold level, TE falls with increase in RDI. Whereas the relationship among NXI as well as TE is adverse, i.e. through more import and thus more modern technology, TE may increase. Again, the effect of product patent on TE compared to the process patent is encouraging. It may suggest that Indian pharmaceutical companies are able to suitably modify their production process for managing the altered permitted situation.

Also, Chapter 3 focuses on productivity of different firms of IPI. TFPG is estimated using firm-level data of IPI using DEA approach considering each firm as a decision-making unit. Then the factors influencing such TFPG are determined.

TFPG is estimated by using the Biennial Malmquist Index (BMI) of DEA employing a computer programme solver in Excel. Two-stage least square methodology under panel regression is employed to identify factors that enhance or hinder TFPG using STATA 15 software.

The factors which are considered as possible causes of TFPG are RDI, NXI as well as advertisement intensity of the previous period. All the variables have been taken in growth terms. A common problem may be that, a simultaneity may involve between TFPG and NXI as well as TFPG and RDI. Therefore, to take care of this problem, the simultaneous panel model has been framed with three equations considering TFPG, NXI and RDI as dependent variables. The proposed model is estimated in a panel set-up showing simultaneous relationships among different variables.

Regarding the productivity issue discussed in Chapter 3, the result can be summed up as follows:

First of all, the overall average annual rate of change of TFPG is 0.712%. In three sub periods (first period from 2000 to 2005, second period covers 2006 to 2010 and third period from 2011 to 2020), the average annual rate of change of TFPG are 0.732, 1.138 and 0.443 respectively. This rate of changes of TFPG is highest in period 2 followed by period 1 and then 3. This maximum change in period 2 may be the immediate effect of complete product patent system in pharmaceuticals. The average annual rate of change of TFPG first increases in period 2 and then falls in period 3. Secondly, decomposing TFPG to changes due to efficiency, scale efficiency as well as technology, it is found that growth in productivity for study period is generally determined by way of technical efficiency change. Therefore, Technical efficiency change (TEC) is the primary cause of productivity rise. The technological variation as well as scale efficiency contributed equally for the productivity growth increase. Thus, better utilisation of factors of production and changes in scale as well as efficiency can move firms to greater level of TFPG during 2000–2001 to 2019–2020. Thirdly, the mean TFPG of the firms varies over the range 0.73 to 1.68. The average of the mean Biennial Malmquist Productivity Index (BMPI) or the grand mean (GRM) is 1.03. Among all the sample firms, 72.97% exhibit mean BMPI below the GRM and the rest 27.03% of firms shows mean BMPI above the GRM. So, the majority of the firms have their mean BMPI below the GRM. The analysis reveals that IPI shows productivity increase at a rate of 3% per annum. During the sample period, the mean technological change (TC) of the firms varies from 0.94 to 1.71. The GRM or average of mean TC of the firms in the sample period is 1.01. The estimated results of mean TEC and mean scale efficiency change (SEC) varies from 0.90 to 1.69 and 0.84 to 1.09 respectively. The GRMs are 1.02 and 1.01 corresponding to TEC and SEC. Finally, it is seen that RDI and AI in the previous period are positively related whereas NXI is negatively related with TFPG. The positive relationship between RDI and TFPG may be due to Research and Development basically includes the examination for numerous new paths as well as skill expansion which enable quicker product expansion thereby encouraging TFPG. The positive relationship between Advertising intensity of previous period and TFPG possibly may be due to firms spending more on advertisement in the previous period may be more prone to introduce novel market product during current period easily, increases sales and thus may increase productivity. But there is an undesirable linkage among net export intensity as well as TFPG. This indicates that import have more favourable impact over export to promote TFPG. The reason may be with more import firms can have access to machineries which may improve its production process thereby shifting the frontier and thus TFPG. Again, the effect of product patent on TFPG compared to the process patent is negative suggesting IPI to be incapable towards suitable modification for managing the changed legal environment.

This chapter addresses the issue of comparison between efficiency and productivity of IPI using firm-level data. It compares technical efficiency and TFPG of IPI using firm-level data based on the results obtained. This chapter also tries to identify the common factors responsible for changes in these two performance indicators.

It suggests the following:

First of all, there is wide variation in TE and TFPG for the sample firms. Secondly, the average TE is highest in period 3 followed by period 2 and then 1. This maximum average TE in period 3 may be the effect of product patent regime in pharmaceuticals. Thus, it is found that TE is more in post-product system relative to pre-product one. Whereas the rate of change of TFPG is highest in period 2 followed by period 1 and then 3. This maximum change in period 2 may be the immediate effect of a complete product patent system in pharmaceuticals. The average annual rate of change of TFPG first increases in period 2 and then falls in period 3. It turns out that in period 3, TE is maximum whereas TFPG is minimum. Thirdly, it is evident that RDI, NXI, AI and MS are the enhancing factors of efficiency. The relationship between AI and TE is found to be U shaped. But MS and TE as well as RDI and TE are inverted U shaped. Whereas the relationship among NXI and Technical Efficiency is undesirable. Again, the effect of product patent on TE compared to the process patent is encouraging. For TFPG, RDI and AI in previous period are factors enhancing TFPG whereas NXI is the retarding factor of TFPG of IPI. Again, the effect of product patent on TFPG compared to the process patent is found to be negative and statistically significant. Finally, for the performance indicators such as TE as well as TFPG, the common determinants turned out to be RDI, AI and NXI. The variables, RDI and AI have a positive relationship with the performance indicators whereas NXI is negatively related to TFPG but positively related to TE. There exist no such structural changes in the series of TFPG in firm-level analysis across the years.

Chapter 4 investigates the performance of the IPI using state-level data. It looks at the performance of pharmaceutical industries in major Indian states. For doing that it estimates technical efficiency and TFPG of Indian states. This chapter helps to compare the Indian states as well as to identify the position of the states in the IPI. This chapter assesses the performance of IPI for 17 major selected states of India considering the period 1983–1984 to 2019–2020. The 17 major selected states considered are Andhra Pradesh (AP), Assam (AS), Bihar (BI), Gujarat (GU), Haryana (HA), Himachal Pradesh (HP), Jammu & Kashmir (JK), Karnataka (KA), Kerala (KE), Maharashtra (MH), Madhya Pradesh (MP), Orissa (OR), Punjab (PU), Rajasthan (RA), Tamil Nadu (TN), Uttar Pradesh (UP) and West Bengal (WB). This section explores two different aspects of pharmaceutical industries of India namely TE and TFPG using state-level data. Another important contribution of this chapter is that it verifies the presence of structural breaks (which may appear due to changes in economic regime over time) in the TFPG series at state level by using panel structural break methodology.

First of all, output-oriented technical efficiency using state-level data are estimated using DEA approach considering each state as a decision-making unit. Then the factors influencing such technical efficiency are determined. TE is estimated by using the BCC model of DEA employing a computer programme solver in Excel. Two-stage least square methodology under panel regression is employed to identify factors that enhance or hinder TE. For that STATA 15 program was used. The possible sources of variation of efficiency score are found by taking into account the simultaneity problem and considering the firm size (MF), degree of mechanisation (K/L), composition of workforce (E/L), relative wage rate (W) and net export intensity $(X\text{-}M)/Y$ as possible determinants. Secondly, TFPG is estimated using state-level data using DEA approach considering each state as a decision-making unit. Then the factors influencing such TFPG are determined. TFPG is estimated by using the BMI of DEA employing a computer programme solver in Excel. Two-stage least square methodology under panel regression are employed to identify factors that enhance or hinder TFPG using STATA 15 software. The factors which are considered as possible causes of TFPG are firm size (MF), degree of mechanisation (K/L), composition of work force (E/L), market share (MS), relative wage rate (W) and net export intensity $(X\text{-}M)/Y$ taking into account the simultaneity problem as before. All the variables have been taken in growth terms. This chapter also verifies the presence of structural breaks, if any, in the TFPG series at the state level by using panel structural break methodology.

The findings of the present chapter can be discussed under two heads: the results of TE of Indian states and the results of TFPG of Indian states.

The results of TE of Indian states are listed as below.

First of all, the mean TE of all the states taken together turns out to be 0.72, implying efficiency level is moderate, on average the industry produces 72% of the maximum producible output. Secondly, mean TE values of all the 17 major selected states reveal that there is wide variation in TE score among the states, the highest being achieved by Maharashtra and the lowest is for Bihar. Finally, the results of determinants of TE shows that all the factors considered such as *MF*, *K*/*L*, *E*/*L* and *W* are found to be statistically significant. All the variables *MF*, *K*/*L*, *E*/*L* and *W* are positively related except degree of mechanisation (*K*/*L*) which is negatively related. TE increases with large sized firms who are technically efficient, may be due to easier access to superior quality of inputs and gain from economic advantages to produce larger value of output. An increase in *K*/*L* induces a lesser efficiency may be due to drawbacks in the management of more capitalistic and sophisticated technology. It may also be possible that Indian pharmaceuticals have installed new plant and machinery recently. Such investment may have been made keeping future opportunities in mind and presently these capitals are not fully utilised (Mazumder et al., 2010). Appropriate combination of work force will promote the industry to operate efficiently. Increase in *W* fosters TE, since with higher *W*, skilled workers are engaged into the production process thus helping to achieve higher TE. Added to that net export intensity will have a favourable impact on TE. An increase in net export intensity may lead to increase in TE due to economies of scale, knowledge spill over from international contacts and spill-over effects from technology diffusion.

Regarding the productivity issue, the result can be summed up as follows.

First, the mean TFPG of all the states taken together turns out to be 0.13. Secondly, mean TFPG values of all the 17 major selected states reveal that there is wide variation in TE score among the states, ranging from 0.0001 to 0.78. Finally, the results of determinants of TFPG shows that that *MF*, *K*/*L*, *E*/*L*, MS and *W* have favourable effect on TFPG. Also, the variables are statistically significant. Large-sized units may become more productive compared to smaller ones, having better access to production opportunities, due to the usage of new technologies and also can utilise economies of scale. Enhancement of *K*/*L* induces higher growth in productivity by encouraging learning by doing. The relation between *E*/*L* and TFPG is positive which shows that the right combination of work force can operate production efficiently and thus boost up TFPG. Producing units having high MS experience a bigger and secure market and also face lesser competition. As a result, productivity may rise. The higher number of skilled workers in the production process can be involved by raising *W* leading to higher TFPG. In addition to it, variable (*X*-*M*/*Y*) also boosts up TFPG. With the rise in net export intensity, TFPG rises may be due to the shift in the frontier because of knowledge spill-over from the international contacts and spill-overs from technology diffusion.

From the result of the panel structural break, the findings are as follows.

The break point is found to be in 2004 in the case of TFPG at the state level. One of the possible reasons for this break may be that IPI has experienced a massive transformation from ‘process patents regime’ in the seventies to a modern and World Trade Organization (WTO)-compatible regime under the TRIPS Agreement in 2005. The ranking of IPI is 3rd in volume and 14th in value in the global pharmaceutical market (Kalani, 2011). Since 2005, India has started a full-fledged product patent regime in pharmaceuticals and is to develop new drugs themselves or to collaborate with the MNCs as manufacturing or marketing partners for the new drugs developed by the MNCs (Chaudhuri 2005).

Chapter 5 focuses on total factor productivity convergence in the pharmaceutical industry across Indian states using the panel data approach. This chapter estimates TFP for the sample states, considering each state as a producing unit, by estimating production function considering three inputs – labour (L), capital (*K*) and material & fuel consumed (*MF*). For estimating the production function, the semi-parametric estimation technique proposed by Levinsohn and Petrin (2003) which addresses the endogeneity problem has been employed. The different approaches used to study convergence of TFP are absolute convergence (sigma convergence), beta convergence, convergence hypothesis using panel unit root tests and convergence hypothesis using Arellano-Bond dynamic panel data estimation as well as convergence hypothesis using system dynamic panel data estimation.

The secondary data employed in this study are obtained from the Annual Survey of Industries (ASI), Summary Results for the Factory Sector published by the Central Statistics Office, Government of India. The variables used are gross value of output; number of workers; fixed capital; materials consumed and fuels consumed covering the period 1983–1984 to 2019–2020. Relevant figures are deflated by appropriate price indices. The sample states are Andhra Pradesh, Assam, Bihar, Gujarat, Haryana, Himachal Pradesh, Jammu and Kashmir, Karnataka, Kerala, Madhya Pradesh, Maharashtra, Orissa, Punjab, Rajasthan, Tamil Nadu, Uttar Pradesh and West Bengal.

The results of this chapter can be summarised as follows:

First of all, it is found that all the three estimated coefficients of labour, capital and material & fuel consumed are positive and statistically significant at 1% level of significance. The sum of the coefficients as obtained is slightly higher than unity. The Wald test fails to reject the null hypothesis of constant returns to scale. Thus, econometric estimation of Cobb–Douglas production function has been done satisfactorily. Hence for calculating TFP, the values of the estimated coefficients of the three inputs, are employed. Secondly, the findings on sigma convergence suggests that the estimated equations show that the coefficients of trend of both the SD and COV are positive and statistically significant. The conclusion, therefore, is that the TFP show significant sigma divergence across the Indian states. Thirdly, the findings on beta convergence from the results of panel unit root tests shows that, in case of Levin-Lin-Chu (LLC) test, the coefficient of the lagged dependent variable is found to be negative in sign and statistically significant; it implies beta convergence for the series of (logarithm) of TFP of all the major Indian states to the all-India average. Exactly the same conclusion on the stationarity of the demeaned series has been obtained by the other tests such as Im–Pesaran–Shin (IPS), ADF-Fisher and PP-Fisher, i.e. the coefficient of the lagged dependent variable is negative and statistically significant. Taking all these test results of LLC, IPS, ADF-Fisher and PP-Fisher, therefore, it can be concluded that the assumption of stationarity of the demeaned series holds for this panel data. Hence, the hypothesis of beta convergence holds for TFP across the 17 major Indian states over the period 1983–1984 to 2019–2020. The results of Dynamic Panel Model Estimation as revealed from the first-differenced Generalised method of moments (GMM)-based results following the Arellano and Bond estimation procedure shows that the coefficient of the lagged dependent variable is statistically significant and is positive. The estimated coefficient is positive and is less than 1 implying prevalence of convergence in TFP of pharmaceutical industry across Indian states over the period 1983–1984 to 2010–2011. The result of system dynamic panel data estimation also shows positive and statistically significant coefficient. The coefficient estimate is also less than 1 in this case. Thus, one may conclude that the time series of TFP of pharmaceutical industry across the 17 Indian states has achieved beta convergence over the period 1983–1984 to 2019–2020. Finally, based on a number of modern as well as conventional statistical tests, beta convergence in TFP of pharmaceutical industries across the Indian states over 1983–1984 to 2019–2020 is an established empirical finding. In view of the fact that all these tests are based on statistically very sound methodologies as opposed to the conventional sigma convergence, conclusion can be made very strongly about the convergence in terms of TFP of pharmaceutical industries across the major states of India.

Chapter 6 examines the move towards a growing IPI based on structural break unit root test. The contribution of the present chapter is that it might be the first attempt to employ endogenous structural break analysis based on unit root test by using Sen (2003) approach taking All India data from the period 1983–1984 to 2019–2020 to find out the nature of growth process of nine major selected variables of IPI. Here, we basically want to test whether there is an improvement in the performance of IPI after 1995, the year when the first version of the product patent started.

IPI is one of the few industries which has been affected in a major way due to TRIPS agreement as from the year 2005 the existing Process Patent regime gave way to the Product Patent regime although the process of establishing a new patent regime in India started since 1995. In such an environment, it will be interesting to examine whether there has been any improvement in the performance of IPI after 1995, i.e. after the period of first version of the product patent regime. For this, an econometric analysis has been carried out for some selected variables like output, employment, productivity of labour, productivity of capital, capital labour ratio, export intensity, export price, import intensity and price by applying a recent development using unit root test to estimate the break point of these major variables using All India level data from the period 1983–1984 to 2019–2020. The distinguishing feature of this method is that the break point is not dependent on the prior belief of the researcher; rather it is endogenously determined depending on time series properties of the variables.

The present chapter uses data on *Y*, *L*, fixed capital and *L* at All India level from the period 1983–1984 to 2019–2020 provided by various issues of 'Annual Survey of Industries, Summary results for the Factory Sector' published by Central Statistical Organisation (CSO), Government of India.

The data on capital stock (*K*) have been obtained by the Perpetual Inventory Accumulation Method. Data on X and M are collected from various issues of Foreign Trade Statistics of India, published by the Directorate General of

Commercial Intelligence and Statistics. Data on the unit value index of exports (P_X) have been collected from the Handbook of Statistics on Indian Economy, Reserve Bank of India. The value of exports and imports has been deflated by unit value index of exports and imports to arrive at the data on the real value of exports and imports.

The results of the present chapter can be summarised as follows.

First of all, for all the variables except Y/L and K/L, i.e. for the seven variables like Y, L, Y/K, X/Y, P_X, M/Y and P the underlying series is of Trend Stationary (TS) type implying convergence towards a stationary process. So for all the seven variables the variability of the series remains constant over time. Secondly, the underlying process is DS for Y/L and K/L suggesting existence of a stochastic trend in the series of productivity of labour and capital labour ratio and the variability of these series is not constant, rather it depends on time. Hence, no definite conclusion can be drawn about the trend of Y/L and K/L or about the break point of these series. Thus, the performance of Y/L and K/L are very poor because first the growth process for these two variables follows a stochastic trend suggesting that no definite conclusion can be made on the extent of growth for these variables and secondly the series does not possess constant variability over time. Moreover, the coefficient of time is negative but not statistically significant in case of K/L showing one cannot infer about the change in the variability of the K/L series but in case of Y/L the coefficient is negative and significant suggesting that the variability has decreased over time, however being of DS type it is not convergent. Thirdly, the break points for Y, L, Y/K and P correspond to the period after 1995 as the break point is 1997–1998 for Y and Y/K and 2000–2001 for L and P. But in case of X/Y and M/Y the break point is 1992–1993, the period after Dunkel Draft submission (1991). Whereas for P_X, the break point is 1989–1990, the period just after India became a net exporter (since 1988–1989). Since the series of Y/L and K/L are of DS type, the rest of the analysis will be discussed excluding these two series. Fourthly, the coefficient of DU_T is positive and significant only in case of P_X showing that the level increases at the break point. For the rest of the series, it is negative and significant implying that the level decreases at the break point. Regarding the coefficient of time, it is found to be positive and significant in case of L implying that there exists an increasing trend for the entire study period but in case of P_X it is negative and significant suggesting that there exists a negative trend for the entire period of analysis. For the rest of the series, the coefficient of time is insignificant and no conclusion can be made regarding the trend for the entire period of analysis. The coefficient of D_T is found to be positive and significant in case of Y, L and P_X implying that the rate of growth increases after the break whereas the rate of growth has fallen in case of X/Y after the break as the coefficient of D_T is negative and significant. For the rest of the series, the coefficient of D_T is insignificant and nothing can be concluded about the rate of growth after the break for these series. Fifthly, based on the above results one can divide the seven variables under the following groups:

Group A: This group consists of only one variable employment, L where the growth increases for the entire period of study as well as after the break point.

However, there is a fall in the level at the break point. Thus, on the whole more or less the performance of *L* is satisfactory in the entire sample period as well as after the break point. Group B: The variable P_X falls under this group. Here trend is negative for the entire period of study but the rate of growth increases after the break point 1989–1990. Also, there is a rise in the level at the break point. Hence, the performance of P_X is moderate as it performed very well after the break point but not for the entire sample period. As for P_X, there is a fall in the growth rate for the entire period. So, it can be said that India is exporting pharmaceuticals at a lesser price (Report of the Task Force, Ministry of Commerce & Industry, December 12, 2008) Also, after the break point, 1989–1990 the increase in the rate of growth of P_X can be explained as: Till 1987–1988, imports were larger than exports except for a few years but with steady increase in exports the country has become a net exporter since 1988–1989 (Chaudhuri 2005). Group C: It consists of only variable output, *Y* where the trend is insignificant for the entire period of study. Also there occurs a fall in the level of output at the time of break but the rate of growth increases after the break 1997–1998. So, for the entire sample period, the performance of this variable is inconclusive but after the break point it acted moderately. Group D: The variables import intensity (*M*/*Y*), productivity of capital (*Y*/*K*) and price (*P*) form this group. Here one cannot surely conclude about their trend for the entire period of analysis and also about the growth of the series after the break point. But there is a fall in the level at the break point. It implies that at their respective break points, 1992–1993, 1997–1998 and 2000–2001 there is a fall in level of *M*/*Y*, *Y*/*K* and *P*. The fall in *M*/*Y* in the year 1992–1993 may be due to the fact that the period during the 1970s to the end of 1990s corresponds to the period of rapid progress of import substitution and then strengthening of export orientation in the IPI (Kamiike and Sato, 2011). Decline in *Y*/*K* at the break 1997–1998 may be due to the fact that for capital, cheaper and easier access in the post-reforms period facilitated its larger use than earlier, but output did not increase proportionately (Virmani & Hashim (2009)). Also, Uchikawa (2001, 2002) has pointed out that there was an investment boom in Indian industry in the mid-1990s and this boom raised production capacities substantially but demand did not rise which led to capacity under-utilisation. At the time of the break (2000–2001), there is a significant decline in the prices of drugs/ medicines. This may be due to the fact that in India, given that pharmaceutical industry was protected only by process patents and not product patents till 2005, the scope for competition was immense and it was this lack of intellectual property rights that brought down the prices of drugs, which were patented elsewhere in the world (Jha, 2010). The consumers have not suffered much because of the new patent regime as drugs/medicines are much more accessible to the consumers (Revised Report Submitted to the UNCTAD, August, 2010). Group-E: Only one variable Export intensity (*X*/*Y*) forms this group. Nothing can be said about the trend for the entire sample period as there occurs a positive but insignificant trend for the entire sample period. But there is a fall in the growth after the break 1992–1993 and there is a fall in the level of the series. Hence, the performance of *X*/*Y* for the entire sample period is inconclusive and bad after the break. For *X*/*Y*, there is a significant fall in the growth rate after the break 1992–1993. Our result is in conformity with Chaudhuri (1993). According to Chaudhuri (1993), one of the implications of Dunkel Draft will be lesser exports. Sixthly, the break points of different variables reveal that the lowest break point year is 1989–1990 for P_X and the highest break point year is 2000–2001 for L and P. Break point year is 1997–1998 for Y and Y/K. So, it is clear that out of the seven variables showing TS process, break point years are after 1995 for four variables Y, L, Y/K and P.

Finally, the variables like Y, L and P_X performed well after the break. Thus, one can say there is an improvement in the performance of employment, output and export price after the break. In the Indian literature, there is a considerable evidence of jobless growth for Indian manufacturing. According to Alessandrini (2009), there is discrepancy between the rate of growth of the economy and the rate of growth of employment. He pointed out that the capability of the Indian economy to generate employment seems to be limited. According to Virmani and Hashim (2009), the manufacturing sector in India performed unsatisfactorily in creating employment. They further pointed out that special policy attention is to be taken for the creation of employment in manufacturing as high growth in output may not guarantee sufficient employment. According to Papola and Sahu (2012), the long-term trend of a decline in the rate of employment growth is a fact that cannot be ignored. Bhalotra (1998) concluded that employment declined in Indian factories in the 1980s.

However, that does not imply all the sectors under manufacturing has experienced a decline in employment. For example, Mehrotra et al. (2013) pointed out that there are certain sectors of manufacturing like textiles; wearing apparel and leather products; paper and paper products, and publishing and reprinting of recorded media; basic metals; motor vehicles and other transport equipment; furniture; and medical and optical instruments, watches and clocks which has experienced reasonable increase in total employment. Our results also show that there is a significant improvement in employment in IPI and hence this result does not support the case of jobless growth for all the sectors of the economy simultaneously.

At the time of the break (2000–2001), it is found that there is a significant decline in P prices of drugs/medicines. So, P performed well at the break point.

The study of the growth of selected major variables of the IPI at All India level by using the modern time series technique clearly identifies the variables whose performance is satisfactory and other variables showing relatively poor performance and hence need special attention. However, it is to be noted that the growth of seven among the nine selected major variables converges towards a deterministic trend. Out of seven, for four variables like Y, L, Y/K and P, the break point corresponds to the period after 1995. Among them three variables Y, L and P performed well. For the entire sample period, the performance of Y is inconclusive but after the break point it acted moderately and the performance of L is satisfactory in the entire sample period as well as after the break point. For P, at the time of the break (2000–2001) there is a significant decline.

Chapter 7 examines the performance of the IPI and pharmaceutical industries of leading countries namely the United States of America, China, Germany, Japan, Ireland, Switzerland, France, Italy, Belgium, United Kingdom, Spain,

Brazil, Canada, South Korea and the Netherlands. This chapter looks at the trends of three lead variables namely output, export and import of the IPI and pharmaceutical industries of leading countries and tries to compare IPI with the other countries in terms of the above three variables and thus helps to identify the position of IPI in the global context. Also, this chapter verifies the presence of structural break in the different series of production, export and import using panel structural break methodology.

The major findings of this chapter can be listed as follows:

First, there are positive growth rates of output for all the countries except the Netherlands and France. The grand, i.e. the average of all countries taken together is 0.034. For six countries namely Ireland, Italy, India, Belgium, Spain, and Switzerland, the growth rate is above average growth rate indicating good performance whereas for the remaining countries such as the United Kingdom, Germany, the Netherlands and France, the growth rate is below the GRM. The result on output suggests that India stands in the fifth position in terms of production of pharmaceuticals. Secondly, all the countries' growth rate in exports and imports is found to be positive. It seems to be a positive trend for all the sample countries in the case of export and import for the sample period. Inter comparison of countries reveals that the growth of export is maximum for Ireland and minimum for the United Kingdom whereas it is maximum for China and minimum for the United Kingdom in the case of import. The GRM, i.e. the average of all countries/taken together of export is 13% and for import it is 12%. In the case of export, six countries namely China, Ireland, India, Belgium, Spain and South Korea have growth rates higher than average growth rate indicating good performance and for the remaining countries the growth rate is less than the average. Whereas in the case of import, for eight countries namely the United States of America, China, Germany, Ireland, India, Belgium, Brazil and South Korea, the growth rate is higher than the average growth rate and for the rest eight countries the growth rate is lower than the average growth rate. It can be seen that India stands in the fourth position for both export and import of pharmaceuticals. Finally, the results of panel structural break analysis show that there exist no such structural changes in the series of output of the countries across the year. In case of export, there exists three breaks in the series. The break points are 2000, 2003 and 2018 in the case of export. If we test the first hypothesis, then from the results one can conclude that existence of three break is very much supported by the results. Now if we run the second hypothesis, then from the results one can conclude that maximum number of breaks is three. Finally, for the third hypothesis, from the results one can conclude that null hypothesis is failed to accept against alternative hypothesis, i.e. there exists three breaks in the series of export. In the case of import, there exist four breaks in the series. The break points are 2000, 2003, 2015 and 2018. As in case of exports if we test the first hypothesis, then from the results it is obvious that existence of four break is very much supported by the results. In case of the second hypothesis, it is found that maximum number of breaks is four. Finally, for the third hypothesis, from the results, it can be concluded that there exist four breaks in the series of import. Now comparing the results of exports and imports one interesting result is that common break points for these two series are 2000, 2003 and 2018.

8.2. Policy Suggestions

The whole study on firm-level data suggests that for raising efficiency and productivity of IPI, any change in policy that leads to research and development growth and also advertisement should be emphasised. Export is to be promoted as it is the enhancing factor for TE.

The whole analysis on state-level data reveals that in order to foster productivity and efficiency of IPI, any policy changes that will lead to an increase in firm size, increase in wage rate and increase in net export intensity should be emphasised. Furthermore, any policy aiming at increase in market share will foster TFPG. Similarly, policy changes leading to right composition of work force will help in promoting TFPG and technical efficiency.

The results of this study can be applied in framing policies for future growth and improvement in the efficiency and productivity of IPI.

8.3. Limitations of the Study

The present study is limited to analysing IPI's efficiency and productivity using firm-level as well as state-level data, so IPI's growth performance is not separately studied using firm-level data as well as state-level data. The role of such an indicator cannot be neglected in determining the performance of the IPI.

Another limitation of the present study is that the estimation of technical efficiency and TFPG is not done in case of the foreign countries. The role of such indicators is very important in determining the position of the IPI in the global context may be the agenda of our future research.

Appendix 1

Panel Analysis: Fixed and Random Effect Model

One of the main advantages of a panel data set over a cross section is that a panel data set will allow the researcher great flexibility in modelling differences in behaviour across individuals. The basic framework for this discussion is a regression model of the form:

$$\begin{aligned} y_{it} &= x_{it}'\beta + z_i'\alpha + \varepsilon_{it} \\ &= x_{it}'\beta + c_i + \varepsilon_i \end{aligned}$$

Let there be K regressors in x_{it}, not including a constant term. The heterogeneity, or individual effect is $z'_i\alpha$ where z_i contains a constant term and a set of individual or group-specific variables, which may be observed and c_i is unobserved. The main objective of the analysis will be consistent and efficient estimation of the partial effects:

$$\beta = \frac{\partial E\left[\frac{y_{it}}{x_{it}}\right]}{\partial x_{it}}$$

Now for estimating the panel regression analysis, one can consider either

I) Fixed effect model

or

II) Random effect model

Fixed Effects: If z_i is unobserved, but correlated with x_{it}, then the least squares estimator of β is biased and inconsistent as a consequence of an omitted variable. In case of fixed-effect model, one can consider the following model:

$$y_{it} = x_{it}'\beta + \alpha_i + \varepsilon_{it}$$

where $\alpha_i = z_i'\alpha$, captures all the observable effects and specifies an estimable conditional mean. In case of fixed effects model, α_i to be a group-specific constant term. It should be noted that the term 'fixed' as used here signifies the correlation of c_i and x_{it} in equation 2, not that c_i is nonstochastic.

Random Effects: When unobserved, individual heterogeneity can be assumed to be uncorrelated with the included variables, then one can consider the following model:

$$y_{it} = x_{it}'\beta + E[z_i'\alpha] + \{z_i'\alpha - E[z_i'\alpha]\} + \varepsilon_{it}$$
$$= x_{it}'\beta + \alpha + u_i + \varepsilon_{it}$$

That is, as a linear regression model with a compound disturbance that may be consistently, albeit inefficiently, estimated by least squares. This random effect approach specifies that u_i is a group-specific random element. The crucial distinction between fixed and random effects is that whether the unobserved individual effect represents elements that are correlated with the regressors in the model or not, not whether these effects are stochastic or not.

Hausman's Test for the Random Effects Model

For estimating the model under panel set-up, one can consider two types of specification, (i) fixed effect model or (ii) random effect model. Now to test which specification is better one have to consider the Hausman's test which says that the random effects are independent of the right-hand side variables. The test is based on the assumption that under the hypothesis of no correlation between the right-hand side variables and the random effects are consistent estimators but fixed effects are inefficient.

The test is based on the following Wald statistic:

$$W = [\beta_{FE} - \beta_{RE}]'\Psi'[\beta_{FE} - \beta_{RE}]$$

$$\text{where } Var[\beta_{FE} - \beta_{RE}] = Var[\beta_{FE}] - Var[\beta_{RE}] = \Psi$$

W is distributed as X^2 with (K-1) degrees of freedom where K is the number of parameters in the model. If W is greater than the critical value then we reject the null hypothesis that both estimators are consistent, i.e. of no correlation between the right-hand side variables and the 'random effects' and in this case the fixed effects model is better.

Seemingly Unrelated Regression (SUR)

SUR is appropriate when all the right-hand side regressors X are assumed to be exogenous, and the errors are heteroscedastic and contemporaneously correlated so that the error variance matrix is given by $V = \Sigma \otimes I_T$.

Zellner's SUR estimator of β takes the following form:

$$b_{SUR} = (X' (\hat{\Sigma} \otimes I_T)^{-1} X)^{-1} X' (\hat{\Sigma} \otimes I_T)^{-1} y$$

where $\hat{\Sigma}$ is a consistent estimate of Σ with typical element s_{ij}, for all i and j.

If autoregressive terms are included in the equation, then the following equation is estimated:

$$y_{jt} = X_{jt}\beta_j + \left[\sum_{r=1}^{p_j} p_{jr}\left(y_{j(t-r)} - X_{j(t-r)}\right)\right] + \epsilon_{jt}$$

where ε_j is assumed to be serially independent, but possibly correlated contemporaneously across equations. Now, one can estimate Generalised Least Squares (GLS) specifications that account for various patterns of correlation between the residuals.

Cross-Section SUR or Contemporaneous Covariances: This class of covariance structures allows for conditional correlation between contemporaneous residuals for cross-section i and j, but restricts residuals in different periods to be uncorrelated, specifically that:

$$E\left(\in_{it}\in_{jt} / x_t^*\right) = \sigma_{ij}, E\left(\in_{is}\in_{jt} / x_t^*\right) = 0 \text{ for all } i, j, s \text{ and } t \text{ with } s \neq t.$$

The error terms may be thought of as cross-sectionally correlated. Alternatively, this error structure is sometimes referred to as clustered by period since observations for a given period are correlated. Using the period-specific residual vectors, one may rewrite this assumption as follows:

$$E\left(\in_t\in_t' / x_t^*\right) = \Omega_M$$

For all t, where

$$\Omega_M = \begin{bmatrix} \sigma_{11} & \cdots & \sigma_{1M} \\ \vdots & \ddots & \vdots \\ \sigma_{M1} & \cdots & \sigma_{MM} \end{bmatrix}$$

This is a cross-section specification because it involves covariances across cross-section as in a SUR type framework. Cross-section SUR generalised least squares on this specification is simply the feasible GLS estimator for systems where the residuals are both cross-sectionally heteroskedastic and contemporaneously correlated.

Eviews employs residual from first stage estimates to form an estimate of Ω_M. In the second stage, they perform feasible GLS.

White Cross-Section or Cross-Section Heteroscedasticity: The White cross-section method assumes that the errors are contemporaneously (cross-sectionally) correlated (period clustered). The method treats the pool regressions as a multivariate regression (with an equation for each cross-section) and computes robust standard errors for the system of equations. The coefficient covariance estimator is as follows:

$$\left(\frac{N^*}{N^* - K^*}\right)\left(\sum_t X_t'X_t\right)^{-1}\left(\sum_t X_t'\widehat{\epsilon}_t\widehat{\epsilon}_t' X_t\right)\left(\sum_t X_t'X_t\right)^{-1}$$

where the leading term is a degrees of freedom adjustment depending on the total number of observations in the stacked data, N^* is the total number of stacked observations and K^* is the total number of estimated parameters.

Appendix 2

Computation of State-Level Data on Export and Import

Data on state-level exports and imports are not readily available and have to be computed.

Method I:

State-level exports and imports figures are constructed in the following way:

Let Y be the output level of the country and let $Y_1, Y_2, \ldots, Y_{17}$ be that of the 17 major states.

Then $s_1 = Y_1/Y$, $s_2 = Y_2/Y$, …, $s_{17} = Y_{17}/Y$, where s_i is the share of each state in total production. Then the data on export of the states are $s_1{}^*X$, $s_2{}^*X$, $s_{17}{}^*X$ and the data on import of the states are $s_1{}^*M$, $s_2{}^*M$, …, $s_{17}{}^*M$, where X and M are data on export and import of All India.

The methodology for such type of data construction can be found in Ray & Ghose (2014).

Method II:

An alternative procedure of state-level data generation on X and M was adopted using the CMIE prowess database.

The method is like this: Data on X for the ith state, $X_i = \sum x_{ij}$ where x_{ij} is the export figure of the jth firm located in the ith state.

Similarly, data on M for the ith state, $M_i = \sum m_{ij}$ where m_{ij} is the import figure of the jth firm located in the ith state.

It may be noted that if the jth firm is found to be located in say, three different states, then the average of the export figure of the jth firm will be taken as the export figure of the jth firm in the three states separately.

A similar methodology can be found in Goldar & Banga (2007).

Appendix 3

Measurement of Different Variables

- Output (Y) measured by gross value added
- Labour (L) measured by number of workers
- Capital (K) obtained from PIAM (discussed in Appendix 4)
- Intermediate inputs (I) measured by the sum of materials consumed and fuels consumed
- Productivity of labour (Y/L)
- Productivity of capital (Y/K)
- Capital labour ratio (K/L)
- Employment (L)
- Relative price (P), i.e. the price of pharmaceutical industry output at All India level relative to the price of output of the overall manufacturing industry at All India level
- Export intensity (X/Y)
- Import intensity (M/Y)
- Firm size (MF) measured by the sum of materials consumed and fuels consumed
- Degree of mechanisation measured by the ratio of capital to labour (K/L)
- Composition of workforce (E/L) measured by (non-production) employees per production worker
- Relative wage rate (W) is the real wage rate in the pharmaceutical industry at state-level relative to real wage rate in overall Indian manufacturing
- *MS* of any state, measured by the ratio of output of that state to output of All India.
- Net export intensity ($(X\text{-}M)/Y$)

Appendix 4

Perpetual Inventory Accumulation Method (PIAM)

Let B_t denote the book value of fixed assets at the end of year t, D_t the depreciation allowances made in that year and P_t the capital goods price index, i.e. machinery and equipment index for that year. Then the series on real fixed investment may be derived as

$$I_t = (B_t - B_{t-1} + D_t) / P_t$$

Then the capital stock series, K can be derived by using the following relationship:

$$K_t = K_{t-1} + I_t \quad \text{(a)}$$

$$\textbf{or } K_t = K_0 + \Sigma I_t \quad \text{(b)}$$

where K_0 is an estimate of real capital stock for a benchmark year.

References and Further Reading

Abdus, S. K., & Sabeerdeen, M. (2016). A study on effective brand promotional strategies influencing customers. *International Journal of Management*, *7*(2), 52–65.

Abramovitz, M. (1956, May). Resources and output trends in United States since 1870. *American Economic Review*, *46*.

Abu, O., & Kirsten, J. F. (2009). Profit efficiency of small- and medium-scale maize milling enterprises in South Africa. *Development Southern Africa*, *26*(3), 353–368.

Acharya, S. (2008). Poverty alleviation and the industrial employment of women (the case of Nepal). *Journal of International Development*, *20*, 670–685.

Acquaah, M. (2005). Enterprise ownership, market competition and manufacturing priorities in a Sub-Saharan African emerging economy: Evidence from Ghana. *Journal of Management and Governance*, *9*, 205–235.

Afriat, S. N. (1972). Efficiency estimation of production functions. *International Economic Review*, *3*(3), 568–598.

Agarwal, A., & Mandelker, G. N. (1987). Managerial incentives and corporate investment and financing decisions. *Journal of Finance*, *42*(4), 823–837.

Agarwal, R. N., & Goldar, B. (1992). *Technical efficiency in the Indian Engineering Industry: Deterministic vs. stochastic frontier production function approach*. [Working Paper, Institute of Economic Growth, Delhi].

Aghion, P., & Howitt, P. A. (1992). A model of growth with creative destruction. *Econometrica*, *60*(2), 323–351.

Aghion, P., & Howitt, P. A. (1998). *Endogenous growth theory*. MIT Press.

Agrawal, P., & Saibaba, P. (2001). TRIPS and India's pharmaceutical industry. *Economic and Political Weekly*, *36*(39), 3787–3790.

Ahluwalia, I. J. (1985). *Industrial growth in India: Stagnation since mid-sixties*. Oxford University Press.

Ahluwalia, I. J. (1991). *Productivity growth in Indian manufacturing*. Oxford University Press.

Aigner, D. J., & Chu, S. F. (1968). On estimating the industry production function. *American Economic Review*, *58*(4), 826–839.

Aigner, D. J., Lovell, C. A. K., & Schmidt, P. (1977). Formulation and estimation of stochastic frontier production function models. *Journal of Econometrics*, *6*(1), 21–37.

Ajibefun, I. A. (2007). Technical efficiency analysis of micro-enterprises: Theoretical and methodological approach of the stochastic frontier production functions applied to Nigerian data. *Journal of African Economies*, *17*(2), 161–206.

Akkemik, K. A. (2006). Patterns of industrialisation, structural changes and productivity in Turkish manufacturing (1970–2000). *Journal of Economic Cooperation*, *27*(1), 71–88.

Akpalu, W., Alnaa, S. E., & Aglobitse, P. B. (2012). Access to microfinance and intra household business decision making: Implication for efficiency of female owned enterprises in Ghana. *Journal of Socio-Economics*, *41*(5), 513–518.

Al Ayouty, I. (2017). R&D performance in the pharmaceutical industry: A case study of Egypt. *European Journal of Sustainable Development*, *6*(2), 121–134. https://doi.org/10.14207/ejsd.2017.v6n2p121

Al Momani, K. M. K., AlWadi, B. M., & Al-Wadi, S. (2023), The nexus of intellectual capital and firm performance: Evidence from Jordanian Pharmaceutical Companies.

In Yaseen, S. G. (Eds.), *Cutting-Edge Business Technologies in the Big Data Era*. Springer. https://doi.org/10.1007/978-3-031-42455-7_16

Alam, T., & Rastgi, R. (2019). Trend analysis of cost efficiency for the pharmaceutical industry: A DEA approach. *Management Science Letters*, *9*(2019), 749–754.

Albin, A. (1990). Manufacturing sector in Kerala: Comparative study of its growth and structure. *Economic and Political Weekly*, *25*(37), 2059–2070.

Aldy, J. E. (2006). Per capita carbon-dioxide emissions: Convergence or divergence? *Environmental and Resource Economics*, *33*(4), 533–555.

Alessandrini, M. (2009). *Jobless growth in Indian manufacturing: A Kaldorian approach*. Conference Proceedings. https://api.semanticscholar.org/CorpusID:73704893

Ali, K., & Hamid, A. (1996). Technical change, technical efficiency, and their impact on input demand in the agricultural and manufacturing sectors of Pakistan. *The Pakistan Development Review*, *35*(3), 215–228.

Alias, R., Abu, M., & Abdullah, A. M. (2008). Technical efficiency of small and medium enterprise in Malaysia: A stochastic frontier production model. *International Journal of Economics and Management*, *2*(2), 395–408.

Allah, A. N. (2012). Social capability deficits and productivity behaviour of African manufacturing firms: Evidence from Lesotho garment producers. *Development Southern Africa*, *29*(2), 317–334.

Alvarez, R., & Crespi, G. (2001). Determinants of technical efficiency in small firms. *Small Business Economics*, *20*, 233–244.

Amiti, M., & Konings, J. (2007). Trade liberalization, intermediate inputs, and productivity: Evidence from Indonesia. *The American Economic Review*, *97*(5), 1611–1638.

Angeriz, A., Mccombie, J., & Roberts, M. (2006). Productivity, efficiency and technological change in European Union regional manufacturing: A data envelopment analysis approach. *The Manchester School*, *74*(4), 500–525.

Annual Report 2011-12, Government of India (GOI), Ministry of Chemicals & Fertilizers, Department of Pharmaceuticals. https://chemicals.gov.in/reports/annual-report-2011-12

Annual Survey of Industries-Summary Results for Factory Sector: Different Issues. https://pib.gov.in/PressReleasePage.aspx?PRID=2069571

Arellano, M., & Bond, S. (1991). Some tests of specification for panel data: Monte Carlo evidence and an application of employment equations. *Review of Economic Studies*, *58*, 277–297.

Ark, B. V., & Piatkowski, M. (2004). Productivity, innovation and ICT in old and new Europe. *International Economics and Economic Policy*, *1*, 215–246.

Aslanogilu, E. (2000). Spillover effects of foreign direct investments on Turkish manufacturing industry. *Journal of International Development*, *12*, 1111–1130.

Atal, S., Deshmankar, B., & Nawaz, S. A. (2016). Cost analysis of commonly used drugs under price control in India: Assessing the effect of drug price control order on brand price. *International Journal of Pharmacy and Pharmaceutical Sciences*, *8*(4), 315–321.

Atkinson, S. E., & Halabi, C. E. (2005). Economic efficiency and productivity growth in the post-privatization Chilean hydroelectric industry. *Journal of Productivity Analysis*, *23*, 245–273.

Audretsch, D. B., & Elston, J. A. (2006). Can institutional change impact high-technology firm growth?: Evidence from Ggermany's Nneuer Markt. *Journal of Productivity Analysis*, *25*, 9–23.

Audretsch, D. B., Santarelli, E., & Vivarelli, M. (1999). Start-up size and industrial dynamics: Some evidence from Italian manufacturing. *International Journal of Industrial Organization*, *17*, 965–983.

Aw, B. Y., Chen, X., & Roberts, M. J. (2001). Firm-level evidence on productivity differentials and turnover in Taiwanese manufacturing. *Journal of Development Economics*, *66*, 51–86.

Ayed-Mouelhi, R. B., & Goaïed, M. (2003). Efficiency measure from dynamic stochastic production frontier: Application to Tunisian textile, clothing, and leather industries. *Econometric Reviews*, *22*(1), 93–11.

Baccouche, R., & Kouki, M. (2003). Stochastic production frontier and technical inefficiency: A sensitivity analysis. *Econometric Reviews*, *22*(1), 79–91.

Badinger, H., & Egger, P. (2007). *Intra- and inter-industry productivity spillovers in OECD manufacturing: A Spatial econometric perspective*. CESifo Working Paper No. 2181.

Bagchi, A. K. (1975). Some characteristics of industrial growth in India. *Economic and Political Weekly*, *10*(5–7), 157–164.

Bagchi, A. K. (1998). Studies on the economy of West Bengal since independence. *Economic and Political Weekly*, *33*(47/48), 2973–2978.

Bai, J., & Perron, P. (2003a). Computation and analysis of multiple structural change models, *Journal of Applied Econometrics*, *18*, 1–22.

Bai, J., & Perron, P. (2003b). Critical values for multiple structural change tests. *Econometrics Journal*, *6*, 72–78.

Bai, J., & Perron, P. (1998). Estimating and testing linear models with multiple structural changes. *Econometrica*, *66*, 47–78.

Balakrishnan, P., & Pushpangadan, K. (1994). Total factor-productivity growth in manufacturing industry: A fresh look. *Economic and Political Weekly*, *29*(31), 2028–2035.

Balakrishnan, P., & Pushpangadan, K. (1998). What do we know about productivity growth in Indian industry? *Economic and Political Weekly*, *33*(33/34), 2241–2246.

Balakrishnan, P., & Pushpangadan, K. (2002). TFPG in manufacturing: The 80s revisited. *Economic and Political Weekly*, *37*(4), 323–325.

Balakrishnan, P., Pushpangadan, K., & Babu, M. S. (2000). Trade liberalization and productivity growth in manufacturing: Evidence from firm-level panel data. *Economic and Political Weekly*, *35*(41), 3679–3682.

Balassa B. (1988). Outward orientation. In H. Chenery & T. N. Srinivasan (Eds.), *Handbook of development economics* (Vol. 2, Ch. 31, pp. 1645–1689). Elsevier.

Baltagi, B. H. (2005). *Econometric analysis of panel data* (3rd ed.). John Wiley & Sons.

Banda, H. S., & Verdugo, L. E. B. (2011). Multifactor productivity and its determinants: An empirical analysis for Mexican manufacturing. *Journal of Productivity Analysis*, *6*, 293–308.

Bandyopadhyay, D. (2001). West Bengal-recipe for industrial revival. *Economic and Political Weekly*, *36*(52), 4788–4789.

Bandyopadhyay, S. (2000). Impact of efficiency indicators on the growth of productivity: A survey and empirical evidence from India. *Margin*, *33*(1), 84–98.

Banerjee, A. (1974). Production functions for selected Indian industries. *Journal of Development Studies*, *10*(2), 213–229.

Banerjee, A. (1975). *Capital intensity and productivity in Indian Industry*. Oxford University Press.

Banerjee, A., Dolado, J., & Galbraith, J. W. (1990). *Recursive tests for unit roots and structural breaks in long annual GNP Series*. [Unpublished Manuscript, University of Florida, Department of Economics].

Banerjee, A., Lumsdaine, R. L., & Stock J. H. (1992). Recursive and sequential tests for a unit root: Theory and international evidence. *Journal of Business and Economic Statistics*, *10*(3), 271–287.

Banerjee, D. (1996). Industrialisation programme in West Bengal: Policy and the problems-some lessons from newly industrialising countries in Asia. In A. Raychaudhuri & D. Sarkar (Eds.), *Economy of West Bengal (Problems and prospects)*. Allied Publishers.

Banerjee, D. (1998). Indian industrial growth and corporate sector behaviour in West Bengal, 1947–97. *Economic and Political Weekly*, *33*(47/48), 3067–3074.

Banga, R., & Goldar, B. N. (2007). Contribution of services to output growth and productivity in Indian manufacturing: Pre and post reforms. *Economic and Political Weekly*, *42*(26), 2769–2777.

Banker, R. D., & Natarajan, R. (2008). Evaluating contextual variables affecting productivity using data envelopment analysis. *Operations Research*, *56*(1), 48–58.

Banker, R. D., Charnes, A., & Cooper, W. W. (1984). Some models for estimating technical and scale efficiencies in data envelopment analysis. *Management Science*, *30*(9), 1078–1092.

Barro, J. R., & Sala-I-Martin, X. (1995). *Economic growth.* McGarw-Hill.

Barro, R. J., & Sala-i-Martin, X. X. (1992). Convergence. *Journal of Political Economy*, *100*, 223–251.

Barua, A., & Leech, D. (1987). *Factor substitution and returns to scale in Indian manufacturing.* [Discussion Paper No. 25, International Trade and Development Division, School of Development Studies, Jawaharlal Nehru University, New Delhi].

Basant, R. (2007). Intellectual property rights regimes: Comparison of pharma prices in India and Pakistan. *Economic and Political Weekly, 42*, 2007, 3969–3977.

Basant, R., & Fikkert, B. (1993). *Impact of R&D, foreign technology purchase and technology spillovers on Indian industrial productivity: Some estimates.* [Working Paper No. 11, Institute of New Technologies, United Nations University, Maastricht].

Basçi, E., Mahmud, S. F., & Yucel, E. M. (2007). Money and productive efficiency evidence from a high-inflation country. *Emerging Markets Finance and Trade*, *43*(1), 64–73.

Basu, S. (1987). West Bengal's economic growth in all-India perspective: With special reference to manufacturing sector. *Economic and Political Weekly*, *22*(30), 1252–1256.

Basuki, B., & Kusumawardhan, T. (2012). Intellectual capital, financial profitability, and productivity: An exploratory study of the Indonesian pharmaceutical industry. *Asian Journal of Business and Accounting*, *5*(2), 41–68. ISSN 1985-4064.

Baten, A., Rana, M., Das, S., & Khaleque, A. (2006). Technical efficiency of some selected manufacturing industries in Bangladesh: A stochastic frontier analysis. *Lahore Journal of Economics*, *11*(2), 23–41.

Baten, A., Rana, M., Das, S., & Nesa, M. K. (2007). Privatization and regional agglomeration effect on technical efficiency of Bangladesh manufacturing industry. *Journal of Economic Cooperation*, *28*(4), 81–104.

Battese, G. E., & Corra, G. S. (1977). Estimation of a production frontier model with application to the pastoral zone of eastern Australia. *Australian Journal of Agricultural Economics*, *21*(3), 169–179.

Battese, G. E., & Borca, S. S. (1997). Functional forms of stochastic frontier production functions and models for technical inefficiency effects: A comparative study for wheat farmers in Pakistan. *Journal of Productivity Analysis*, *8*(4), 395–414.

Battese, G. E., & Coelli, T. J. (1995). A model for technical inefficiency effects in a stochastic frontier production function for panel data. *Empirical Economics*, *20*(2), 325–332.

Battese, G. E., & Coelli, T. J. (1988). Prediction of firm-level technical efficiencies with a generalized frontier production function and panel data. *Journal of Econometrics*, *38*(3), 387–399.

Battese, G. E., & Coelli, T. J. (1992). Frontier production functions, technical efficiency and panel data. *Journal of Productivity Analysis*, *3*(1/2), 153–169.

Battese, G. E., & Coelli, T. J. (1993). *A stochastic frontier production function incorporating a model for technical inefficiency effects* [Working Paper No. 69, Department of Econometrics, University of New England, Australia].

Becchetti, L., & Sierra J. (2003). Bankruptcy risk and productive efficiency in manufacturing firms. *Journal of Banking and Finance*, *27*(11), 2099–2120.

Becchetti, L., & Santoro, M. I. M. (2001). The determinants of small and medium-sized firm internationalization and its relationship with productive efficiency. *Weltwirtschaftliches Archive, Bd*, *137*, 297–319.

Bergoeing, R., & Repetto, A. (2006). Micro efficiency and aggregate growth in Chile. *Cuadernos De Economia, 43*, 169–191.

Bergström, F. (2000). Capital subsidies and the performance of firms. *Small Business Economics, 14*, 183–193.

Bermen, E. (2000). *Does factor-based technological change stifle international convergence? Evidence from manufacturing* [Working Paper: 7964, National Bureau of Economic Research].

Bernard, A. B., & Jensen, J. B. (2004). Exporting and productivity in the USA. *Oxford Review of Economic Policy, 20*(3), 343–357.

Bernard, A., & Durlauf, S. (1996). Interpreting tests of the convergence hypothesis. *Journal of Econometrics, 71*, 161–173.

Bernard, A., & Jones, C. (1996a, March). Productivity and convergence across U.S. states and industries. *Empirical Economics, 21*, 113–135.

Bernard, A., & Jones, C. (1996b, December). Comparing apples to oranges: Productivity convergence and measurement across industries and countries. *American Economic Review, 86*, 1216–1238.

Berndt, E. R. (2001). The us pharmaceutical industry: Why major growth in times of cost containment? *Health Affairs, 20*(2), 100–114.

Bernstein, J. I., Mamuneas, T. P., & Pashardes, P. (2004). Technical efficiency and US. Manufacturing productivity growth. *The Review of Economics and Statistics, 86*(I), 402–412.

Bhagwati, J. N. (1988). Export-promoting trade strategy: Issues and evidence. *The World Bank Research Observer, 3*(1), 27–58.

Bhalotra, S. R. (1998). Changes in utilization and productivity in a deregulating economy. *Journal of Development Economics, 57*, 391–420.

Bhandari, A. K., & Maiti P. (2007, April). Efficiency of Indian manufacturing firms: Textile industry as a case study. *International Journal of Business and Economics, 6*(1), 71–88.

Bhandari, A. K., & Maiti, P. (2012). Efficiency of Indian leather firms: Some results obtained using two conventional methods. *Journal of Productivity Analysis, 37*, 73–93.

Bhandari, A. K., & Ray, S. C. (2011). Technical efficiency in Indian textile industry: A non-parametric analysis of firm-level data. *Bulletin of Economic Research, 64*(1), 109–124.

Bhasa, M. P. (2006). Does ownership affect performance? Empirical evidence from the Indian pharmaceutical industry. *Finance India, 20*(3), 913–940.

Bhasin, V. K., & Seth, V. K. (1977). Estimation of production function for Indian manufacturing sector: Pooling of cross-section and time-series data. *Artha Vijanana, 19*(2), 113–128.

Bhattacharjea, A., & Sindhwani, F. (2014). *Competition issues in the Indian pharmaceuticals sector*. Centre for Development Economics, Delhi School of Economics.

Bhattacharya, B. B., & Mitra, A. (1989). Industry-agriculture growth rates: Widening disparity: An explanation. *Economic and Political Weekly, 24*(34), 1963–1970.

Bhattacharya, M. (2002). Group profit, market share and efficiency: Evidence from Australian manufacturing. *Review of Industrial Organization, 20*, 187–199.

Bhattacharyya, A. (2012). Adjustment of inputs and measurement of technical efficiency: A dynamic panel data analysis of the Egyptian manufacturing sectors. *Empirical Economics, 42*, 863–880.

Bhaumik, S. K., & Kumbhakar, S. C. (2010). Is the post-reform growth of the Indian manufacturing sector efficiency driven? Empirical evidence from plant-level data. *Journal of Asian Economics, 21*, 219–232.

Bhavani, T. A. (1991a). Factor substitution and factor demand in Indian modern small enterprises: A case study of metal products. *Artha Vijanan, 33*(1), 41–55.

Bhavani, T. A. (1991b). Technical efficiency in Indian modern small scale sector: An application of frontier production function. *Indian Economic Review*, *26*(2), 149–166.

Bielenberg, A., & Geary, F. (2006). Growth in manufacturing output in Ireland between the union and the famine: Some evidence. *Explorations in Economic History*, *43*, 119–152.

Biesebroeck, J. V. (2005). Firm size matters: Growth and productivity growth in African manufacturing. *Economic Development and Cultural Change*, *53*(3), 545–583.

Blanchard, O. J., & Summers, L. H. (1986). Hysterics and the European unemployment problem. In S. Fisher (Ed.), *NBER Macroeconomics Annual 1986* (pp. 15–77). The MIT Press.

Blazek, D., & Sickles, R. C. (2010). The impact of knowledge accumulation and geographical spillovers on productivity and efficiency: The case of U. S. Shipbuilding during WWII. *Economic Modelling*, *27*(6), 1484–1497.

Blomstrom, M., & Persson, H. (1983). Foreign investment and spillover efficiency in an underdeveloped economy: Evidence from the Mexican manufacturing industry. *World Development*, *11*(6), 493–501.

Böckerman, P., & Maliranta, M. (2007). The micro-level dynamics of regional productivity growth: The source of divergence in Finland. *Regional Science and Urban Economics*, *37*, 165–182.

Bollard, A., Klenowb, P. J., & Sharma, G. (2013). India's mysterious manufacturing miracle. *Review of Economic Dynamics*, *16*, 59–85.

Bond, S., & Blundell, R. (1998). Initial condition and moment restrictions in dynamic panel data models. *Journal of Econometrics*, *87*, 115–143.

Boreinsztein, E., De Gregorio, J., & Lee, J. W. (1998). How does foreign direct investment affect economic growth. *Journal of International Economics*, *45*(1), 115–135.

Bottazzi, G., & Secchi, A. (2003). Why are distributions of firm growth rates tent-shaped? *Economics Letters*, *80*, 415–420.

Bottazzi, G., & Secchi, A. (2005). Growth and diversification patterns of the worldwide pharmaceutical industry. *Review of Industrial Organization*, *26*, 195–216.

Box, G. E. P., & Tiao, G. C. (1975). Intervention analysis with applications to economic and environmental problems. *Journal of the American Statistical Association*, *70*(349), 70–79.

Boyd, G., McDonald, J. F., Ross, M., & Hanson, D. A. (1987). Separating the changing composition of U.S. Manufacturing production from energy efficiency improvements: A divisia index approach. *The Energy Journal*, *8*(2), 77–96.

Braga, H., & Willmore, L. (1991). Technological imports and technological effort: An analysis of their determinants in Brazilian firms. *The Journal of Industrial Economics*, *39*(4), 421–432

Brand, H. (1974). Productivity in the pharmaceutical industry. *Monthly Labour Review*, *97*, 9–13.

Braun, M., & Larrain, B. (2005). Finance and the business cycle: International, inter-industry evidence. *The Journal of Finance*, *LX*(3), 1097–1128.

Breitung, J. (2000). The local power of some unit root test for panel data. *Advances in Econometrics*, *15*, 161–177.

Breitung, J., & Mayer, W. (1994). Testing for unit roots in panel data: Are wages on different bargaining levels cointegrated? *Applied Economics*, *26*, 353–361.

Breitung, J., & Das, S. (2005). Panel unit root tests under cross sectional dependence. *Stat Neerl*, *52*, 1–20.

Burange, L. G. (1999). Industrial growth and structure: Manufacturing sector in Maharashtra. *Economic and Political Weekly*, *34*(44), M39–M48.

Burange, L. G. (2004). *Energy and labour use in the organised manufacturing sector of Maharashtra*. [Working Paper No. UDE14/2/2004006, Department of Economics, University of Mumbai].

Burki, A. A., Khan, M. A., & Bratsberg, B. (1997). Parametric tests of allocative efficiency in the manufacturing sectors of India and Pakistan. *Applied Economics, 29*, 11–22.

Byun, T., Kim, K., & Choi, H. (2012). Comparative analysis of the total factor productivity of manufacturing in northeast Asian metropolitan areas. *Growth and Change, 43*(1), 167–177.

Calabrese, A., Campisi, D., & Mancuso, P. (2010). *Telecommunication industry and productivity convergence in the OECD countries*. The University of Rome Tor Vergata. Retrieved January 12, 2013, from http://userpage.fu berlin.de/~jmueller/its/conf/dub01/papers/mancuso.pdf

Carod, J. M. A., & Blasco, A. S. (2005). The determinants of entry are not independent of start-up size: Some evidence from Spanish manufacturing. *Review of Industrial Organization, 27*, 147–165.

Carod, J. M. A., Solís, D. L., & Bofarull, M. M. (2008). New business formation and employment growth: Some evidence for the Spanish manufacturing industry. *Small Business Economics, 30*, 73–84.

Carreira, C., & Teixeira, P. (2008). Internal and external restructuring over the cycle: A firm-based analysis of gross flows and productivity growth in Portugal. *Journal of Productivity Analysis, 29*, 211–220.

Caselli, M. (2013). Credit constraints, inequality and the growth gains from trade. *Economics Letters, 121*, 43–47.

Castany, L., Bazo, E. L., & Moreno, R. (2007). *Decomposing differences in total factor productivity across firm size* [Working Papers2007/5, Research Institute of Applied Economics].

Castany, L., Bazo, E. L., & Moreno, R. (2005). *Differences in total factor productivity across firm size: A distributional analysis*. In 45th Congress of the European Regional Science Association, August 23-27, Vrije Universiteit, Amsterdam.

Castiglione, C. (2012). Technical efficiency and ICT investment in Italian manufacturing firms. *Applied Economics, 44*, 1749–1763.

Caves, D., Laurits, W., Christensen, R., & Diewert, W. E. (1982). The economic theory of index numbers and the measurement of input, output and productivity. *Econometrica, 50*(6), 1393–1414.

Caves, R. E., & Barton, D. (1990). *Efficiency in US manufacturing industries*. The MIT Press.

Central Statistical Organization (Kolkata). https://mospi.gov.in/central-statistical-office-cso

Chadha, A. (2009). TRIPS and patenting activity: Evidence from the Indian pharmaceutical industry. *Economic Modelling, 26*(2), 499–505.

Chakraborty, C. (2017). Regional disparity and convergence of the growth of output, employment and productivity of labour of Indian pharmaceutical industry. *Vidyasagar University Journal of Economics, XIX*, 76–91 (ISSN 0975-8003).

Chakraborty, C., & Ghose, A. (2010). Growth performance of Indian pharmaceutical industry: Evidence from structural break unit root test. *Vidyasagar University Journal of Economics, XV*, 115–124 (ISSN 0975-8003).

Chakraborty, C., & Ghose, A. (2011). Interstate variation of the growth process of Indian pharmaceutical industry: Evidence from structural break unit root test. *Vidyasagar University Journal of Economics, XVI*, 2011–2012.

Chakraborty, C., & Ghose, A. (2013). Regional disparity and convergence of the growth of output of Indian pharmaceutical industry: Evidence based on structural break unit root test. *The Journal of Industrial Statistics, 2(2)*, 195–207. (ISSN 2278-4667)

Chakraborty, C., & Ghose, A. (2014, April). Input oriented technical efficiency and input slack of Indian Pharmaceutical Industry: Evidence from non parametric data envelopment analysis. In A. Emrouznejad, R. Banker, S. M. Doraisamy, & B. Arabi (Eds.),

Recent developments in data envelopment analysis and its applications, Proceedings of the 12th International Conference of DEA, Kuala Lumpur, Malaysia (pp. 256–261). ISBN: 978 1 85449 487 0.

Chakraborty, C., & Ghose, A. (2014, July-December). Efficiency and its determinants of Indian pharmaceutical industry: Evidence from stochastic frontier production analysis. *CBS Journal of Management Practices*, *1*(2), 47–58. (ISSN 2349-5073)

Chakraborty, C., & Ghose, A. (2015, August). Performance of Indian pharmaceutical industry in the post-liberalization era: Evidence based on structural break unit root test. *Suprayaga, No. 5*, 261–270. (ISBN 978-81-924236-4-7)

Chakraborty, C., & Ghose, A. (2017, March). Growth of output and its determinants in Indian pharmaceutical industry: Evidence from a panel regression. *The Journal of Industrial Statistics*, *6*(1), 108–122. (ISSN 2278-4667).

Chakraborty, C., & Ghose, A. (2018). The interstate variation of technical efficiency of Indian pharmaceutical industry: Stochastic frontier production function approach. In S. K. Jana & D. Mondal (Eds.), *Contemporary issues of economic development in India*. Concept Publication Company.

Chakraborty, C., & Ghose, A. (2019). The relative role of exports and imports in explaining technical efficiency of Indian Pharmaceutical Industry: An interstate variation. In B. Jana, P. Pal, & A. Chakraborty (Eds.), (Eds.), *India's economic development: Some issues and challenges* (pp. 74–95). Kumud Publication. ISBN 978-93-82974-45-0.

Chakraborty, C., & Pal, D. (2020a, June). Efficiency of Indian pharmaceutical industry: A non-parametric approach. *Artha Beekshan*, *29*(1), 24–34 (ISSN 0972-1185). https://www.arthabeekshan.com/Arthbikhan%20June,%202020.pdf

Chakraborty, C., & Pal, D. (2020b, October 1). Total factor productivity growth of Indian pharmaceutical industry: A non-parametric approach. *Vidyasagar University Journal of Economics*, *XXIV*, 129–142. http://inet.vidyasagar.ac.in:8080/jspui/handle/123456789/6352

Chakravarty, S. (1974). *Reflections on the growth process in the Indian Economy.* Hyderabad Administrative Staff College of India.

Chakravarty, S. (1979). On the question of home market and prospects for Indian growth. *Economic and Political Weekly*, *14*(30–32) (special number), 1231–1242.

Chambell, J. Y., & Mankiw, N. G. (1987). Permanent and transitory components in macroeconomic fluctuations. *American Economic Review: Papers and Proceedings*, *77*(2), 111–117.

Chambell, J. Y., & Mankiw, N. G. (1988). Are output fluctuations transitory?. *Quarterly Journal of Economics*, *102*(4), 875–880.

Chan, C.-P., & Lee, C.-C. (2008). Are per capita carbon dioxide emissions converging among industrialized countries? New time series evidence with structural breaks. *Environment and Development Economics*, *13*(4), 497–515.

Chan, L., & Daim, T. U. (2011). Multi-perspective analysis of the Chinese pharmaceutical sector: Policy, enterprise and technology. *Journal of Technology Management in China*, *2*, 171–190.

Chand, S., & Sen, K. (2002). Trade-liberalization and productivity growth: Evidence from Indian manufacturing. *Review of Development Economics*, *6*(1), 120–132.

Chandan, S., & Sanjay, S. (2010). Impact of infrastructure on output, productivity and efficiency: Evidence from the Indian manufacturing industry. *Indian Growth and Development Review*, *3*(2), 100–121.

Chandran, V. G. R., & Pandiyan, V. (2008). Technical efficiency and technological change in Malaysian service industries. *Applied Economics Letters*, *15*(7–9), 655–657.

Chandrasekhar, C. P., & Purkayastha, P. (1982). Transfer pricing in the Indian drug industry: An estimate and it's implications. *Social Scientist*, 3–10.

Chandulal. (2021). *Journal of Advanced Research in Economics and Administrative Sciences*. https://bcsdjournals.com/index.php/jareas ISSN 2708-9320 (Print) and 2709-0965 (Online) Vol.2, Issue 3. https://doi.org/10.47631/jareas.v2i3.300

Chapelle, K., & Plane, P. (2005). Productive efficiency in the Ivorian manufacturing sector: An exploratory study using a data envelopment analysis approach. *The Developing Economies*, *XLIII-4*, 450–471.

Chapelle, K., & Plane, P. (2005). Technical efficiency measurement within the manufacturing sector in côte d'ivoire: A stochastic frontier approach. *The Journal of Development Studies*, *41*(7), 1303–1324.

Charnes, A., Cooper, W. W., & Rhodes, E. L. (1978). Measuring the efficiency of decision-making units. *European Journal of Operational Research*, *2*(6), 429–444.

Charnes, A., Cooper, W. W., & Rhodes, E. L. (1981). Data envelopment analysis: Approach for evaluating program and managerial efficiency-with an application to the program follow through experiment in us public school education. *Management Science*, *27*(6), 668–697.

Chattopadhyay, S. K. (2004) Trends in total factor productivity of manufacturing sector in West Bengal: A sectoral and temporal analysis. *Reserve Bank of India Occasional Papers*, *25*(1–3), 75–103.

Chaudhuri, K., & Das, S. (2006). WTO, the TRIPS and Indian pharmaceutical industry. *Journal of Quantitative Economics*, *4*(1), 97–110.

Chaudhuri, S. (1984). Manufacturing drugs without TNCS: Status of indigenous sector in India. *Economic and Political Weekly*, *19*(31,32,33), 1341–1383.

Chaudhuri, S. (1993, September 4). Dunkhel draft on drug patents, background and implications. *Economic and Political Weekly, 8*(36), 1833–1888.

Chaudhuri, S. (1999). Growth and structural changes in Pharmaceutical industry in India. In S. Anindya, G. Subir, & V. Rajendra (Eds.), *The structure of the Indian industry.* Oxford University Press.

Chaudhuri, S. (2002, August 10). TRIPS agreement and amendment of patents act in India. *Economic and Political Weekly*, *37*(32), 3354–3360.

Chaudhuri, S. (2005). *The WTO and India's Pharmaceuticals Industry; Patent Protections, TRIPS and developing countries.* Oxford University Press.

Chaudhuri, S. (2007, March). The gap between successful innovation and access to its benefits: Indian pharmaceuticals. *European Journal of Development Research, 19*(1), 49–65.

Chaudhuri, S. (2008, July 19). Ranbaxy sell-out: Reversal of fortunes. *Economic & Political Weekly*, *43*(29), 11–13.

Chaudhuri, S. (2011). *Multinationals and Monopolies Pharmaceutical Industry in India after TRIPS WPS No. 685/November 2011*. Indian Institute of Management.

Chaudhuri, S. (2012, March 24). Multinationals and monopolies pharmaceutical industry in India after TRIPS. *Economic & Political Weekly*, *xlviI*(12), 46–54.

Chaudhuri, S. (2013, April 27). The larger implications of the novartis-glivec judgment. *Economic & Political Weekly*, *xlviII*(17), 10–12.

Chaudhuri, S., Goldberg, P. K., & Jia, P. (2006). Estimating the effects of global patent protection in pharmaceuticals: A case study of quinolones in India. *The American Economic Review*, *96*(5), 1477–1514.

Chen, B., & Zadrozny, P. A. (2013). Further model-based estimates of us total manufacturing production capital and technology, 1949–2005. *Journal of Productivity Analysis*, *39*, 61–73.

Chen, T., & Tang, D. (1987). Comparing technical efficiency between import-substitution-oriented and export-oriented foreign firms in a developing economy. *Journal of Development Economics*, *26*(2), 277–289.

Chen, T., & Tang, D. (1996). Export performance and productivity growth: The case of Taiwan. *Economic Development and Cultural Change*, *38*(3), 577–585.

Chenery, H., Robinson, S., & Syrquin, M. (1986). *Industrialization and growth: A comparative study*. Oxford University Press.

Cheng, Y. S., & Lo, D. (2004). *Firm size, technical efficiency and productivity growth in Chinese industry* [Working Paper No. 144, School of Oriental and African Studies, University of London].

Cheri, G. (2004). *The effect of changing intellectual property on pharmaceutical industry prospects in India and China: Considerations for access to medicines*. DFID Health Systems Resource Centre.

Chilingerian, J. A. (1995). Evaluating physician efficiency in hospitals: A multivariate analysis of best practices. *European Journal of Operational Research*, *80*(3), 548–574.

Chintrakarn, P., & Chen, Y. (2011). Do unions impact efficiency?: Evidence from the U.S. Manufacturing sector. *Contemporary Economic Policy*, *29*(3), 431–440.

Chirwa, E. W. (2001). Privatization and technical efficiency: Evidence from the manufacturing sector in Malawi. *African Development Review*, *13*(2), 277–307.

Chirwa, E. W. (2004). Industry and firm effects of privatization in Malawian oligopolistic manufacturing. *The Journal of Industrial Economics*, *LII*(2), 277–290.

Christensen, L. R., & Jorgenson, D. W. (1969). The measurement of us real capital input, 1929-1967. *Review of Income and Wealth*, *15*(4), 293–320.

Christensen, L. R., & Jorgenson, D. W. (1970). Us real product and real factor input, 1929-1967. *Review of Income and Wealth*, *16*(1), 19–50.

Christiano, L. J. (1992). Searching for a break in GNP. *Journal of Business and Economic Statistics*, *10*(3), 237–250.

Christiano, L. J., & Eichenbaum, M. (1989). *Unit roots in real GNP: Do we know and do we care?* [Discussion Paper 18, Federal Reserve Bank of Minneapolis, Institute for Empirical Macroeconomics].

Christopoulos, D. K., & Tsionas, E. G. (2002). Allocative inefficiency and the capital-energy controversy. *Energy Economics*, *24*(4), 305–318.

Chuang, Y. C. (1999). The role of human capital in economic development: Evidence from Taiwan. *Asian Economic Journal*, *13*(2), 117–144.

Chun, H., & Nadiri, M. I. (2002). *Decomposing productivity growth in the US Computer Industry* [Working Paper No. 9267, National Bureau of Economic Research, Cambridge].

Cihan, B. (1993, October). Inflation, growth, and import bottlenecks in the Turkish manufacturing industry. *Journal of Development Economics*, *42*(1), 111–131.

Clark, P. K. (1987). The cyclical component of U.S. ECONOMIC activity. *Quarterly Journal of Economics*, *102*(4), 797–814.

Clerides, S. K., Lach, S., & Tybout, J. R. (1998, August). Is learning by exporting important? Micro-dynamic evidence from Colombia, Mexico, and Morocco. *Quarterly Journal of Economics*, *113*(3), 903–948.

Cochrane, J. H. (1988). How big is the random walk in GNP? *Journal of Political Economy*, *96*(5), 893–920.

Coelli, T. J. (1994). A guide to frontier version 4.1: A computer program for stochastic frontier production and cost function estimation, mimeo. CEPA Working Paper 96/7. Department of Econometrics, University of New England, Armidale NSW Australia.

Coelli, T. J. (1996). *A guide to FRONTIER Version 4.1*. CEPA, University of New England.

Coelli, T. J., Rao, D. S. P., & Battese, G. E. (1998). *An introduction to efficiency and productivity analysis*. Kluwer Academic Publishers.

Çolak, M., & Kara, O. (2012). The effect of privatization on efficiency and work values: Turkey's cement industry example. *Journal of Labour Relations*, *3*(1), 86–104.

Collins, B., McDonald, T., & Mousa, J. A. (2007). The rise and decline of auto parts manufacturing in the midwest. *Monthly Labor Review*, *130*, 14–20.

Corden, W. M. (1966). The structure of a tariff system and the effective protective rate. *The Journal of Political Economy*, *74*(3), 221–237.

Cornwell, C., Schmidt, P., & Sickles, R. C. (1990). Production frontiers with cross- sectional and time-series variation in efficiency levels. *Journal of Econometrics*, *46*(1/2), 185–200.

Coto, M. P., Inglada, V., Rey, L. B., & Rodriguez, A. A. (2004). Changes in the world air industry: An analysis of technical efficiency. *International Journal of Transport Economics*, *31*(3), 341–354.

Covich, M. P., & Aggarwal, A. (2010). Reform and efficiency: An application to Iranian regional electricity companies. *Iranian Economic Review*, *15*(26), 83–104.

Cozza, C., Malerba, F., & Mancusi, M. L., Perani, G., & Vezzulli, A. (2012). Innovation, profitability and growth in medium and high-tech manufacturing industries: Evidence from Italy. *Applied Economics*, *44*, 1963–1976.

Cullet, P. (2001, October 27). Patents bill, TRIPS and right to health. *Economic and Political Weekly*, *36*(43), 4049–4051.

Das, D. K. (2002). *Trade liberalization and industrial productivity: An assessment of developing country experiences* [Working Paper No. 77, Indian Council for Research on International Economic Relations, New Delhi].

Das, D. K. (2003). *Manufacturing productivity under varying trade regimes: India in the 1980s and 1990s* [Working Paper No. 107, Indian Council for Research on International Economic Relations].

Das, D. K. (2004). Manufacturing productivity under varying trade regimes, 1980–2000. *Economic and Political Weekly*, *39*(5), 423–433.

Das, D. K. (2008). *Trade liberalization, employment, labor productivity and real wages: A study of the organized manufacturing industry in India in the 1980s and 1990s*. International Labor Organization Asia-Pacific Working Paper Series, ILO Sub regional office for South Asia, New Delhi.

Das, S., & Bhattacharya, K. (2008). Price convergence across regions in India. *Empirical Economics*, *34*, 299–313.

Das, S., Baten, Md. A., Rana, Md. M., & Khaleque, Md. A. (2008). Analysis of the growth of manufacturing industries in Bangladesh. *South Asia Economic Journal*, *9*(1), 85–108.

Dasgupta, S. (1998). West Bengal and industry: A regional perspective. *Economic and Political Weekly*, *33*(47/48), 3049–3060.

Datta, C. T., & Kumar, P. (2009). *The Indian pharmaceutical industry: Fundamentals vis-à-vis market perception*. Mimeo. Indian School of Business.

Daveri, F., & Lasinio, C. J. (2008). Off-shoring and productivity growth in the Italian manufacturing industries. *CESifo Economic Studies*, *54*, 414–450.

David, P. A., & Rosenbloom, J. L. (1990). Marshallian factor market externalities and the dynamics of industrial localization. *Journal of Urban Economics*, *28*(3), 349–370.

Dayal, G. A., & Husain, A. M. (2002). Centripetal forces in China's economic takeoff. *IMF Staff Papers*, *49*(3), 364–393.

De Carolis, D. M. (2003). Competencies and imitability in the pharmaceutical industry: An analysis of their relationship with firm performance. *Journal of Management*, *29*(1), 27–50.

De Melo, J., & Robinson, S. (1992). Productivity and externalities: Models of export-led growth. *Journal of International Trade & Economic Development*, *1*(1), 41–68.

De Oliveira, L. S., Shayani, R. A., & De Oliveira, M. A. G. (2013). Proposed business plan for energy efficiency in Brazil. *Energy Policy*, *61*, 523–531.

Debreu, G. (1951). The coefficient of resource utilization. *Econometrica*, *19*(3), 273–292. https://doi.org/10.2307/1906814

Demirel, P., & Mazzucato, M. (2010). The evolution of firm growth dynamics in the us pharmaceutical industry. *Regional Studies*, *44*(8), 1053–1066.

Denison, E. F. (1962). *The source of growth in the United States, and alternative before US*. Committee of Economic Development.

Denison, E. F. (1967). *Why growth rates differ. Post war experience in nine western countries.* The Brooking Institution.

Denison, E. F. (1985). *Trends in American economic growth: 1929–1982.* The Brooking Institution.

Denney, G. D., Fuss, M. A., & Waverman, L. (1981). Measurement and interpretation of total factor productivity in regulated industries with an application of Canadian Telecommunications. In T. G. Cowing & R. E. Stevenson (Eds.), *Productivity measurement in regulated industries.* Academic Press.

Deolalikar, A. B., & Roller, L. H. (1989). Patenting by manufacturing firms in India: Its production and impact. *Journal of Industrial Economics*, *37*(3), 303–314.

Deraniyagala, S. (2001). The impact of technology accumulation on technical efficiency: An analysis of the Sri Lankan clothing and agricultural machinery industries. *Oxford Development Studies*, *29*(1), 101–114.

Desai, A. V. (1981). Factors underlying the slow growth of Indian industry. *Economic and Political Weekly*, *16*(10-12), 381–392.

Destefanis, S., & Sena, V. (2007). Patterns of corporate governance and technical efficiency in Italian manufacturing. *Managerial and Decision Economics*, *28*(1), 27–40.

Dhanora, M., Sharma, R., & Park, W. G. (2021). Technological innovations and market power: A study of Indian pharmaceutical industry. *Millennial Asia*, *12*(1), 5–34. https://doi.org/10.1177/0976399620944272

Dholakia, B. H., & Dholakia, R. H. (1994). Total factor productivity growth in Indian manufacturing. *Economic and Political Weekly*, *29*(53), 3342–3344.

Diaz, M. A., & Sanchez, R. (2008). Firm size and productivity in Spain: A stochastic frontier analysis. *Small Business Economics*, *30*(3), 315–323.

Dickey, D. A. (1976). *Estimation and hypothesis testing in non stationary time series* [Unpublished Doctoral Dissertation, IOWA State University, AMES, IA].

Dickey, D. A., & Fuller, W. A. (1979). Distribution of the estimators for autoregressive time series with the unit root. *Journal of American Statistical Association*, *74*, 427–431.

Dickey, D. A., & Fuller, W. A. (1981). Likelihood ratio statistics for autoregressive time series with a unit root. *Econometrica*, *49*(4), 1057–1072.

Diewert, E. (2000). *The challenge of total factor productivity measurement.* Department of Economics, University of British Columbia.

Dijkstra, A. G. (2000). Trade liberalization and the industrial development in Latin America. *World Development*, *28*(9), 1567–1582.

Dimelis, S., & Louriy, H. (2002). Foreign ownership and production efficiency: A quantile regression analysis. *Oxford Economic Papers*, *54*, 449–469.

Dimitriu, M. C., & Savu, B. M. (2010). Econometric analysis of efficiency in the Indian manufacturing sector. *Romanian Journal of Economic Forecasting*, *1*, 182–197.

Din, M., Ghani, E. & Mahmood, T. (2007). Technical efficiency of Pakistan's manufacturing sector: A stochastic frontier and data envelopment analysis. *The Pakistan Development Review*, *46*(1), 1–18.

Ditzen, J. (2018). Estimating dynamic common-correlated effects in stata. *The Stata Journal*, *18*(3), 585–617.

Ditzen, J. (2021). Estimating long run effects and the exponent of cross-sectional dependence: An update to xtdcce2. *The Stata Journal*, *21*(3), 687–707. https://ideas.repec.org/p/bzn/wpaper/bemps81.html

Ditzen, J., Karavias, Y., & Westerlund, J. (2021a). Testing for multiple structural breaks in panel data. arXiv:2110.14550v2 [econ.EM] 28 Oct 2021. https://arxiv.org/abs/2110.14550v2

Ditzen, J., Karavias, Y., & Westerlund, J. (2021b). Testing and estimating structural breaks in time series and panel data in stata. *arxiv* [econ.EM] 2110.14550. https://arxiv.org/abs/2110.14550

Diwan, R. K., & Gujarati, D. (1968). Employment and productivities in industries. *Artha Vijnana, 10*(2), 29–66.

Doi, N. (1992). The efficiency of small manufacturing firms in Japan. *Small Business Economics, 4*, 29–35.

Domazlicky, B. R., & Weber, W. L. (2003). Does environmental protection lead to slower productivity growth in the chemical industry?. *Environmental and Resource Economics, 28*, 1–24.

Driffield, N., & Munday, M. (2001). Foreign manufacturing, regional agglomeration and technical efficiency in UK industries: A stochastic production frontier approach. *Regional Studies, 35*(5), 391–399.

Driffield, N. L., & Kambhampati, U. S. (2003). Trade liberalization and the efficiency of firms in Indian manufacturing. *Review of Development Economics, 7*(3), 419–430.

Driffield, N., Munday, M., & Roberts, A. (2005). Foreign direct investment, transactions linkages, and the performance of the domestic sector. *International Journal of the Economics of Business, 9*(3), 335–351.

Duggan, M., Garthwaite, C., & Goyal, A. (2016). The market impacts of pharmaceutical product patents in developing countries: Evidence from India. *The American Economic Review, 106*(1), 99–135.

Dunne, T., Roberts, M. J., & Samuelson, L. (1988). Patterns of firm entry and exit in U.S. Manufacturing industries. *RAND Journal of Economics, 19*(4), 495–515.

Economidou, C., & Murshid, A. P. (2008). Testing the linkages between trade and productivity growth. *Review of Development Economics, 12*(4), 845–860.

El-Akhdar, S., Mardhy, A., & Kerak, E. (2015). Strategic analysis of the pharmaceutical sector in morocco and quality approach, International Journal of Science and Research (IJSR), *5*(11), 876–885.

Elbadawi, I., Mengistae, T., Temesge, T., & Zeufack, A. (2099). Economic geography and manufacturing productivity in Africa: An analysis of firm level data. *The Journal of Developing Areas, 42*(2), 223–252.

Elizabeth, M. C., Ghosh, M., & Kelton, C. M. L. (1994). Pricing behavior of United States manufacturing industries: A statistical study using disaggregated data. *Review of Industrial Organization, 9*(6), 745–771.

Endri, E., Susanti, D., Hutabarat, L., Simanjuntak, T. P., & Handayani, S. (2020). Financial performance evaluation: Empirical evidence of pharmaceutical companies in Indonesia. *Systematic Reviews in Pharmacy, 11*(6), 803–816.

Enyinda, C. I., Mbah, C. H., & Ogbuehi, A. (2010). An empirical analysis of risk mitigation in the pharmaceutical industry supply chain: A developing-country perspective. *Thunderbird International Business Review, 52*(1), 45–54.

Epstein, R. J. (2007). Growth of the Asian health-care market: Global implications for the pharmaceutical industry. *Nature Reviews Drug Discovery, 6*(10), 785–792.

Evans, P. (1997a). How fast do economies converge? *Review of Economics and Statistics, 36*, 219–225.

Evans, P. (1997b). *Consistent estimation of growth regressions* [Working Paper, Ohio State University].

Evans, P., & Karras, G. (1996a). Do economies converge? Evidence from a panel of U.S. states. *Review of Economics and Statistics, 78*, 384–388.

Evans, P., & Karras, G. (1996b). Convergence revisited. *Journal of Monetary Economics, 37*, 249–265.

Färe, R., Grifell-Taté, E., Grosskopf, S., & Lovell, C. A. K. (1997). Biased technical change and the Malmquist productivity index. *The Scandinavian Journal of Economics, 99*(1), 119–127.

Färe, R., Grosskopf, S., & Lovell, C. A. K. (1994). *Production frontiers*. Cambridge University Press.

Färe, R., Grosskopf, S., Lindgren, B., & Roos, P. (1992). Productivity changes in Swedish pharmacies 1980-89, a non-parametric Malmquist approach. *Journal of Productivity Analysis*, *3*(1/2), 85–101.

Färe, R., Grosskopf, S., Norris, M., & Zhang, Z. (1994). Productivity growth, technical progress and efficiency changes in industrial countries. *American Economic Review*, *84*(1), 66–83.

Färe, R., Grosskopf, S., & Margaritis, D. (2001). Productivity trends in Australian and New Zealand manufacturing. *The Australian Economic Review*, *34*(2), 125–134.

Faria, A., Fenn, P., & Bruce, A. (2005). Production technologies and technical efficiency: Evidence from Portuguese manufacturing industry. *Applied Economics*, *37*, 1037–1046.

Farrell, M. J. (1957). The measurement of productive efficiency. *Journal of the Royal Statistical Society, Series A, General*, *120*(3), 253–281.

Faruq, H. A., & Yi, D. T. (2010). The determinants of technical efficiency of manufacturing firms in Ghana. *Global Economy Journal*, *10*(3), Art. 7, 0–21.

Feder, G. (1982). On exports and economic growth. *Journal of Development Economics*, *12*(1–2), 59–73.

Federico, S., & Minerva, G. A. (2008). Outward FDI and local employment growth in Italy. *Review of World Economics*, *144*(2), 295–324.

Feinberg, S. E., & Majumdar, S. K. (2001). Technology spillovers from foreign direct investment in the Indian pharmaceutical industry. *Journal of International Business Studies*, *32*(3), 421–437.

Felipe, J., & McCombie, J. S. L. (2001). Biased technical change, growth accounting and the conundrum of the East Asian miracle. *Journal of Comparative Economics*, *29*(3), 542–565.

Felipe, J., & McCombie, J. S. L. (2001). Biased technical change, growth accounting and the conundrum of the East Asian miracle. *Journal of Comparative Economics*, *29*(3), 542–565.

Feng, G., & Serletis, A. (2008). Productivity trends in U.S. manufacturing: Evidence from the NQ and aim cost functions. *Journal of Econometrics*, *142*, 281–311.

Feng, Y., Liu, K., Lyu, L., Sun, G., & Hu, Y. (2022). The financial impact of patents on SMEs in China: Empirical evidence from pharmaceutical sector. *Science, Technology and Society*, *27*(1), 46–65.

Fernandes, A. M. (2008). Structure and performance of the service sector in transition economies. *Economics of Transition*, *17*(3), 467–501.

Ferrantino, M. J., Ferrier, G. D., & Linvill, C. B. (1995). Organizational form and efficiency: Evidence from Indian sugar manufacturing. *Journal of Comparative Economics*, *21*(1), 29–53.

Festa, G., Kolte, A., Carli, M. R., & Rossi, M. (2022). Envisioning the challenges of the pharmaceutical sector in the Indian health-care industry: A scenario analysis. *Journal of Business & Industrial Marketing*, *37*(8), 1662–1674. https://doi.org/10.1108/JBIM-07-2020-0365

Findlay, R. (1978). Relative backwardness, direct foreign investment, and the transfer of technology: A simple dynamic model. *Quarterly Journal of Economics*, *92*(1), 1–16.

Fisher, R. A. (1932). *Statistical methods for research workers* (4th ed.). Oliver & Boyd.

Fousekis, P. (2003). Productivity growth in the large-scale manufacturing of Greece: A non-parametric approach. *Global Business and Economic Review*, *5*(2), 265–283.

Franke, J. A., & Romer, D. H. (1999, June). Does trade cause growth? *The American Economic Review*, *89*(3), 379–399.

Frantzen, D. (2003). Technical diffusion, productivity convergence and specialisation in OECD manufacturing. *International Review of Applied Economics*, *21*(1), 75–98.

Fried, H., Lovell, C., & Schmidt, S. (Eds.) (1994). *The measurement of productive efficiency: Techniques and applications*. Oxford University Press.

Fujimori, A., Kamiike, A., & Sato, T. (2010). Technical efficiency of the small scale pharmaceutical industry in India: Evidence from firm level survey. *Journal of Economics & Business Administration*.

Fuller, W. A. (1976). *Introduction to statistical time series*. Wiley.

Gagnon, M.-A., & Lexchin, J. (2008). The cost of pushing pills: A new estimate of pharmaceutical promotion expenditures in the United States. *PLoS Medicine*, *5*(1), e1. http://dx.doi.org/10.1371/journal.pmed.0050001

Galbraith, J. K., Roy Chowdhury, D., & Shrivastava, S. (2004). Pay inequality in manufacturing, 1979-98. *Economic and Political Weekly*, *39*(28), 3139–3148.

Gangopadhyay, S. (1996). Prospective industrial sectors of West Bengal and the recent industrial drive – An empirical assessment. In A. Raychaudhuri & D. Sarkar (Eds.), *Economy of West Bengal (Problems and prospects)*. Allied Publishers.

Gangopadhyay, S., & Wadhwa, W. (1998). *Labor costs and productivity in Indian Industry: A disaggregated analysis*. Report for the International Labor Organization.

Gascón, F., Lozano, J., Ponte, B., & de la Fuente, D. (2017). Measuring the efficiency of large pharmaceutical companies: An industry analysis. *The European Journal of Health Economics*, *18*, 587–608.

Gebreeyesus, M. (2008). Firm turnover and productivity differentials in Ethiopian manufacturing. *Journal of Productivity Analysis*, *29*, 113–129.

Getachew, L., & Sickles, R. C. (2007). The policy environment and relative price efficiency of Egyptian private sector. *Journal of Applied Econometrics*, *22*(4), 703–728.

Ghose, A., & Pal, D. (2007, March). Growth of food grains production: An interdistrict comparison of West Bengal. *Artha Beekashan*, *15*(4), 216–233.

Ghose, A., & Pal, D. (2013). Regional disparity and convergence of the growth processes of Indian agricultural sector: evidence based on structural break unit root test; development policy issues in India 2: Studies on Disparity and Displeasure; Published by *acb publication in collaboration with Planning and Development Unit (A Unit of Planning Commission of India) Jadavpur University*; ISBN 81-87500-65-4.

Ghose, A., & Chakraborti, C. (2013). The relative role of imports and exports in explaining productivity of Indian bio-pharmaceutical firms: Evidence from non parametric data envelopment analysis. *Foreign Trade Review*, *48*(2), 165–201.

Ghose, A., & Chakraborty, C. (2008, October). The effect of trade liberalisation on the growth process of Indian Pharmaceutical Industry. *Vaanijya*, 15–21.

Ghose, A., & Chakraborty, C. (2012, September). Total factor productivity growth in pharmaceutical industry: A look using modern time series approach with Indian data. *The Journal of Industrial Statistics*, *1*(2), 250–268.

Ghose, A., & Roy Biswas, P. (2011). Inter-industrial variation in total factor productivity growth of manufacturing sector of West Bengal: Evidence from non-parametric approach. *Indian Economic Journal*, *59*(2), 29–50.

Ghose, A., & Roy Biswas, P. (2012). Inter-industrial variation of productivity growth in Indian manufacturing sector: Evidence from a non-parametric approach. *Journal of Industrial Statistics*, *1*(1), 57–81.

Ghosh, S. (2013). Do economic reforms matter for manufacturing productivity? Evidence from the Indian experience. *Economic Modeling*, *31*(2013), 723–733.

Godfrey, Y., & Vincent, M. (2008). Iso 9000 certification and technical efficiency of foreign-financed manufacturing firms in southern China: A stochastic frontier approach. *Journal of Economic Studies*, *35*(5–6), 385–404.

Goedhuys, M., Janz, N., & Mohnen, P. (2008, June). What drives productivity in Tanzanian manufacturing firms: Technology or business environment? *The European Journal of Development Research*, *20*(2), 199–218.

Goldar, B. (1985). Unit size and economic efficiency in small-scale washing soap industry in India. *Artha Vijnana*, *27*(1), 21–40.

Goldar, B. (1986). Econometrics of Indian Industry. In K. L. Krishna (Ed.), *Econometric application in India*. Oxford University Press.
Goldar, B. (1986). Employment growth in Indian industry. *Indian Journal of Industrial Relations*, *22*(3), 271–285.
Goldar, B. (1986). *Productivity growth in Indian Industry*. Allied Publishers Pvt. Ltd.
Goldar, B. (1988). Relative efficiency of modern small scale industries in India. In K. B. Suri (Ed.), *Small scale enterprise in industrial development*. SAGE Publications.
Goldar, B. (1989). Inter-state variations in industrial consumption of energy. In V. K. Seth (Ed.), *Themes in spatial perspective*. Commonwealth Publishers.
Goldar, B. (2004). *Productivity trends in Indian manufacturing in the pre- and post-reform periods* [Working Paper No. 137, Indian Council for Research on International Economic Relations].
Goldar, B. (2006). Productivity Growth in Indian Manufacturing in the 1980s and 1990s. In S. D. Tendulkar, A. Mitra, K. Narayanan, & D. K. Das (Eds.), *India: Industrialization in a reforming economy*. Academic Foundation.
Goldar, B. (2013). R&D intensity and exports: A study of Indian pharmaceutical firms. *Innovation and Development*, *3*(2), 151–167.
Goldar, B., & Kumari, A. (2003). Import liberalization and productivity growth in Indian manufacturing industries in the 1990s. *The Developing Economies*, *61*(4), 436–460.
Goldar, B., & Kumari, A. (1999). Technology imports and employment in large engineering firms in India: Pre- and post-reforms scenario. *Indian Journal of Labor Economics*, *42*(4), 943–955.
Goldar, B., & Banga, R. (2007, June). *Impact of trade liberalization on foreign direct investment in Indian Industries* [Working Paper Series, No. 36, Asia-Pacific Research and Training Network on Trade].
Goldar, B., & Aggarwal, S. C. (2005). Trade liberalization and price-cost margin in Indian industries. *The Developing Economies*, *XLIII-3*, 346–373.
Goldar, B., & Seth, V. (1989). Spatial variation in the rate of industrial growth in India. *Economic and Political Weekly*, *24*(22), 1237–1240.
Goldar, B., & Ranganathan, V. S. (1991). Capacity utilization in Indian industries. *Indian Economic Journal*, *39*(2), 82–92.
Goldar, B., Ranganathan, V. S., & Banga, R. (2004). Ownership and efficiency in engineering firms: 1990–91 to 1999–2000. *Economic and Political Weekly*, *39*(5), 441–447.
Gomes, de M. A. (2005). Demand shocks and productivity growth. *Portuguese Economic Journal*, *4*, 15–45.
González, E., & Gascón, F. (2004). Sources of productivity growth in the Spanish pharmaceutical industry (1994–2000). *Research Policy*, *33*(5), 735–745.
Gopinath, M., Pickz, D., & Li, Y. (2004). An empirical analysis of productivity growth and industrial concentration in US manufacturing. *Applied Economics*, *36*, 1–7.
Gould, J. P., & Nelson, C. R. (1974). The stochastic structure of the velocity of money. *American Economic Review*, *64*(3), 405–418.
Goyal, A. (1996). Industrial pricing and growth fluctuations: Some tests. *Economic and Political Weekly*, *31*(48), M54–M62.
Goyal, J., & Kaur, H. (2017, July-Dec). Assessing the financial efficiency in Indian pharmaceutical industry: An application of data envelopment analysis. *International Journal of Business Management & Research*, *7*(2), 47–62.
Grace, C. (2004). The effect of changing intellectual property on pharmaceutical industry prospects in India and china. *DFID Health Systems Resource Centre*, 1–68.
Granér, M., & Isaksson, A. (2009). Firm efficiency and the destination of exports: Evidence from Kenyan plant-level data. *The Developing Economies*, *47*(3), 279–306.
Greenaway, D. (1986). *Characteristics of industrialization and economic performance under alternative development strategies. Background Paper to 1987 World Development Report*. Oxford University Press.

Greenaway, D., & Sapsford, D. (1994). What does liberalization do for exports and growth? *Weltwirtschaftliches Archiv*, *130*, 152–174.

Greene, W. (2007). The emergence of India's pharmaceutical industry and implications for the U.S. Generic drug market (working paper no. 2007-05-a). Office of Economics Working Papers, US International Trade Commission. https://www.usitc.gov/publications/332/EC200705A.pdf

Greene, W. H. (1990). A gamma-distributed stochastic frontier model. *Journal of Econometrics*, *46*(1/2), 141–163.

Grossman, G., & Helpman, E. (1991). *Innovation and growth in the global economy.* MIT Press.

Guillaumont, P. (1994). Politique d'ouverture et croissance économique: Les effetsde la croissance et de l'instabilité des exportations. *Revue d'économie du développement*, *1*(1), 91–114.

Gupta, U. G. K., & Kapoor, R. (2017). An inquiry into the productivity of the Indian pharmaceutical industry: Application of data envelopment analysis. *Brazilian Journal of Operations & Production Management*, *14*(2), 145–152. https://doi.org/10.14488/BJOPM.2017.v14.n2.a2

Gupta, A. (2010). *Indian manufacturing productivity: What caused the growth stagnation before the 1990s?* International Productivity Monitor, No. 2 0, 85–102.

Gupta, K. L. (1989). *Industrialization and employment in developing countries: A comparative study.* Routledge.

Gupta, N. C. (1987). *Productivity, investment and import substitution in Indian Industries*. Anmol Publications.

Gupta, V. K., & Gupta, R. (2021, January–February). literature review on pharmaceutical industry in India comparison of post reform and pre reform period and policy, *International Journal of Scientific Research & Engineering Trends*, *7*(1), 2395–566X.

Gurumurthy, P. S., & Iyer, V. C. (2012). A study on enhancing efficiency of unorganized powerloom sector with special reference to powerloom sector in India. *International Journal of Research in Commerce Economics & Management*, *2*(11), 113–118.

Haddad, M. (1993). *How trade-liberalization affected productivity in Morocco* [World Bank Policy Research & External Affairs Working Paper No. 1096, Washington DC].

Hadri, K. (1998). *Testing for stationarity in heterogeneous panel data*. Mimeo.

Haidar, J. I. (2012). Trade and productivity: Self-selection or learning-by-exporting in India. *Economic Modelling*, *29*(2012), 1766–1773.

Haley, G. T., & Haley, U. C. (2012). The effects of patent-law changes on innovation: The case of India's pharmaceutical industry. *Technological Forecasting and Social Change*, *79*(4), 607–619.

Halkos, G. E., & Tzeremes, N. G. (2010). The effect of foreign ownership on SMEs performance: An efficiency analysis perspective. *Journal of Productivity Analysis*, *34*, 167–180.

Hall, R. E. (1978). Stochastic implication of the life cycle – permanent income hypothesis: Theory and evidence. *Journal of Political Economy*, *86*(6), 971–987.

Haller, S. A. (2008). The distribution of productivity in Irish manufacturing between 1995 and 2004 – determinants, changes and implications. *The Economic and Social Review*, *39*(1), 13–38.

Han, G., Kalirajan, K., & Singh, N. (2002). Productivity and economic growth in East Asia: Innovation, efficiency and accumulation. *Japan and the World Economy*, *14*(4), 401–424.

Hanggraeni, D. (2011). Analysis of the efficiency and productivity of Indonesian pharmaceutical public companies using data envelopment analysis. *Indonesian Capital Market Review*, *6*(2), 98–112.

Hanna, B. G. (2008). An empirical study of income growth and manufacturing industry pollution in new England, 1980–1990. *Ecological Economics*, *67*(2008), 75–82.

Hanson, J. A., & Lieberman, S. (1989). India: Poverty, employment and social services. Conference Proceedings, World Bank, Washington DC, ISBN-10: 082131419X.

Haouas, I., Yagoubi, M., & Heshmati, A. (2003). Labor-use efficiency in Tunisian manufacturing industries. *Review of Middle East Economics and Finance, 1*(3), 195–214.

Hare, D. (1999). Spatial patterns in China's rural industrial growth and prospects for the alleviation of regional income inequality. *Journal of Comparative Economics, 27*, 475–497.

Harris, R., & Sollis, R. (2003). *Applied time series modelling and forecasting*. Wiley.

Harris, R. I. D. (1991). Measuring efficiency in Northern Ireland manufacturing using a frontier production function approach. *Scottish Journal of Political Economy, 38*(4), 386–397.

Harris, R. I. D. (2001). Comparing regional technical efficiency in UK manufacturing plants: The case of Northern Ireland 1974-1995. *Regional Studies, 35*(6), 519–534.

Harrison, A. (1996). Openness and growth: A time-series, cross-country analysis for developing countries. *Journal of Development Economics, 48*, 419–447. https://doi.org/10.1016/0304-3878(95)00042-9

Harrison, A. E., Martin, L. A. & Nataraj, S. (2012). Learning versus stealing: How important are market-share reallocations to India's productivity growth? *The World Bank Economic Review, 27*(2), 202–228.

Hasan, R. (2002). The impact of imported and domestic technologies on the productivity of firms: Panel data evidence from Indian manufacturing firms. *Journal of Development Economics, 69*, 23–49.

Hashim, B. R., & Dadi, M. M. (1973). *Capital-output relations in Indian Manufacturing (1946-64)*. M.S. University of Baroda.

Hashimoto, A., & Haneda, S. (2008). Measuring the change in R&D efficiency of the Japanese pharmaceutical industry. *Research Policy, 37*(10), 1829–1836.

Havrylyshyn, O. (1990). Trade policy and productivity gains in developing countries: A survey of literature. *The World Bank Research Observer, 5*(1), 1–24.

Hayami, Y., Vemon, W. R., & Southword, H. M. (1979). *Agricultural growth in Japan, Taiwan, Korea and Philippines.* The University Press of Hawaii.

Hazell, P. (1982). *Instability in Indian foodgrain production*. Research Report 30. International Food Policy Research Institute.

He, F., Zhang, Q., Lei, J., Fu, W., & Xu, X. (2013). Energy efficiency and productivity change of China's iron and steel industry: Accounting for undesirable outputs. *Energy Policy, 54*(1), 204–213.

He, H., & Weng, Q. (2012). Ownership, autonomy, incentives and efficiency: Evidence from the forest product processing industry in China. *Journal of Forest Economics, 18*(3), 177–193

Hendry, D. F. (1986). Econometric modeling with co-integrated variables: An overview. *Oxford Bulletin of Economics and Statistics, 48*(3), 201–212.

Hidalgo, J., & Schafgans, M. (2017). Inference and testing breaks in large dynamic panels with strong cross sectional dependence, *Journal of Econometrics, 196*(2), 259–274.

Hirashima, S. (2000). Issues in agricultural reforms: Public investment and land market development. *Economic and Political Weekly, 35*(43 & 44), 3879–3884.

Ho, C. Y., Li, X., & Zhou, W. (2017). *Foreign direct investment spillovers and pharmaceutical innovation: The role of intellectual property rights* (No. 775). ADBI Working Paper.

Hodges, H., & Østbye, S. (2010). Is small firm gardening good for local economic growth? *Applied Economics Letters, 17*, 809–813.

Holzl, W., & Reinstaller, A. (2005). Sectoral and aggregate technology shocks: Is there a relationship? *Empirica, 32*, 45–72.

Honjo, Y. (2004). Growth of new start-up firms: Evidence from the Japanese manufacturing industry. *Applied Economics, 36*, 343–355.

Hoque, A., & Das, S. (2021). Trends in productivity growth of Indian pharmaceutical industry: A growth accounting analysis. *Journal of Pharmaceutical Research International, 33*(47A), 437–446. https://doi.org/10.9734/jpri/2021/v33i47A33031

Horn, H., Lang, H., & Lundgren, S. (1995). Managerial effort incentives, x-efficiency and international trade. *European Economic Review, 39*(1), 117–138.

Horner, R. (2013, August 3). The global relevance of India's pharmaceutical patent laws. *Economic & Political Weekly, xlviii*(31), 16–18.

Hossain, M. A., & Karunaratne, N. D. (2004). Trade liberalisation and technical efficiency: Evidence from Bangladesh manufacturing industries. *The Journal of Development Studies, 40*(3), 87–114.

Hsieh, C. T. (1998). *What explains the industrial revolution in East Asia? Evidence from factor markets*. Princeton University Discussion Papers in Economics NO. 196, Woodrow Wilson School of Public and International Affairs.

https://finance.yahoo.com/news/top-16-medicine-producing-countries-120134464.html?guccounter=1&guce_referrer=aHR0cHM6Ly93d3cuZ29vZ2xlLmNvbS8&guce_referrer_sig=AQAAAHeNaOAwukGrG9QsTUl4wNBjZfQgqTtRXbpqJl4Wz3mvqIoWbKTikbT_l4TirFOsSQHWpAkR_BGKVDbotch8ramgVU1Xt-hxUuSOFIrieqG3uzvVAZ6gyTotHdXEPw1kQ1t559fZ0jrDodlWTE6UObMYL2N5mVO8EvEz3IwhooiW

https://microdata.gov.in/nada43/index.php/catalog/ASI

https://oec.world/en/profile/hs/pharmaceutical-products

https://www.efpia.eu

Hu, A. G. Z., & Png, I. P. L. (2013). Patent rights and economic growth: Evidence from cross-country panels of manufacturing industries. *Oxford Economic Papers, 65*(3), 675–698.

Huang, C. J., & Liu, J. T. (1994). Estimation of a non-neutral frontier production function. *Journal of Productivity Analysis, 5*(2), 171–180.

Huang, R. R. (2008). Tolerance for uncertainty and the growth of informationally opaque industries. *Journal of Development Economics, 87*, 333–353.

Hurlin, C. (2004). *Testing Granger causality in heterogenous panel data models with fixed coefficients*. Document de recherche LEO, 2004-4, University of Orleans.

Hurwitz, M. A., & Caves, R. E. (1988). persuasion or information? Promotion and the shares of brand name and generic pharmaceuticals. *Journal of Law and Economics, 31*(2), 299–320.

Hussain, A., Yang, X., Yali, L., & Nazir, M. S. (2020). Foreign direct investment (FDI) by Asian and European Union (EU) countries: The investment effects of pharmaceutical sector. *International Journal of Economics and Finance, 12*(4), 1–16.

Hwang, A. R. (2003). Exports, returns to scale, and total factor productivity: The case of Taiwanese manufacturing industries. *Review of Development Economics, 7*(2), 204–216.

Ibrahim, M. H. (1997). Efficiency performance in Malaysian manufacturing industries. *Pakistan Journal of Applied Economics, 13*(2), 227–243.

Ikshan, M. (2007). Total factor productivity growth in Indonesian manufacturing: A stochastic frontier approach. *Global Economic Review, 34*(4), 321–342.

Im, K. S., Pesaran, M. H., & Shin, Y. (1997). *Testing for unit roots in heterogeneous panels*. [Manuscript, Department of Applied Economics, University of Cambridge].

Institute of Economic Growth. (2010). *Effects of New patents regime on Consumers and Products of Drugs/Medicines in India*. Revised Report Submitted to the UNCTAD.

Jacobzone, S. (2000). *Pharmaceutical policies in OECD countries*. http://dx.doi.org/10.1787/323807375536

Jaforullah, M. (1996). Technical efficiencies of some manufacturing industries of Bangladesh: An application of the stochastic production function approach. *Bangladesh Development Studies, 24*(1/2), 131–149.

Jaforullah, M., & David, N. J. (1996). Technical efficiency in the New Zealand dairy industry: A frontier production function approach. *New Zealand Economic Papers*, *30*(1), 1–17.

Jagadeesh, H., & Sasidharan, S. (2014). Do stronger IPR regimes influence R&D efforts? Evidence from the Indian pharmaceutical industry. *Global Business Review*, *15*(2), 189–204.

Javorcik, B. S., & Li, Y. (2013). Do the biggest aisles serve a brighter future? Global retail chains and their implications for Romania. *Journal of International Economics*, *90*(2013), 348–363.

Jeanneney, S. G., & Hua, P. (2003). *Real exchange rate and productivity in China* (37 pages) [Working Papers no. 200328, CERDI, France].

Jha, R. (2007, September 29). Options for Indian pharmaceutical industry in the changing environment. *Economic and Political Weekly*, *42*(39), 3958–3967.

Jha, R. (2010, March 6). Prices of new pharmaceuticals in India: Across section study. *Economic & Political Weekly*, *xlv*(*10*), 71–78.

Jiankang, M. U. (2014). SCP analysis of biopharmaceutical industry in China. *Journal of Chemical and Pharmaceutical Research*, *6*(3), 522–529.

Johnson, H. G. (1960). The cost of protection and the scientific tariff. *The Journal of Political Economy*, *68*(4), 327–345.

Jondrow, J., Lovell, C. A. K., Materov, S., & Schmidt, P. (1982). On estimation of technical inefficiency in the stochastic frontier production function model. *Journal of Econometrics*, *19*(2/3), 233–238.

Jorgenson, D. W., & Griliches, Z. (1967). The explanation of productivity change. *Review of Economic Studies*, *34*(3), 249–283.

Joseph, R. K (2012, May 5). Policy reforms in the Indian pharmaceutical sector since 1994 impact on exports and imports. *Economic & Political Weekly*, *XlVII*(18), 62–72.

Joshi, H. N. (2003). Analysis of the Indian pharmaceutical industry: With emphasis on opportunities in 2005. *Pharmaceutical Technology*, *27*, 74–94.

Kalani, S. (2011). Emerging role of it in Indian pharmaceutical industry and its implications for the education system. *Pharma Times*, *43*(05), 25–27.

Kale, D., & Little, S. (2007). From imitation to innovation: The evolution of R&D capabilities and learning processes in the Indian pharmaceutical industry. *Technology Analysis & Strategic Management*, *19*(5), 589–609.

Kalirajan, K. P. (1981). The economic efficiency of farmers growing high-yielding, irrigated rice in India. *American Journal of Agricultural Economics*, *63*(3), 566–570.

Kalirajan, K. P. (1997). A measure of economic efficiency using returns to scale. *Economics Letters*, *56*(3), 253–257.

Kalirajan, K. P., & Shand, R. T. (1994). *Economics in disequilibrium: An approach from the frontier*. Macmillan India Ltd.

Kambhampati, U. S. (2003). Trade reforms and the efficiency of firms in India. *Oxford Development Studies*, *31*(2), 219–233.

Kambhampati, U. S. (2006). Financial liberalisation, corporate governance and the efficiency of firms in Indian manufacturing. *Structural Change and Economic Dynamics*, *17*, 46–69.

Kamiike, A., Sato, T., & Aggarwal, A. (2012). *Productivity dynamics in the Indian pharmaceutical industry: Evidences from plant-level panel data* [Working Papers id: 4445, eSocialSciences].

Kanjilal, K., & Ghosh, S. (2002). Future industrial CO_2 emission and consequences of CO_2 abatement on the Indian economy. *Pacific and Asian Journal of Energy*, *12*(2), 123–128.

Kao, C. (1999). Spurious regression and residual-based tests for cointegration in panel data. *Journal of Econometrics*, *90*, 1–44.

Kao, Y. H., Chang, H. H., & Lee, M. J. (2006). Tea, obesity, and diabetes. *Molecular Nutrition & Food Research*, *50*, 188–210. https://doi.org/10.1002/mnfr.200500109

Kaplan, W., & Laing, R. (2005). local production of pharmaceuticals: Industrial policy and access to medicines an overview of key concepts, issues and opportunities for future research. *Health, Nutrition and Population (HNP)*. Washington, DC.

Kar, J., & Chakraborty, D. (1986). Inter-fuel substitution possibilities in Indian manufacturing industries – A traslog approach. *Artha Vijnana, 28*(2), 133–151.

Karamehic, J., Ridic, O., Ridic, G., Jukic, T., Coric, J., Subasic, D., … Masic, I. (2013). Financial aspects and the future of the pharmaceutical industry in the United States of America. *Materia Socio-Medica, 25*(4), 286.

Karavias, Y., Narayan, P. K., & Westerlund, J. (2022). Structural breaks in interactive effects panels and the stock market reaction to covid-19. *Journal of Business & Economic Statistics, 41*(3), 653–666. https://doi.org/10.1080/07350015.2022.2053690

Karin, I. (2003, October). Material accounting in a macroeconomic framework: Forecast of waste generated in manufacturing industries in Norway. *Environmental and Resource Economics, 26*(2), 227–248.

Karunaratne, N. D. (2001). *Microeconomic reforms and technical efficiency in Australian Manufacturing Mimeo*. School of Economics, University of Queensland.

Karunaratne, N. D. (2007, April). *Microeconomic reform and technical efficiency in Australian Manufacturing* [Discussion Paper No. 345, School of Economics, The University of Queensland. Australia].

Kathuria, V. (2000). Productivity spillovers from technology transfer to Indian manufacturing firms. *Journal of International Development, 12*, 343–369.

Kathuria, V. (2002). Liberalisation, FDI, and productivity spillovers – An analysis of Indian manufacturing firms. *Oxford Economic Papers, 54*, 688–718.

Kathuria, V., Natarajan, S. N. R., & Sen, K. (2013). The effects of economic reforms on manufacturing dualism: Evidence from India. *Journal of Comparative Economics, 41*(2013), 1240–1262.

Kato, A. (2009). Product market competition and productivity in the Indian manufacturing industry. *Journal of Development Studies, 45*(10), 1579–1593.

Katrak, H. (1985). Imported technology, enterprise size and R&D in a newly industrialized country: The Indian experience. *Oxford Bulletin of Economics and Statistics, 47*(3), 213–229.

Katz, J. M. (1969). *Production function, foreign investment and growth*. North-Holland Publishing Company.

Kazi, U.A. (1980). The variable elasticity of substitution production function: A case study for Indian manufacturing industries. *Oxford Economics Papers, 32*(1), 163–175.

Kazzazi, F., Pollard, C., Tern, P., et al. (2017). Evaluating the impact of brexit on the pharmaceutical industry. *Journal of Pharmaceutical Policy and Practice, 10*, 32. https://doi.org/10.1186/s40545-017-0120-z

Kazzazi, F., Pollard, C., Tern, P., Ayuso-Garcia, A., Gillespie, J., & Thomsen, I. (2017). Evaluating the impact of brexit on the pharmaceutical industry. *Journal of Pharmaceutical Policy and Practice, 10*, 1–12.

Kee, H. L. (2005). Productivity or endowments? Sectoral evidence for Hong Kong's aggregate growth. *Asian Economic Journal, 19*(1), 51–81.

Keller, W. (2000). Do trade pattern and technology flows affect productivity growth? *World Bank Economic Review, 14*(1), 17–47.

Kendrick, J. W. (1956). Productivity trends: Capital and labor. *Review of Economics and Statistics, 38*(3), 248–257.

Kendrick, J. W. (1961). *Productivity trends in the United States.* National Bureau of Economic Research.

Kendrick, J. W. (1973). *Post war productivity trends in the United States,* 1947-1969. National Bureau of Economic Research.

Kesič, D. (2011). Strategic development trends in the world pharmaceutical industry. *Managing Global Transitions: International Research Journal, 9*(3), 207–223.

Kian, M. J., Hadian, M., & Ghaffari, S. (2020). Factors affecting pharmaceutical industry enforcements in Iran and selected countries. *Archives of Pharmacy Practice, 11*(S4), 95–102.

Kim, E. (2000). Trade liberalization and productivity growth in Korean manufacturing industries: Price protection, market power, and scale efficiency. *Journal of Development Economics, 62,* 55–83.

Kim, S., & Han, G. (2001). A decomposition of total factor productivity growth in Korean manufacturing industries: A stochastic frontier approach. *Journal of Productivity Analysis, 16*, 269–281.

Kim, S., & Saravanakumar, M. (2012). Economic reform and total factor productivity growth in Indian manufacturing industries. *Review of Development Economics, 16*(1), 152–166.

Kim, S., & Shafi'I, M. (2009). Factor determinants of total factor productivity growth in Malaysian manufacturing industries: A decomposition analysis. *Asian-Pacific Economic Literature, 23*(1), 48–65.

Kim, S., Park, D., & Park J. H. (2012). Productivity growth in different plant-size groups in the Malaysian manufacturing sector. *Asian Economic Journal, 26*(1), 25–42.

Kim, T., & Park, C. (2003). R&D, trade, and productivity growth in Korean manufacturing? *Review of World Economics, 139*(3), 460–483.

Kim, T., & Park, C. (2006). Productivity growth in Korea: Efficiency improvement or technical progress? *Applied Economics, 38*, 943–954.

Kiran, R., & Mishra, S. (2009a). Performance of the Indian pharmaceutical industry in post- TRIPS period: A firm level analysis. *International Review of Business Research Papers, 5*(6), 148–160.

Kiran, R., & Mishra, S. (2009b). Research and development, export and patenting in Indian pharmaceutical industry: A post TRIPS analysis. *Eurasian Journal of Business Economics, 4*(7), 53–67.

Klapper, L. F., & Parker, S. C. (2011). Gender and the business environment for new firm creation. *The World Bank Research Observer, 26*(2), 237–257.

Klein, B., & Leffler, K. B. (1981). The role of market forces in assuring contractual performance. *Journal of Political Economy, 89*, 615–641. https://doi.org/10.1086/260996

Klenow, P. J. (1996). Industry innovation: Where and why. *Carnegie-Rochester Conference Series on Public Policy, 44*, 125–150.

Kodde, D. A., & Palm, F. C. (1986). Wald criteria for jointly testing equality and inequality restrictions. *Econometrica, 54*(5), 1243–1248.

Kolasa, M. (2008). Productivity, innovation and convergence in Poland. Economics of Transition, *16*(3), 467–501.

Kolte, A., Mal, H., Fulambrikar, M., & Jagtap, A. (2021). Impact of price control on pharmaceutical sector with reference to India. *International Journal of Intelligent Enterprise, 8*(1), 90–104.

Kong, X., Marks, R. E., & Wan, G. H. (1999). Technical efficiency, technological change and total factor productivity growth in Chinese state-owned enterprises in the early 1990s. *Asian Economic Journal, 13*(3), 267–281.

Koopmans, T. C. (1951). An analysis of production as an efficient combination of activities. In Cowlles Commission for Research in Economics (Ed.), *Activity analysis of production and allocation.* Monograph No. 13, Wiley.

Kounetas, K., & Tsekouras, K. (2010, January). Are the energy efficiency technologies efficient? *Economic Modeling, 27*(1), 274–283.

Krüger, J. J. (2008). The sources of aggregate productivity growth: US manufacturing industries, 1958–1996. *Bulletin of Economic Research, 60*(4), 405–427.

Kravtsova, V. (2008). Foreign presence and efficiency in transition economies. *Journal of Productivity Analysis, 29*, 91–102.

Krishna, K. L. (1974). A model for the manufacturing sector: Some preliminary results. In N. K. Choudhury et al. (Eds.), *Towards an econometric model of the Indian Economy, pt. III*. Indian Council of Social Science Research.

Krishna, K. L. (1987). Industrial growth and productivity in Indian. In P. R. Brahman & V. R. Panchamukhi (Eds.), *The development process of the Indian Economy.* Himalaya Publishing House.

Krishna, K. L., & Sahota, G. S. (1991). Technical efficiency in Bangladesh manufacturing industries. *Bangladesh Development Studies*, *1*(2), 89–105.

Krishna, P., & Mitral, D. (1998). Trade liberalization, market discipline and productivity growth: New evidence from India. *Journal of Development Economics*, *56*(2), 447–462.

Krishna, R. (1982). Some aspects of agricultural growth, price policy and equity in developing countries. *Food Research Institute Studies*, *18*(3), 219–260.

Krishnamurty, K., & Sastry, D. U. (1975). *Investment and financing in the corporate sector in India.* Tata McGraw-Hill Publication.

Krueger, A. O. (1974). The political economy of the rent-seeking society. *American Economic Review*, *64*(3), 291–303.

Krueger, J. J. (2003). The global trends of total factor productivity: Evidence from the nonparametric Malmquist index approach. *Oxford Economic Papers*, *55*(2), 265–286.

Kruger, J. J. (2003). Productivity transitions in the us manufacturing sector. *Applied Economics Letters*, *11*, 935–937.

Krugman, P. (1989). Surévaluation et accélération des productivités: un modèle spéculatif in Laussel D. et Montet C. Commerce international et concurrence parfait, Paris. *Economica*, 121–135.

Krugman, P. R. (1987). Is trade policy passe?. *Economic Perspectives*, *1*(2), 131–144.

Kumar, A., Soni, R., Hawaldar, I. T., Vyas, M., & Yadav, V. (2020). The testing of efficient market hypotheses: A study of Indian pharmaceutical industry. *International Journal of Economics and Financial Issues*, *10*(3), 208–216. https://www.econjournals.com/index.php/ijefi/article/view/9764

Kumar, N. (1987). Technology imports and local research and development in Indian manufacturing. *Developing Economies*, *25*(3), 220–233.

Kumar, N. (2003). Intellectual property rights, technology and economic development: Experiences of Asian countries. *Economic and Political Weekly*, *January 18*, 209–226.

Kumar, N., & Saqib, M. (1996). Schumpeter Opportunities for Adaptation and In-house R&D Activity in a Developing Country: The Indian Experience. *Mimeo, Research and Information System for the Non-aligned and Other Developing Countries*, New Delhi.

Kumar, S., & Arora, N. (2012). Evaluation of technical efficiency in Indian sugar industry: An application of full cumulative data envelopment analysis. *Eurasian Journal of Business and Economics*, *5*(9), 57–78.

Kumari, A. (2007, March). Liberalisation, TRIPS and technological behaviour of firms in Indian pharmaceutical industry. *International Review of Business Research Papers*, *3*(1), 12–22.

Kumbhakar, S. C. (1990). Production frontiers, panel data and time-varying technical inefficiency. *Journal of Econometrics*, *46*(1/2), 201–211.

Kumbhakar, S. C. (2003). Factor productivity and technical change. *Applied Economics Letters*, *10*(5), 291–297.

Kumbhakar, S. C., & Bhattacharyya, A. (1996). Productivity growth in passenger-bus transportation: A heteroskedastic error component model with unbalanced panel data. *Empirical Economics*, *21*(4), 557–573.

Kumbhakar, S. C., & Lovell, C. A. K. (2000). *Stochastic frontier analysis*. Cambridge University Press.

Kumbhakar, S. C., Ghosh, S., & McGuckin, J. T. (1991). A generalized production frontier approach for estimating determinant of inefficiency in us dairy farms. *Journal of Business and Economic Statistics*, *9*(3), 279–286.

Kumbhakar, S. C., Heshmati, A., & Hjalmarsson, L. (1999). Parametric approaches to productivity measurement: A comparison among alternative models. *Scandinavian Journal of Economics*, *101*(3), 405–424.

Kumbhakar, S. C., Ortega-Argilés, R., Potters, L., Vivarelli, M., & Voigt, P. (2009). *Corporate R&D and firm efficiency: Evidence from Europe's Top R&D investors*. Discussion Paper No. 4657, Institute for the Study of Labor (IZA), Bonn, Germany.

Kumbhakar, S. C., Shinichiro, N., & Heshmati, A. (2000). Estimation of firm-specific technological bias, technical change and total factor productivity growth: A dual approach. *Econometric Reviews*, *19*(4), 493–515.

Kwaitkowski, D., Phillips, P. C. B., Schmidt, P., & Shin, Y. (1992). Testing the null hypothesis of stationary against the alternative of a unit root. *Journal of Econometrics*, *54*(1–3), 159–178.

Kwiatkowski, D., Phillips, P. C. B., Schmidt, P., & Shin, Y. (1992). Testing the null hypothesis of stationarity against the alternative of a unit root: How sure are we that economic time series have a unit root. *Journal of Econometrics*, *54*, 159–178.

Kwon, J. (1986). Capital utilization, economies of scale and technical change in the growth of total factor productivity. *Journal of Development Economics*, *24*, 75–89.

Kyle, M. K., & McGahan, A. M. (2012). Investments in pharmaceuticals before and after TRIPS. *Review of Economics and Statistics*, *94*(4), 1157–1172.

Lahiri, A., & Yi, K. (2005). A tale of two states: Maharashtra and West Bengal. *Review of Economic Dynamics*, *12*(3), 523–542.

Lalitha, N. (2002, August 24). Indian pharmaceutical industry in WTO regime: A SWOT analysis. *Economic and Political Weekly*, *37*(34), 3542–3555.

Lall, S. (1974, August). The international pharmaceutical industry and less developed countries with special reference to India. *Oxford Bulletin of Economics and Statistics*, *36*(3), 143–172.

Lall, S. V., & Rodrigo, G. C. (2001). Perspectives on the heterogeneity in Indian industry. *World Development*, *29*(12), 2127–2143.

Lawrence, Z. R., & Weinstein, D. E. (2001). Trade and growth: Import-led or Export-led? Evidence from Japan and Korea. In J. Stiglitz & S. Yusuf (Eds.), *Rethinking the East Asian miracle*. Oxford University Press for the World Bank.

Lee, B. S., K. S., & Hong, S. H. (2005). Sectoral manufacturing productivity growth in Korean regions. *Urban Studies*, *42*(7), 1201–1219.

Lee, C. C., & Chang, C. P. (2009). Stochastic convergence of per capita carbon-dioxide emissions and multiple structural breaks in OECD countries. *Economic Modeling*, *26*(6), 1375–1381.

Lee, C. C., Chang, C. P., & Chen, P. F. (2008). Do CO_2 emission levels converge among 21 OECD countries? New evidence from unit root structural break tests. *Applied Economics Letters*, *15*(7), 551–556.

Lee, F. C., & Tang, J. (2001). Multifactor productivity disparity between Canadian and U.S. Manufacturing firms. *Journal of Productivity Analysis*, *15*, 115–128.

Lee, K., & Kang, S. M. (2007). Innovation types and productivity growth: Evidence from Korean manufacturing firms. *Global Economic Review*, *36*(4), 343–359.

Lee, M., & Zhang, N. (2012). Technical efficiency, shadow price of carbon dioxide emissions, and substitutability for energy in the Chinese manufacturing industries. *Energy Economics*, *34*, 1492–1497.

Leibenstein, H. (1976). Allocative efficiency v. x-efficiency. *American Economic Review*, *56*(3), 392–415.

Levin, A., & Lin, C. F. (1993). *Unit root tests in panel data: New results*. University of California.

Levin, A., & Lin, C. F. (1992). Unit root test in panel data: Asymptotic and finite-sample properties [Discussion Paper 92-93, San Diego, CA: Department of Economics, University of California].

Levin, A., Lin, C. F., & Chu, C.S. J. (2002). Unit root tests in panel data: Asymptotic and finite-sample properties. *Journal of Econometrics, 108*, 1–24. https://doi.org/10.1016/S0304-4076(01)00098-7

Levinsohn, J., & Petrin, A. (2003). Estimating production functions using inputs to control for unobservables. *Review of Economic Studies, 70*, 317–341.

Liang, S., & Zhang, T. (2011). What is driving CO_2 emissions in a typical manufacturing center of south china? The case of Jiangsu province. *Energy Policy, 39*(11), 7078–7083.

Liao, H., Liu, X., Holmes, M., & Weyman-Jones, T. (2009, March). The impact of foreign R&D on total factor productivity in the east Asian manufacturing industry. *The Manchester School, 77*(2), 224–270.

Liao, H., Liu, X., & Wang, C. (2012, July). Knowledge spillovers, absorptive capacity and total factor productivity in China's manufacturing firms. *International Review of Applied Economics, 26*(4), 533–547.

Lin, C. V., Cheung, C. B. L., & Nam, K. (1995, October). External economies in Taiwan's manufacturing industries. *Contemporary Economic Policy, 13*(4), 118–130.

Lin, C., Ma, Y., & Su, D. (2009). Corporate governance and firm efficiency: Evidence from China's publicly listed firms. *Managerial and Decision Economics, 30*, 193–209.

Lin, J. T., Chen, T. L., & Lin, Y. T. (2009). Critical material planning for TFT-LCD production industry. *International Journal of Production Economics, 122*, 639–655.

Ling, W., & Adam, S. (2005, March-April). Comparative analysis of capital productivity in china's high-tech industries. *China and World Economy, 13*(2), 93–105.

Little, I. M. D., Majumder, D., & Page, J. M. Jr. (1987). *Small manufacturing enterprises – A comparative analysis of India and other economies.* Oxford University Press.

Liu, T., & Li, K. W. (2012). Analyzing china's productivity growth: Evidence from manufacturing industries. *Economic Systems, 36*, 531–551.

Liu, Z. (2002). Foreign direct investment and technology spillover: Evidence from china. *Journal of Comparative Economics, 30*, 579–602.

Liu, Z., & Liu, G. S. (1996). The efficiency impact of the Chinese industrial reforms in the 1980's. *Journal of Comparative Economics, 23*(3), 237–255.

Liu, Z., & Lyu, J. (2020). Measuring the innovation efficiency of the Chinese pharmaceutical industry based on a dynamic network DEA model. *Applied Economics Letters, 27*(1), 35–40.

Ljung, G. M., & Box, G. E. P. (1978). On a measure of lack of fit in time series models. *Biometrika, 65*(2), 297–303.

Lo, D., & Li, G. (2011). China's economic growth, 1978–2007: Structural-institutional changes and efficiency attributes. Journal of *Post Keynesian Economics, 34*(1), 59–83.

Lovell, C. A. K. (1993). Production Frontiers and Productive Efficiency. In H. O. Fried, C. A. K. Lovell, & S. S. Schmidt (Eds.), *The measurement of productive efficiency: Techniques and applications.* Oxford University Press.

Lu, Y., Ni, J., Tao, Z., & Yu, L. (2013). City–industry growth in china. *China Economic Review, 27*, 135–147.

Lucas, R. E. (1988). On the mechanics of economic development. *Journal of Monetary Economics, 22*(1), 3–42.

Lumsdaine, R. L., & Papell, D. H. (1997). Multiple trend breaks and the unit root hypothesis. *The Review of Economics and Statistics, 79*(2), 212–218.

Lundvall, K., & Battese, G. E. (2000). Firm size, age and efficiency: Evidence from Kenyan manufacturing firms. *Journal of Development Studies, 36*(3), 146–163.

Lynk, E. L. (1982). Factor demand, substitution and biased technical change in Indian industry. *Manchester School*, *1*(2), 126–138.

MacKinnon, J. G. (1990). Critical values for co-integration tests. *UC San Diego Discussion Paper*, 90–94. Queen's Economics Department Working Paper No. 1227, http://www.econ.queensu.ca/faculty/mackinnon/

MacKinnon, J. (1991). Critical values for cointegration tests. University of California, San Diego, Economics Working Paper Series no. 90-4, Department of Economics, UCSD.

Madanmohan, T. R. (1997). Exit strategies: Experience of Indian pharmaceutical firms. *Economic and Political Weekly*, *32*(48), M107–M110.

Maddala, G. S., & Kim, I. M. (1998). *Unit roots, cointegration and structural change*. Cambridge University Press.

Maddala, G. S., & Wu, S. (1999). A comparative study of unit root tests with panel data and a new simple test. *Oxford Bulletin of Economics and Statistics*, *61*, 631–652. http://dx.doi.org/10.1111/1468-0084.61.s1.13

Madden, G., & Savage, S. J. (1999). Telecommunications productivity, catch-up and innovation. *Telecommunications Policy*, *23*(1), 65–81.

Madheswaran, S., Liao, H., & Rath, B. N. (2007). Productivity growth of Indian manufacturing sector: Panel estimation of stochastic production frontier and technical inefficiency. *The Journal of Developing Areas*, *40*(2), 35–50.

Mahadevan, R. (2000). A frontier approach to measuring total factor productivity growth in Singapore's service sector. *Journal of Economic Studies*, *29*(1), 48–58.

Mahadevan, R. (2002). *New currents in productivity analysis – Where to now?* Asian Productivity Organisation.

Mahadevan, R. (2003). To measure or not to measure total factor productivity growth? *Oxford Development Studies*, *31*(3), 365–378.

Mahajan, V. (2020). Is productivity of Indian pharmaceutical industry affected with the introduction of product patent act? *Indian Growth and Development Review*, *13*(1), 227–258. https://doi.org/10.1108/IGDR-11-2018-0116

Mahajan, V., Nauriyal, D. K., & Singh, S. P. (2014). Efficiency and ranking of Indian pharmaceutical industry: Does type of ownership matter?. *Eurasian Journal of Business and Economics*, *7*(14), 29–50. https://doi.org/10.17015/ejbe.2014.014.02

Mahajan, V., Nauriyal, D. K., & Singh, S. P. (2018, January 29). Efficiency and its determinants: Panel data evidence from the Indian pharmaceutical industry. *Margin: The Journal of Applied Economic Research*, *12*(1), 19–40. https://doi.org/10.1177/0973801017738416

Maher, J. M., & Gordon, S. (2008). Learning, forecasting and structural breaks. *Journal of Applied Econometrics*, *23*(5), 553–583.

Mahmood, T., Ghani, E., & Din, M. (2006). Efficiency of large-scale manufacturing in Pakistan: A production frontier approach. *The Pakistan Development Review*, *45*(4), 689–700.

Majeed, S., Ahmed, Q. M., & Butt, M. S. (2010). Trade liberalization and total factor productivity growth (1971-2007). *Pakistan Economic and Social Review*, *48*(1), 61–84.

Majumdar, M., & Rajeev, M. (2009). Comparing the efficiency and productivity of Indian pharmaceutical firms: A malmquist-meta-frontier approach. *International Journal of Business and Economics*, *8*(2), 159–181.

Majumdar, M., Rajeev, M., & Ray, S. C. (2009). *Output and Input efficiency of manufacturing firms in India: A case of the Indian pharmaceutical sector*. Working Paper 219. Institute for Social and Economic Change, Bangalore.

Majumdar, S. K. (1994). Assessing firms capabilities – theory and measurement – A study of Indian pharmaceutical-industry. *Economic and Political Weekly*, *29*(22), 83–89.

Majumder, S. K. (1997). The impact of size and age on firm-level performance: Some evidence from India. *Review of Industrial Organization*, *12*(2), 231–241.

Mandal, S. K., & Madheswaran, S. (2010). Environmental efficiency of the Indian cement industry: An interstate analysis. *Energy Policy*, *38*(2), 1108–1118.

Mani, S. (2006). *The sectoral system of innovation of Indian pharmaceutical industry*. [Working Paper 382]. The Institute of Development Studies and partner organisations. Report. https://hdl.handle.net/20.500.12413/3108

Manjappa, D. H., & Mahesha, M. (2008). Measurement of productivity growth, efficiency change and technical progress of selected capital-intensive and labor- intensive industries during reform period in India. *Indian Journal of Economics and Business*, *7*(1), 167–178.

Mankiw, N. G., Romer, D., & Weil, D. N. (1992). A contribution to the empirics of economic growth. *Quarterly Journal of Economics*, *107*, 407–438.

Marcos, M., Suarez, A., & Galvez, C. (2000). Technical efficiency of Spanish manufacturing firms: A panel data approach. *Applied Economics*, *32*(10), 1249–1258.

Margono, H., & Sharma, S. C. (2006). Efficiency and productivity analyses of Indonesian manufacturing industries. *Journal of Asian Economics*, *17*, 979–995.

Marnuneas, T. E., & Ishaq Nadiri, M. (1996). Public R&D policies and cost behavior of the US manufacturing industries. *Journal of Public Economics*, *63*, 57–81.

Maté-Sánchez-Val, M. L., & Guijarro, A. M. (2011). A spatial efficiency index proposal: An empirical application to SMEs productivity. *Annals of Regional Science*, *47*, 353–371.

Mathew, G., & Unnikrishnan, M. K. (2012, May 5). The emerging environmental burden from pharmaceuticals. *Economic & Political Weekly*, *xlviI*(18), 31–34.

Mazumdar, M., & Rajeev, M. (2009). Comparing the efficiency and productivity of the Indian pharmaceutical firms: A malmquist-meta-frontier approach. *International Journal of Business and Economics*, *8*(2), 159–181.

Mazumdar, M., & Rajeev, M. (2007). TRIPS agreement and the emerging in-house R&D activity of the Indian pharmaceutical companies: A panel data analysis of the firm level data. *PES Business Review*, *3*(1), 3–23.

Mazumder, M., Rajeev, M., & Ray, S. C. (2010). *Sources of heterogeneity in the efficiency of Indian pharmaceutical firms* [CSH Occasional papers N°27/2010].

Mazzucato, M., & Parris, S. (2015). High-growth firms in changing competitive environments: The us pharmaceutical industry (1963 to 2002). *Small Business Economics*, *44*(1), 145–170.

McKinnon, J. G. (1990). Critical values for co-integration tests. *UC San Diego Discussion Paper*, 90–94.

Meade, J. E. (1951). *Theory of international economic policy*. Oxford University Press.

Meeusen, W., & van den Broeck, J. (1977). Efficiency estimation from Cobb-Douglas production function with composed error. *International Economic Review*, *18*(2), 435–444.

Mehrotra, S., Gandhi, A., Saha, P., & Sahoo, B. K. (2013). Turnaround in India's employment story silver lining amidst joblessness and informalisation? *Economic & Political Weekly*, *48*(35), 87–96.

Mehta, K., Rai, A., & Bhanot, N. (2013, April 13). Dictated by pharma companies. *Economic & Political Weekly*, *xlviiI*(15), 15–17.

Mellor, J. W. (1976). *The new economics of growth: A strategy for India and the developing world*. Cornell University Press.

Mengistae, T. (1995). *Age-size effects in productive efficiency: A second test of the passive learning model*. WPS/96-2, Centre for the Study of African Economies, Institute of Economics and Statistics, University of Oxford, Oxford, UK.

Mengistae, T. (1998). *Age-size effects in firm growth and productive efficiency: The case of manufacturing establishments in Ethiopia*. World Bank. worldbank.org/DEC/Resources/age-size.pdf

Milner, C., Vencappa, D., & Wright, P. (2007). Trade policy and productivity growth in Indian manufacturing. *The World Economy, 30*(2), 249–266.

Minangsari, F., Robiani, B., & Mukhlis (2019). The efficiency of the pharmaceutical industry in Indonesia: A stochastic frontier approach. *Jurnal Ekonomi Pembangunan, 17*(2), 49–58. https://doi.org/10.29259/jep.v17i2.8949

Mini, F., & Rodriguez, E. (2000). Technical efficiency indicators in a Philippine manufacturing sector. *International Review of Applied Economics, 14*(4),461–173.

Mion, G., & Zhu, L. (2013). Import competition from and offshoring to China: A curse or blessing for firms? *Journal of International Economics, 89*(2013), 202–215.

Mirmozaffari, M., Yazdani, R., Shadkam, E., Khalili, S. M., Mahjoob, M., & Boskabadi, A. (2022). An integrated artificial intelligence model for efficiency assessment in pharmaceutical companies during the covid-19 pandemic. *Sustainable Operations and Computers, 3*, 156–167. https://doi.org/10.1016/j.susoc.2022.01.003. Epub 2022 Jan 4. PMCID: PMC8724018.

Mishra, P., & Chandra, T. (2010). Mergers, acquisitions and firms' performance: Experience of Indian pharmaceutical industry. *Eurasian Journal of Business and Economics, 3*(5), 111–126.

Misra, S. K., & Puri, V. K. (2002). *Indian economy – Its development experience*. Himalaya Publishing House.

Mitchell, J., Smith, R. J., & Weale, M. R. (2002). Quantification of qualitative firm-level survey data. *The Economic Journal, 112*, C117–C135.

Mitchell, M. F. (2002). Technological change and the scale of production. *Review of Economic Dynamics, 5*, 477–488.

Mitra, A. (1977). *Terms of trade and class relations*. Frank Cass.

Mitra, A. (1999). Total factor productivity growth and technical efficiency in Indian industries. *Economic and Political Weekly, 34*(31), M98–M105.

Mitra, A. (2000). Total factor productivity growth and urbanization economies: A case of Indian industries. *Review of Urban and Regional Development Studies, 12*(2), 97–108.

Mitra, A., & Sato, H. (2007). Agglomeration economics in japan: Technical efficiency, growth and unemployment. *Review of Urban and Regional Development Studies, 19*(3), 197–209.

Mitra, A., Sharma, C., & Véganzonés-Varoudakis, M. A. (2012). Estimating impact of infrastructure on productivity and efficiency of Indian manufacturing. *Applied Economics Letters, 19*, 779–783.

Mitra, D., & Ural, B. P. (2008). Indian manufacturing: A slow sector in a rapidly growing economy. *The Journal of International Trade & Economic Development, 17*(4), 525–559.

Mohan, M. (1989). *Advertising management: Concepts and cases*. Tata McGrawHill Education, ISBN: 978007451780.

Mok, V., Yeung, G., Han, Z., & Li, Z. (2010). Export orientation and technical efficiency: Clothing firms in china. *Managerial and Decision Economics, 31*, 453–463.

Moshi, G. (2013, June). Convergence in industry efficiency and technology adoption in African telecommunications: An empirical study. *European Scientific Journal, 9*(18), 55–73.

Motohashi, K. (2008). It, enterprise reform, and productivity in Chinese manufacturing firms. *Journal of Asian Economics, 19*, 325–333.

Mühlau, P., & Lindenberg, S. (2003). Efficiency wages: Signals or incentives? An empirical study of the relationship between wage and commitment. *Journal of Management and Governance, 7*, 385–400.

Mukherjee, G. P. (1963). On size-productivity relationship in Indian industries. *The Journal of Industrial Economics, 2*(2), 141–159.

Mukherjee, K. (2008). Energy use efficiency in U.S. Manufacturing: A nonparametric analysis. *Energy Economics, 30*, 76–96.

Mukherjee, K., & Ray, S. C. (2004). *Technical efficiency and its dynamics in Indian manufacturing: An inter-state analysis* [Working Paper, No. 18, USA: University of Connecticut].

Mukherjee, K., & Ray, S. C. (2005). Technical efficiency and its dynamics in Indian manufacturing: An inter-state analysis. *Indian Economic Review, New Series, 40*(2), 101–125.

Mukherjee, R., Das, P. K., & Bhattacharya, U. K. (1999). Small-scale industries in West Bengal, 1971-97: Data analysis for study of growth. *Economic and Political Weekly, 34*(48), M157–M162.

Mukhopadhyay, D., & Sarkar, N. (2001). Has there been an acceleration in the growth of agriculture in West Bengal? A fresh look using modern time series techniques. Sankhy*a: The Indian Journal of Statistics, Series B, 63*(1), 89–107.

Mukhopadhyay, K., & Paul, P. (2018). Pharmaceutical growth versus health equity in India: When markets fail. *Journal of Public Health: From Theory to Practice, 27*(4), 473–489. https://doi.org/10.1007/s10389-018-0969-6

Mullen, J. K. (2001). Long-run technical change and multifactor productivity growth in us manufacturing. *Applied Economics, 33*(3), 301–308.

Mullen, J. K., Williams, M., & Moomaw, R. L. (1996). Public capital stock and interstate variations in manufacturing efficiency. *Journal of Policy Analysis and Management, 15*(1), 51–67.

Muratoğlu, G. (2017). Does pharmaceutical industry boost economic growth? A competitiveness-related approach. *Yaşar Üniversitesi E-Dergisi, 12*(48), 296–314.

Murray, C. J. (1998). *Essays on the decomposition of macroeconomic time series into permanent and transitory components* [Unpublished Ph.D Dissertation, Department of Economics, Washington].

Murray, C. J., & Zivot, E. (1998). *Inference on unit roots and trend breaks in macroeconomic time series* [Manuscript, Department of Economics, University of Houston].

Murty, M. N. (1986). Inter-fuel substitution and derived demand for inputs in the manufacturing sector of India. *Journal of Quantitative Economics, 2*(1), 119–135.

Muthuswamy, V. V., & Nithya, N. (2023). Predictors of quality of work in the Indian pharma industry: A perceptual study among medical representatives. *The Journal of Modern Project Management, 11*(2), 1–13. https://journalmodernpm.com/manuscript/index.php/jmpm/article/view/652

Nag, B. (2005). Impact of capacity utilisation and slow adjustments of quasi-fixed factors on productivity and efficiency measurement: An experiment with Indian pharmaceutical industry. *Journal of Pharmaceutical Finance, Economics & Policy, 14*(4), 69–97.

Nagaraj, R. (1989). Growth in manufacturing output since 1980: Some preliminary findings. *Economic and Political Weekly, 24*(26), 1481–1484.

Nagaraj, R. (2003). Industrial policy and performance since 1980: Which way now. *Economic and Political Weekly, 38*(35), 3707–3715.

Nagarajan, M., & Barthwal, R. R. (1990, Oct–Dec). Profitability and structure: A firm level study of the Indian pharmaceutical industry. *Indian Economic Journal, 38*(2), 70–81.

Nandy, S., & Sussan, F. (2021). R&D intensity and export: The case of Indian pharmaceutical industry, *Review of Integrative Business and Economics Research, 10*, Supplementary Issue 3, 1–16.

Narashimham, G. V. L., & Fabrycy, M. Z. (1974). Relative efficiencies of organized industries in India, 1949-1958. *Journal of Development Studies, 12*(2), 230–241.

Nataraj, S. (2011). The impact of trade liberalization on productivity: Evidence from India's formal and informal manufacturing sectors. *Journal of International Economics, 85*, 292–301.

Nayyar, D. (1978). Industrial development in India: Some reflections on growth and stagnation. *Economic and Political Weekly, 13*(31–33), 1265–1278.

Nazari, J., & Herremans, I. (2007). Extended VAIC model: Measuring intellectual capital components. *Journal of Intellectual Capital*, *8*, 595–609. https://doi.org/10.1108/14691930710830774

Nelson, C. R., & Plosser, C. I. (1982). Trends and random walks in macroeconomic time series: Some evidence and implications. *Journal of Monetary Economics*, *10*(2), 139–162.

Nelson, C. R., & Kang, H. (1981). Spurious productivity in inappropriately de-trended time series. *Econometrica*, *49*(3), 741–751.

Nelson, C. R., & Kang. H. (1984). Pitfalls in the use of time as an explanatory variable in the regression. *Journal of Business Economics and Statistics*, *2*(1), 73–82.

Nelson, C. R., & Pack, H. (1999). The Asian miracle and modern growth theory. *Economic Journal*, *109*(457), 416–436.

Nelson, R. A. (1990). Productivity growth, scale economics and the schumpeterian hypothesis. *Southern Economic Journal*, *57*(2), 521–527.

Neogi, C., & Ghosh, B. (1998). Impact of liberalization on performance of Indian industries: A firm-level study. *Economic and Political Weekly*, *33*(9), M16–M24.

Neogi, C., & Ghosh, B. (1994). Intertemporal efficiency variations in Indian manufacturing industries. *The Journal of Productivity Analysis*, *5*, 301–324.

Neogi, C., Kamiike, A., & Sato, T. (2012). *Identification of factors behind performance of pharmaceutical industries in India*. DP, Research Institute for Economics and Business Administration, Kobe University.

Ng, Y. C., & Wei, L. Q. (2012). Efficiency of Chinese enterprises: Does human resource management matter?. *Applied Economics Letters*, *19*, 35–39.

Ngwuluka, N. C., Ochekpe, N. A., & Odumosu, P. O. (2011). An assessment of pharmaceutical waste management in some Nigerian pharmaceutical industries. *African Journal of Biotechnology*, *10*(54), 11259–11264.

Nikaido, Y. (2004). Technical efficiency of small-scale industry: Application of stochastic production frontier model. *Economic and Political Weekly*, *39*(6), 592–597.

Nishimizu, M., & Page, J. M. (1982). Total factor productivity growth, technological progress and technical efficiency change: Dimensions of productivity change in Yugoslavia. *Economic Journal*, *92*(368), 920–936.

Nishimizu, M., & Page, J. (1982). Total factor productivity growth, technological progress and technical efficiency changes. *Economic Journal*, *92*, 920–936. https://doi.org/10.2307/2232675

Nouraei Motlagh, S., Lotfi, F., Hadian, M., Safari, H., & Rezapour, A. (2014). Factors influencing pharmaceutical demand in Iran: Results from a regression study. *International Journal of Hospital Research*, *2*, 93–96.

O'hUallacháin, B. (1984). Input-output linkages and foreign direct investment in Ireland. *International Regional Science Review*, *9*(3), 185–200.

Obukohwo, E. O., Olele, E. H., & Buzugbe, P. N. (2018). Assessing efficiency in the pharmaceutical sector of Nigeria. *CBN Journal of Applied Statistics*, *9*(2), 131–148.

Oczkowski, E., & K. Sharma (2005). Determinants of efficiency in least developed countries: Further evidence from Nepalese manufacturing firms. *The Journal of Development Studies*, *41*(4), 617–630.

Oh, D. H. (2011). Productivity growth, efficiency change and technical progress of the Korean manufacturing industry. *Journal of the Asia Pacific Economy*, *16*(1), 50–70.

Oh, D., Heshmati, A., & Loof, H. (2012). Technical change and total factor productivity growth for Swedish manufacturing and service industries. *Applied Economics*, *44*, 2373–2391.

Oh, I., Lee, J. D., & Hesmati, A. (2008). Total factor productivity in Korean manufacturing industries, *Global economic Review*, *37*(1), 23–50.

Okamoto, Y., & Sjoholm, F. (2005). FDI and the dynamics of productivity in Indonesian manufacturing. *The Journal of Development Studies*, *41*(1), 160–182.

Önder, A. Ö., Deliktas, E., & Lenger, A. (2003). Efficiency in the manufacturing industry of selected provinces in turkey a stochastic frontier analysis. *Emerging Markets Finance and Trade*, *39*(2), 98–113.

Osorio, L. L. D. R., Flórez-López, E., & Grande-Tovar, C. D. (2021). The potential of selected agri-food loss and waste to contribute to a circular economy: Applications in the food, cosmetic and pharmaceutical industries. *Molecules*, *26*(2), 515.

Ozler, S., & Yilmaz, K. (2009). Productivity response to reduction in trade barriers: Evidence from Turkish manufacturing plants. *Review of World Economics*, *145*, 339–360. https://doi.org/10.1007/s10290-009-0019-0

Pack, H. (1988). Industrialization and trade. In H. B. Chenery & T. N. Srinivassan (Eds.), *Handbook of development economics.* North Holland.

Page, J. M. Jr. (1984). Firm size and technical efficiency: Application of production frontier to Indian survey data. *Journal of Development Economics*, *16*(1/2), 129–152.

Pal, D., Chakraborty, C., & Ghose, A. (2018, September). Is there improvement in total factor productivity growth of the Indian pharmaceutical industry after TRIPS agreement? Evidence from biennial malmquist index in the Central European Review of Economics and Management (ISSN 2543-9472; eISSN 2544-0365) *2,* No. *3*, pp. 53–77.

Palangkaraya, A., Stierwald, A., & Yong, J. (2005). Is firm productivity related to firm size and age? The case of large Australian firms. *The Melbourne Institute of Applied Economic and Social Research*, The University of Melbourne, Revised Version.

Pannu, H. S., Kumar, U. D., & Farooquie, J. A. (2010). Impact of Innovation on the Performance of Indian Pharmaceutical Industry using Data Envelopment Analysis. *IIMB WORKING PAPER NO.2010-02-302.* https://papers.ssrn.com/sol3/papers.cfm?abstract_id=2125785

Parameswaran, M. (2009). International trade, R&D spillovers and productivity: Evidence from Indian manufacturing industry. *Journal of Development Studies*, *45*(8), 1249–1266.

Parameswaran, M., & Prameswaran, M. (2004). Economic reforms, technical change and efficiency change: Firm level evidence from capital goods industries in India. *Indian Economic Review, New Series*, *39*(1), 239–260.

Parasiya, S., Balamuralidhara, V., Kumar, P., Dave, A., Gujrati, R., & Shukla, A. (2013). Need for drug price control in India. *International Journal of Drug Regulatory Affairs*, *1*(4), 12–18.

Park, Y., Shin, J., & Kim, T. (2010). Firm size, age, industrial networking, and growth: A case of the Korean manufacturing industry. *Small Business Economics*, *35*, 153–168.

Parron, P. (1989). The great crash, the oil price shock and the unit root hypothesis. *Econometrica*, *57*(6), 1361–1401.

Pastor, J. T., Asmild, M., & Lovell, C. (2011). The biennial malmquist productivity change index. *Socio-Economic Planning Sciences*, *45*, 10–15.

Paternostro, S., Marchetti, D., & L. Barbone, Jr. (1999). *Structural adjustment, ownership transformation and size in Polish industry*. The World Bank Policy Research Working Paper Series No. 1624.

Patnaik, P. (1981). An explanatory hypothesis on the Indian Industrial Stagnation. In A. K. Bagchi & N. Banerjee (Eds.), *Changes and choice in Indian Industry.*

Patra, S., & Nayak, S. R. (2012). A theoretical study on the relationship between wages and labor productivity in industries. *International Journal of Economics Research*, *313*, 157–163.

Paul, S. (1974). Industrial performance and government controls. In J. C. Sandesara (Ed.), *The Indian economy: Performance and prospects.* University of Bombay.

Pavcnik, N. (2004, March). Review of the economics of essential medicines. *Journal of Economic Literature*, *42*(1), 195–197.

Perron, P. (1990). *Further evidence on breaking trend functions in macroeconomic variables* [Unpublished Manuscript, Department of Economics, Princeton University].

Perron, P. (1997). Further evidence on breaking trend functions in macroeconomic variables. *Journal of Econometrics*, *80*(2), 355–385.

Perron, P., & Vogelsang, T. J. (1991). *The great crash, the oil price shock and the unit root hypothesis: corrections and extensions of some asymptotic results* [Unpublished Manuscript, Department of Economics, Princeton University].

Pesaran, M. H. (2004). *General diagnostic tests for cross section dependence in panels. University of Cambridge* [Faculty of Economics, Cambridge Working Papers in Economics No. 0435].

Pesaran, M. H., Pettenuzzo, D., & Timmermann, A. (2006). Forecasting time series subject to multiple structural breaks. *Review of Economic Studies*, *73*(4), 1057–1084.

Petrin, A., & Levinsohn, J. (2012). Measuring aggregate productivity growth using plant-level data. *RAND Journal of Economics*, *43*(4), 705–725.

Pham, H. T., Dao, T. L., & Reilly, B. (2010). Technical efficiency in the Vietnamese manufacturing sector. *Journal of International Development*, *22*, 503–520.

Phillips, P. C. B. (1987). Time series regression with a unit root. *Econometrica*, *55*, 277–302.

Phillips, P. C. B., & Perron, P. (1988). Testing for a unit root in time series regression. *Biometrika*, *75*, 335–346.

Phillips, P. C. B., & Durlauf, S. N. (1986). Multiple time series regression with integrated process. *Review of Economic Studies*, *53*(4), 473–495.

Pinell-Siles, A. (1979). *Determinants of private industrial investment in India* [World Bank Staff Working Paper, No. 33].

Pitt, M. M., & Lee, L. F. (1981). The measurement and sources of technical inefficiency in the Indonesian weaving industry. *Journal of Development Economics*, *9*(1), 43–64.

Pombo, C., & Taborda, R. (2006). Performance and efficiency in Colombia's power distribution system: Effects of the 1994 reform. *Energy Economics*, *28*(3), 339–369.

Ponce, M. F. (2019). An overview of the global pharma industry's new trends. Elsevier. http://dx.doi.org/10.2139/ssrn.3397618

Porter, M. E. (1990). *The competitive advantage of nations.* Harvard University Press.

Pradeep, V., & Chen, J. R. (2012). Measuring productivity growth, efficiency change and technical progress in small scale firms in India during pre and post-reform periods. *Journal of Economic Policy Reform*, *15*(2), 153–169.

Pradhan, G., & Barik, K. (1998). Fluctuating total factor productivity in India: Evidence form selected polluting industries. *Economic and Political Weekly*, *34*(31), M92–M97.

Pradhan, J. P. (2006). *Global competitiveness of Indian Pharmaceutical Industry: Trends and strategies* [Working Paper, No. 2006/05SID, Institute for Studies in Industrial Development].

Prasad, & Bhatt, S. (1993). Strengthening India's patent system, implications for pharmaceutical sector. *Economic and Political Weekly*, *28*(21), 1037–1058.

Primont, D. F., & Domazlicky, B. R. (2005). Which matters most to the estimation of efficiency and productivity growth in state manufacturing: Method or measurement? *The Review of Regional Studies*, *35*(2), 117–138.

Quah, D. T. (1993). Galton's fallacy and the convergence hypothesis. *Scandinavian Journal of Economics*, *95*, 427–443.

Quah, D. T. (1994). Exploiting cross-section variations for unit root inference in dynamic data. *Economics Letters*, *44*(1-2), 9–19.

Quah, D. T. (1996). Empirics for economic growth and convergence. *European Economic Review*, *40*, 1353–1375.

Quatraro, F. (2009). Innovation, structural change and productivity growth: Evidence from Italian regions, 1980–2003. *Cambridge Journal of Economics*, *33*, 1001–1022.

Quiros, R., Rodriguez, C., & Rodriguez, D. (2010). E-commerce and efficiency at the firm level. *International Journal of Production Economics*, *126*(2), 299–305.

Raheman, A., Qayyum, A., & Afza, T. (2008). Efficiency dynamics of Sugar Industry of Pakistan. *The Pakistan Development Review*, *48*, 4 Part II (Winter 2009), 921–938.

Raj, K. N. (1976). Growth and stagnation in Indian industrial development. *Economic and Political Weekly, 11*(5–7), 223–236.

Raj, S. N. R. (2011). Structure, employment and productivity growth in the Indian unorganized manufacturing sector: An industry level analysis. *The Singapore Economic Review, 56*(3), 349–376.

Ramani, S. V., & Maria, A. (2005). TRIPS: Its possible impact on biotech segment of the Indian pharmaceutical industry. *Economic & Political Weekly, 40*, 675–683.

Ramaswamy, V. K. (1990). *Technical efficiency in modern small industry in India* [Ph. D. Dissertation, Department of Economics, University of Delhi].

Ramaswamy, V. K. (1994). Technical efficiency in modern small-scale firms in Indian industry: Applications of stochastic production frontier. *Journal of Quantitative Economics, 10*(2), 309–324.

Ramaswamy, V. K. (1999). Productivity growth, protection and plant entry in a deregulating economy: The case of India. *Small Business Economics, 13*(2), 131–139.

Ramondo, N. (2009). Foreign plants and industry productivity: Evidence from Chile. *Scandinavian Journal of Economics, 111*(4), 789–809.

Rangarajan, C. (1982). Industrial growth: Another look. *Economic and Political Weekly, 17*(14–16), 589–604.

Rangnekar, D. (2006, February 4). No pills for poor people? Understanding the disembowelment of India's patent regime. *Economic and Political Weekly, 41*(5), 409–416.

Rao, J. M. (1996a). Manufacturing productivity growth: Method and measurement. *Economic and Political Weekly, 31*(44), 2927–2936.

Rao, J. M. (1996b). Indices of industrial productivity growth. *Economic and Political weekly, 31*(49), 3177–3188.

Rao, S. C., Raghavan, P., & Gupta, K. (2003). Maharashtra's success in manufacturing. *Margin, 35*(4), 97–103.

Rappoport, P. (1990). *Testing for the frequency of permanent shifts in time series* [Unpublished Manuscript, Department of Economics, Rutgers University].

Rappoport, P., & Reichlin, L. (1989). Segmented trends and non-stationary time series. *Economic Journal, 99*(395), 168–177.

Rasekh, H. R., Mehralian, G., & Vatankhah-Mohammadabadi, A. A. (2012). Situation analysis of R&D activities: An empirical study in Iranian pharmaceutical companies. *Iranian Journal of Pharmaceutical Research: IJPR, 11*(4), 1013.

Raut, L. (1995). R&D spillover and productivity growth: Evidence from Indian private firms. *Journal of Development Economics, 48*, 1–23. https://doi.org/10.1016/0304-3878(95)00028-3

Ray, A. S. (1996). A statistical profile of West Bengal Industry: Trends and structural changes (1971-91). In A. Raychaudhuri & D. Sarkar (Eds.), *Economy of West Bengal (Problem and prospects)*. Allied Publishers.

Ray, S. (2006). The changing role of technological factors in explaining efficiency in Indian firms. *Journal of Developing Areas, 40*(1), 127–140.

Ray, S. C. (1997). Regional variation in productivity growth in Indian manufacturing: A nonparametric analysis. *Journal of Quantitative Economics, B*(1), 73–94.

Ray, S. C. (2002). Did India's economic reforms improve efficiency and productivity? A nonparametric analysis of the initial evidence from manufacturing. *Indian Economic Review, New Series, 37*(1), 23–57.

Ray, S. C. (2004). *Data envelopment analysis: Theory and techniques for economics and operations research.* Cambridge University Press.

Ray, S. C. (2006). The changing role of technological factors in explaining efficiency in Indian firms. *Journal of Developing Areas, 40*(1), 127–140.

Ray, S. C. (2009). Are Indian firms too small? A nonparametric analysis of cost efficiency and the optimal organization of the Indian manufacturing industry. *Indian Economic Review, New Series, 44*(1), 49–67.

Ray, S. C., & Desli, E. (1997). Productivity growth, technical progress and efficiency changes in industrialized countries: Comment. *American Economic Review*, *85*(5), 1033–1039.

Ray, S. C., & Ghose, A. (2014). Production efficiency in Indian agriculture: An assessment of the post green revolution years. *Omega*, *44*, 58–69.

Ray, S. C., & Mukherjee, K. (1996). Decomposition of the fisher ideal index of productivity: A nonparametric analysis of U.S. Airline data. *Economic Journal*, *106*(439), 1659–1678.

Raychaudhuri, A., & Chatterjee, B. (1998). Pattern of industrial growth in West Bengal during last two decades: Some policy suggestions. *Economic and Political Weekly*, *33*(47/48), 3060–3065.

Rebick, M. E. (1999). Trade and the wage structure in the presence of price differentials in the product market: The Japanese labor market 1965–1990. *Journal of the Japanese and International Economies*, *13*, 22–43.

Reddy, A. V. J., & Rao, B. M. (2017, April–June). opportunities and challenges for Indian pharmaceutical companies in overseas markets and need of digital tools for sustainable success, *Indian Journal of Pharmaceutical Education and Research*, *51*(2).

Reddy, M., & Yanagida, J. F. (1999). Technical efficiency analysis of Fiji's sugar industry: An application of the stochastic frontier production function approach. *South African Journal of Economics*, *2*(1), 77–92.

Reichlia, L. (1989). Structural change and unit root econometrics. *Economics Letters*, *31*(3), 231–233.

Reifschneider, D., & Stevenson, R. (1991). Systematic departures from the frontier: Framework for the analysis of firm inefficiency. *International Economic Review*, *32*(3), 715–723.

Report of the Task Force, Ministry of Commerce & Industry, December 12, 2008.

Resende, M., & Facë Anha, L. O. (2002). Privatization and efficiency in Brazilian telecommunications: An empirical study. *Applied Economics Letters*, *9*, 823–826.

Rice, P. G. (1990, December). Relative labour costs and the growth of part-time employment in British manufacturing industries. *The Economic Journal*, 1138–1146.

Richmond, J. (1974). Estimating the efficiency of production. *International Economic Review*, *15*(2), 515–521.

Rodrik, D. (1988). *Imperfect competition, scale economies and trade policy in developing countries. Mimeo*, Harvard University.

Rodrik, D. (1992). Closing the technology gap: Does trade liberalization really help? In G. K. Helleiner (Ed.), *Trade policy, industrialization and development: New Perspectives*. Claredon Press.

Rodrik, D. (2011). *Unconditional convergence* [Working Paper 17546, National Bureau of Economic Research Working Paper Series].

Rodrik, D., & Subramanian, A. (2004). *From 'Hindu Growth' to productivity surge: The mystery of the Indian Growth Transition* [IMF Working Paper WP/04/77, International Monetary Fund, Washington DC].

Romer, P. (1990). Endogenous technical change. *Journal of Political Economy*, *98*(5), Part-2, 71–102.

Rosario, S., & Mazumdar, C. S. (2022). A study of the impact of value-added efficiency on profitability and market value in the Indian pharma industry. *Academic Journal of Interdisciplinary Studies*, *11*(1), 212.

Roudaut, N., & Vanhems, A. (2012). Explaining firms efficiency in the Ivorian manufacturing sector: A robust nonparametric approach. *Journal of Productivity Analysis*, *37*, 155–169.

Roy Biswas, P., & Ghose, A. (2012). *Growth, efficiency & productivity of Indian Manufacturing Industries: An econometric analysis*. LAP Lambert Academic Publishing.

Roy Chaudhury, U. D. (1977). Industrial breakdown of capital stock in India. *The Journal of Income and Wealth*, *3*(2), 144–163.

Ruane, F., & Ugur, A. (2004). Foreign direct investment and productivity spillovers in Irish manufacturing industry: Evidence from plant level panel data. *International Journal of the Economics of Business*, *11*(3), 53–66.

Rudra, A. (1967). *Relative rates of growth – Agriculture and industry*. Department of Economics, University of Bombay.

Saal, D. S. (2001). The impact of procurement-driven technological change on US manufacturing productivity growth. *Defense and Peace Economics*, *12*(6), 537–568.

Safari, H., Arab, M., Rashidian, A., Kebriaee-Zadeh, A., & Gorji, H. A. (2018). A comparative study on different pharmaceutical industries and proposing a model for the context of Iran. *Iranian Journal of Pharmaceutical Research: IJPR*, *17*(4), 1593.

Sahin, R. A., & Kalirajan, K. P. (1999). Sources of output growth in Bangladesh food processing industries: A decomposition analysis, *Developing Economies*, *37*(3), 355–374.

Sahinöz, S., & Cosar, E. E. (2009). Understanding sectoral growth cycles and the impact of monetary policy in the turkish manufacturing industry. *OECD Journal: Journal of Business Cycle Measurement and Analysis, 2009*(1), 43–69.

Said, S. E., & Dickey, D. A. (1980). Testing the unit roots in ARMA models of unknown order. *Biometrika*, *71*, 599–607.

Said, S. E., & Dickey, D. A. (1985). Hypothesis testing in ARIMA (p, 1, q) models. *Journal of the American Statistical Association*, *80*(390), 369–374.

Saini, L., & Agarwal, P. K. (2023). Challenges Of Establishing Pharmaceutical Company In India. *Journal of Xidian University*, *17*(5), 697–702, https://doi.org/10.37896/jxu17.5/071

Sala-i-Martin, X. (1996). The classical approach to convergence analysis. *The Economic Journal*, *106*(437), 1019–1036. https://doi.org/10.2307/2235375

Samad, Q. A., & Patwary, F. K. (2002). Technical efficiency and technical change in the major manufacturing industries of Bangladesh. *Bangladesh Development Studies*, *28*(1–2), 113–135.

Samad, Q. A., & Patwary, F. K. (2003). Technical efficiency in the textile industry in Bangladesh: An application of frontier production function. *International Journal of Information and Management Sciences*, *14*(1), 19–30.

Samuelson, P. A. (1973). Proof that properly discounted present values of assets vibrate randomly. *The Bell Journal of Economics and Management Science*, *4*(2), 369–374.

Sandhya, G. D., Mrinalini, N., & Nath, P. (2014, July 26). Sector and cluster effects of FDI in R&D in India emerging trends. *Economic & Political Weekly*, *xlix*(30), 182–190.

Sankar, U. (1970). Elasticity of substitution and returns to scale in Indian manufacturing industries. *International Economic Review*, *11*(3), 399–411.

Santarelli, E., & Vivarelli, M. (2002). Is subsidizing entry an optimal policy? *Industrial and Corporate Change, 11*(1), 39–52.

Saranga, H., & Phani, B. V. (2009). Determinants of operational efficiencies in the Indian pharmaceutical industry. *International Transactions in Operational Research*, *16*(1), 109–130.

Saranga, H., & Banker, R. D. (2010). Productivity and technical changes in the Indian pharmaceutical industry. *Journal of the Operational Research Society, 61*, 1777–1788.

Saranga, H., & Phani, B. V. (2003). *The Indian pharmaceutical industry – An overview of cost efficiency using DEA*. www.iitk.ac.in

Sarangi, H. (2007). Multiple objective data envelopment analysis as applied to the Indian pharmaceutical industry. *Journal of the Operational Research Society*, *58*(11), 1480–1493. https://doi.org/10.1057/palgrave.jors.2602280

Sarma, J. V. M. (1988). Investment allowance and private corporate investment in India. *Economic and Political Weekly*, *22*(5), 2235–2238.

Sasaki, H. (2007). The rise of service employment and its impact on aggregate productivity growth. *Structural Change and Economic Dynamics,18*, 438–459.

Savvides, A., & Zachariadis, M. (2005). International technology diffusion and the growth of TFP in the manufacturing sector of developing economies. *Review of Development Economics*, *9*(4), 482–501.

Scherer, F. M. (2000). The pharmaceutical industry. In *Handbook of health economics* (Vol. 1, Part B, 1297–1336). Elsevier.

Schimmelpfennig, D., & Thirtle, C. (1994). Cointegration and causality: Exploring the relationship between agriculture R&D and productivity. *Journal of Agricultural Economics*, *45*(2), 220–231.

Schmidt, P., & Lovell, C. A. K. (1979). Estimating technical and allocative inefficiency relative to stochastic production and cost frontiers. *Journal of Econometrics*, *9*(3), 343–366.

Schmidt, P., & Sickles, R. C. (1984). Production frontiers and panel data. *Journal of Business and Economic Statistics*, *2*(4), 367–374.

Schwarz, G. (1978). Estimating the dimension of a model. *The Annals of Statistics*, *6*(2), 461–464. http://www.jstor.org/stable/2958889

Scott, J. T., & Pascoe, G. (1986, May). Beyond firm and industry effects on profitability in imperfect markets. *Review of Economics and Statistics*, *68*, 284–292.

See, K. F., & Coelli, T. (2012). An analysis of factors that influence the technical efficiency of Malaysian thermal power plants. *Energy Economics*, *34*(3), 677–685.

Sen Gupta, D. N. (1993). Indian manufacturing industry: Growth episode of the eighties. *Economic and Political Weekly*, *28*(22), M54–M62.

Sen, A. (2003). On unit-root tests when the alternative is a trend-break stationary process. *Journal of Business and Economics Statistics*, *21*(1), 174–184.

Sen, A. (2009). On Perron's unit root tests in the presence of an innovation variance break. *Applied Mathematical Sciences*, *3*(27), 1341–1360.

Sengupta, M., Ghose, A., & Pal, D. (2009). Impact of liberalization on growth of output in the agricultural sector: A fresh look using modern time series approach. Paper presented at the *45th Annual Conference of The Indian Econometric Society*, Guwahati, January 9-10, 2009.

Seth, V. K., & Seth, A. K. (1991). Labor absorption in the Indian manufacturing sector. *Indian Journal of Industrial Relations*, *27*(1), 19–38.

Shah, M. B., & Patel, A. S. (2003). Drug price control in India –an overview. In A. I. Wertheimer (Ed.), *International Drug Regulatory Mechanisms* (1st edn.). CRC press. https://doi.org/10.1201/9781003063858

Shand, R., & Bhide, S. (2000). Sources of economic growth, regional dimensions of reforms. *Economic and Political Weekly*, *35*(42), 3747–3757.

Shapiro, M., & Watson, M. W. (1988). Sources of business cycle fluctuations. *NBER, Macroeconomics Annual 3*, 111–148.

Sharma, C. (2012). R&D and firm performance: Evidence from the Indian pharmaceutical industry. *Journal of the Asia Pacific Economy*, *17*(2), 332–342.

Sharma, C., & Mishra, R. K. (2011, November). Does export and productivity growth linkage exist? Evidence from the Indian manufacturing industry. *International Review of Applied Economics*, *25*(6), 633–652.

Sharma, D., Patel, P., & Shah, M. (2023). Comprehensive study on industry 4.0 in the pharmaceutical industry for sustainable development. *Environmental Science and Pollution Research*, *30*, 90088–90098. https://doi.org/10.1007/s11356-023-26856-y

Shashikanth, K., Mamatha, K., & Rao, T. S. (2018). A project report on sales and advertising. *International Journal of Management, Technology and Engineering*, *8*(VII), 648–652.

Shendy, R. (2012). Efficiency gains from trade reform: Foreign input technology or import competition? Evidence from south Africa. *The International Trade Journal*, *26*, 385–412.

Shepherd, W. G. (1986). Tobin q and the structure-performance relationship: Comment. *American Economic Review*, *76*(5), 1205–1210.

Shin, K., Lee, D., Shin, K., & Kim, E. (2018). Measuring the efficiency of us pharmaceutical companies based on open innovation types. *Journal of Open Innovation: Technology, Market, and Complexity*, *4*(3), 34.

Shiraishi, M., & Yano, G. (2004). Efficiency of Chinese township and village enterprises in the 1990s based on micro data for Wuxi city, 1991–97. *The Developing Economies*, *XLII-3*, 421–452.

Shivdas, A. P. (2012). *Resource based view of performance measurement of pharmaceutical companies in India: Sales versus efficiency* [Working Paper No.120, Amrita School of Business].

Siddharthan, N. S. (1988). In –house R&D, imported technology and firm-size: Lessons from Indian experience. *Developing Economies*, *26*(3), 212–221.

Siddharthan, N. S. (1992). Transaction costs, technology transfer, and in-house R&D: A study of the Indian private corporate sector. *Journal of Economic Behavior and Organization*, *18*(2), 265–271.

Siddharthan, N. S., & Aggarwal, R. N. (1992). Determinants of R&D decisions: A cross-section study of Indian private corporate firms. *Economics of Innovation and New Technology*, *2*(2), 103–110.

Siddharthan, N. S., Pandit, B. L., & Agarwal, R. N. (1992). *Growth and profit behavior of large Indian firms* [Working Paper, Institute of Economic Growth, Delhi].

Siegel, D. (1995). Errors of measurement and the recent acceleration in manufacturing productivity growth. *The Journal of Productivity Analysis*, *6*, 297–320.

Siggel, E. (1992). Productivity measurement from a deficient data base: An empirical study of Kenya's manufacturing sector. *Journal of Productivity Analysis*, *3*(4), 365–379.

Singh, N. (1989, January–June). Trade behaviour of firms: An empirical study of the size and foreign collaboration effects. *Indian Economic Review*, *24*(1), 45–65.

Singh, N. (1990). Profitability, growth and indebtedness of firms: The effects of size, foreign ownership and MNE-size. *Journal of Quantitative Economics*, *6*(1), 127–149.

Singh, P., & John, S. (2022). Analysis of the Indian pharmaceutical sector: Current status, challenges and opportunities. *IJFANS*, *11*(7).

Singhal, S., Gupta, S., & Gupta, V. K. (2022). Study of intellectual capital on drugs and pharmaceutical industry of India: Using panel data analysis. *Finance: Theory and Practice*, *26*(1), 66–78. https://doi.org/10.26794/2587-5671-2022-26-1-66-78

Sleuwaegen, L., & Goedhuys, M. (2003). Technical efficiency, market share and profitability of manufacturing firms in Côte D'ivoire: The Technology Trap. *Cambridge Journal of Economics*, *27*, 851–866.

Smith, P. J. (1999). Do knowledge spillovers contribute to U.S. State output and growth? *Journal of Urban Economics*, *45*, 331–353.

Söderbom, M., & Teal, F. (2004). Size and efficiency in African manufacturing firms: Evidence from firm-level panel data. *Journal of Development Economics*, *73*, 369–394.

Solow, R. M. (1957). Technical change and the aggregate production function. *Review of Economics and Statistics*, *39*(3), 312–332.

Soo, K. T. (2008). From license raj to market forces: The determinants of industrial structure in India after reform. *Economica*, *75*(298), 222–243.

Sorensen, A. (2001, September). Comparing apples and oranges: Productivity convergence and measurement across industries and countries: Comment. *American Economic Review*, *91*(4), 1160–1167.

Sorte Junior, W. F. (2012). The production and R&D structure of the Brazilian pharmaceutical industry: The role of public procurement and public drug production. *Global Public Health*, *7*(10), 1062–1079.

Srinivasan, P. V. (1992). Determinants of capacity utilization in Indian industries. *Journal of Quantitative Economics*, *8*(1), 139–156.

Srinivasan, S. (1999, February 27). How many aspirins to the rupee? Runaway drug prices, *Economic and Political Weekly*, *34*(9), 514–518.

Srinivasan, S. (2011, June 11). Medicines for all, the pharma industry and the Indian state. *Economic & Political Weekly, XLVI*(24), 43–50.

Srinivasan, S., & Phadke, A. (2013, January 5). Pharma policy 2012 and its discontents. *Economic & Political Weekly, xlviII*(1), 38–42.

Srinivasan, S., & Srikrishna, T. (2005, October 8). Making medicines available at reasonable prices the task force report. *Economic and Political Weekly, 40*(41), 4401–4406.

Srinivasan, S., Srikrishna, T., & Aisola, M. (2014, August 23). Pharma price control policy unrealistic and unfair. *Economic & Political Weekly, xlIX(34)*, 13–15.

Srivastava, V. (1996). *Liberalization, productivity and competition: A panel study of Indian manufacturing*. Oxford University Press.

Srivastava, V. (2000). *The impact of India's economic reforms on industrial productivity, efficiency and competitiveness (Report of a project sponsored by the Industrial Development Bank of India)*. National Council of Applied Economic Research, New Delhi.

Sterlacchini, A., & Venturini, F. (2013). Boosting manufacturing productivity through R&D: International comparisons with special focus on Italy. *Journal of Industry, Competition and Trade, 13*, 187–208.

Sterner, T. (1990). Energy efficiency and capital embodied technical change: The case of Mexican cement manufacturing. *Energy Journal, 11*(2), 155–167.

Stevenson, R. E. (1980). Likelihood function for generalized stochastic frontier estimation. *Journal of Econometrics, 13*(1), 57–66.

Stock, J. H., & Watson, M. W. (1988a). Testing for common trends. *Journal of the American Statistical Association, 83*(404), 1097–1107.

Stock, J. H., & Watson, M. W. (1988b). Variable trends in economic series. *Journal of Economic Perspective, 2*(3), 147–174.

Strazicich, M. C., & List, J. A. (2003). Are CO_2 emission levels converging among industrial countries. *Environmental and Resource Economics, 24*(3), 263–271.

Stulz, R. M., & Wasserfallen, W. (1985). Macroeconomic time series, business cycles and macroeconomic policies. In K. Brunner & A. H. Metzler (Eds.), *Understanding monetary regimes* (pp. 9–54). Carnegie-Rochester Conference Series on Public Policy.

Su, D., & He, X. (2012). Ownership structure, corporate governance and productive efficiency in China. *Journal of Productivity Analysis, 38*, 303–318.

Sun, C. (2004). Imperfect competition, economic miracle, and manufacturing productivity growth: Empirical evidence from Taiwan. *Atlantic Economic Journal, 34*, 341–359.

Sun, C. H. (2007). Economic integration, efficiency change and technological progress. *Applied Economics, 39*, 653–662.

Sun, C. H., & Kalirajan, K. P. (2005). *Gauging the sources of growth of high-tech and low-tech industries: The case of Korean manufacturing* (pp. 170–185). Australian economic paper, Blackwell Publishing Ltd/University of Adelaide and Flinders University.

Sun, C.-H. (2007). The conundrum of economic miracles: Manufacturing growth without total factor productivity growth. *Journal of Developing Areas, 40*(2), 157–158.

Sun, C.-H. (2007). The growth process in East Asian manufacturing industries: A re-examination. *The Developing Economies, 45*(1), 130–134.

Sun, H., Hone, P., & Doucouliagos, H. (1999). Economic openness and technical efficiency. *Economics of Transition, 7*(3), 615–636.

Sun, L., & Wang, M. (1996). Global warming and global dioxide emission: An empirical study. *Journal of Environmental Management, 46*(4), 327–343.

Suyanto, R., & Salim, A. (2010). Sources of productivity gains from FDI in Indonesia: Is it efficiency improvement or technological progress?. *The Developing Economies, 48*(4), 450–472.

Tan, G. K. R. (2006). Efficiency estimates for Singapore manufacturing: New evidence from the malmquist index. *Applied Economics Letters, 13*, 715–721.

Tanuwidjaja, E., & Thangavelu, S. (2007). Structural change and productivity growth in the Japanese manufacturing industry. *Global Economic Review, 36*(4), 385–405.

Tata Services Limited. (2003). *Reforms and productivity trends in Indian manufacturing sector.* Department of Economics and Statistics, Tata Services.

Taymaz, E. (2005). Are small firms really less productive? *Small Business Economic, 25,* 429–445.

Taymaz, E., & Saatci, G. (1997). Technical change and efficiency in Ttirkish manufacturing industries. *Journal of Productivity Analysis, 8,* 461–475.

Temouri, Y, Driffield, N. L., & AñónHigón, D. (2008). Analysis of productivity differences among foreign and domestic firms: Evidence from Germany. *Review of World Economics, 144*(1), 32–54.

Timmer, M. P. (2002). Climbing the technology ladder too fast? New evidence on comparative productivity performance in Asian manufacturing. *Journal of the Japanese and International Economies, 16,* 50–72.

Tinbergen, J. (1942). Zur theorie der langfristigen wirtschaftsentwicklung (on the theory of trend movement). *Weltwirtschafliches Archiv, 55*(1), 511–549.

Tran, T. B., Grafton, R. Q.,& Kompas, T. (2008a). Firm efficiency in a transitional economy: Evidence from Vietnam. *Asian Economic Journal, 22*(1), 47–66.

Tran, T. B., & Grafton, R. Q., & Kompas, T. (2008b). Institutions matter: The case of Vietnam. *The Journal of Socio-Economics, 38,* 1–12.

Trianni, A., Cagno, E., & Worrell, E. (2013). Innovation and adoption of energy efficient technologies: An exploratory analysis of Italian primary metal manufacturing SMEs. *Energy Policy, 61,* 430–440.

Trivedi, P. (2004). An inter-state perspective on manufacturing productivity in India: 1980-81 to 2000-01. *Indian Economic Review, 39*(1), 203–237.

Trivedi, P., Prakash, A., & Sinate, D. (2000). *Productivity in major manufacturing industries in India: 1973-74 to 1997-98* [Developing Research Group No. 20, Department of Economic Analysis and Policy, Reserve Bank of India, Mumbai].

Truett, D. B., & Truett, L. J. (2009). Firm-size and efficiency in the South African motor vehicle industry. *Australian Economic Papers,* 333–341.

Tsai, K. H., & Wang, J. C. (2004). R&D productivity and the spillover effects of high-tech industry on the traditional manufacturing sector: The case of Taiwan. *World Economy,* 1555–1570.

Tsekouras, K. D., & Daskalopoulou, I. F. (2006). Market concentration and multifaceted productive efficiency. *Journal of Productivity Analysis, 25,* 79–91.

Tsen, W. H. (2005). The determinants of foreign direct investment in the manufacturing industry of Malaysia. *Journal of Economic Cooperation, 26*(2), 91–110.

Tsionas, E. G. (2000). Regional growth and convergence: Evidence from the united states. *Regional Studies, 34,* 231–238.

Tyagi, S., Mahajan, V., & Nauriyal, D. K. (2014). Innovations in Indian drug and pharmaceutical industry: Have they impacted exports? *Journal of Intellectual Property Rights, 19*(July), 243–252.

Tyagi, S., Nauriyal, D. K., & Gulati, R. (2016). Firm level R&D intensity: Evidence from Indian drugs and pharmaceutical industry. *Review of Managerial Science, 1–36.* https://doi.org/10.1007/s11846-016-0218-8

Tybout, J. R. (1992). Linking trade and productivity: New research directions. *The World Bank Economic Review, 6*(2), 189–211.

Tybout, J. R. (2000, March). Manufacturing firms in developing countries: How well do they do and why? *Journal of Economic Literature, 38*(1), 11–44.

Tybout, J. R., & Westbrook, M. D. (1995). Trade liberalization and the dimensions of efficiency change in Mexican manufacturing industries. *Journal of International Economics, 39*(1-2), 53–78.

Tybout, J. R., de Melo, J., & Corbo, V. (1991). The effects of trade reforms on scale and technical efficiency: New evidence from Chile. *Journal of International Economics, 31*(3/4), 231–250.

Uaur, A. (2004). *Technical efficiency in Irish Manufacturing Industry, 1991-99* [Economic Papers, Economics Department, Trinity College, Dublin].

Uchikawa, S. (2001, August 25). Investment boom and underutilisation of capacity in the 1990s. *Economic and Political Weekly*, *36*(34), 3247–3254.

Uchikawa, S. (2002). Investment boom and the capital goods industry. In S. Uchikawa (Ed.), *Economic reforms and industrial structure in India*. Manohar Publishers.

Unel, B. (2003). *Productivity trends in India's manufacturing sector in the last two decades* [IMF Working Paper, WP/03/22, International Monetary Fund, Washington DC].

Unni, J., Lalitha, N., & Rani, U. (2001). Economic reform and productivity trends in Indian manufacturing. *Economic and Political Weekly*, *36*(41), 3914–3922.

Upendranath, C., Vijayabaskar, M., & Vyasulu, V. (1994). Industrial growth and structure: Analysis of manufacturing sector in Karnataka. *Economic and Political Weekly*, *29*(48), M157–M164.

Urata, S., & Kawai, H. (2002). Technological progress by small and medium enterprises in Japan. *Small Business Economics*, *18*(1-3), 53–67.

Vijayalalitha, V., Garg, P., Kiradoo, G., & Ashifa, K. M. (2022). Measurement of total factor productivity and its components in Indian pharmaceutical firms: An application of DEA. *European Chemical Bulletin*, *11*(10), 82–94. https://doi.org/10.31838/ecb/2022.11.10.011

Vahtra, P., & Liuhto, K. (2005). *An overview of Russia's largest corporations abroad*. http://www.haworthpress.com/web/JEB

Valadhkani, A., Lyton, A. P., & Pahlavani, M. (2005). *Multiple structural breaks in Australia's macroeconomic data: An application of the Lumsdaine and Papell Test* [Economic Working Paper number WP05-17, School of Economics, University of Wollongong, NSW, Australia].

Valdemar, S., Hansenz, M. D., Eriksson, T., & Madsen, E. S. (2004). R&D and productivity in Danish firms: Some empirical evidence. *Applied Economics*, *36*, 1797–1806.

Valodia, I., & Velia, M. (2006). Macro–micro linkages in trade: Trade, efficiency and competitiveness of manufacturing firms in Durban, south Africa. *Journal of African Economies*, *15*(4), 688–721.

Varien, H. (1984). The non-parametric approach to production analysis. *Econometrica*, *52*(3), 579–599.

Varshney, A. (1984). Political economy of slow industrial growth in India. *Economic and Political Weekly*, *19*(35), 1511–1517.

Varum, C. A., & Rocha, V. C. (2013). Employment and SMEs during crises. *Small Business Economics*, *40*, 9–25.

Vashist, D. C. (1984). Substitution possibilities and price sensitivity of energy demand in Indian manufacturing. *Indian Economic Journal*, *32*(1), 84–97.

Venturini, F. (2012). Looking into the black box of Schumpeteri an growth theories: An empirical assessment of R&D races. *European Economic Review*, *56*, 1530–1545.

Vial, V. (2008). How much does turnover matter? Evidence from Indonesian manufacturing total factor productivity growth, 1975-95. *Oxford Development Studies*, *36*(3), 295–322.

Virmani, A., & Hashim, D. A. (2009). *Factor employment, sources and sustainability of output growth: Analysis of Indian manufacturing* [Ministry of Finance, Government of India, Working Paper No.3/2009-DEA].

Visalakshi, S., & Sandhya, G. D. (2000, November 25). R and D in pharma industry in context of biotech commercialisation. *Economic and Political Weekly*, 4223–4233.

Vithalani, C. A., Brijesh, H., & Joshi, P. M. (2016, June). A comparative study of profitability of selected pharma companies of India. *Global Journal for Research Analysis*, *5*(6), 45–47.

Vixathep, S., & Matsunaga, N. (2012). Firm efficiency in Cambodia's garment industry on the eve of the multi-fiber arrangement termination. *Asian Economic Journal*, *26*(4), 359–380.

Vogelsang, T. J., & Perron, P. (1998). Additional tests for a unit root allowing for a break in the trend function at an unknown time. *International Economic Review, 39*(4), 1073–1100.

Vyas, V., Narayanan, K., & Ramanathan, A. (2012). Determinants of mergers and acquisitions in Indian pharmaceutical industry. *Eurasian Journal of Business and Economics, 5*(9),79–102.

Wachter, S. D., & Tzavalis, E. (2012). Detection of structural breaks in linear dynamic panel data models. *Computational Statistics & Data Analysis, 56*(11), 3020–3034, ISSN 0167-9473. https://doi.org/10.1016/j.csda.2012.02.025

Wagner, J. (2008). Export entry, export exit and productivity in German manufacturing industries. *International. Journal of the Economics of Business, 15*(2), 169–180.

Wakeel, A. I., & Ekundayo, P. M. (2016). Determinants of pharmaceutical industry's performance in Nigeria. *Managing Global Transitions, 14*(3), 267–282.

Walujadi, D. (2004). Age, export orientation and technical efficiency: Evidence from garment firms in DKI Jakarta. *Makara of Social Sciences and Humanities Series, 8*(3), 97–104.

Wang, H., & Schmidt, P. (2002). One-step and two-step estimation of the effects of exogenous variables on technical efficiency levels. *Journal of Productivity Analysis, 18*(2), 129–144.

Wang, J. Y. (1990). Growth, technology transfer, and the long-run theory of international capital movements. *Journal of International Economics, 29*(3/4), 255–271

Wasserfallen, W. (1986). Non-stationarities in macro-economic time series – Further evidence and implications. *Canadian Journal of Economics, 19*(3), 498–510.

Watal, J. (1997). Implementing the TRIPS agreement, policy options open to India. *Economic and Political Weekly, 32*(39), 2461–2468.

Weber, W. L., & Domazlicky, B. R. (1999). Total factor productivity growth in manufacturing: A regional approach using linear programming. *Regional Science and Urban Economics, 29*(1), 105–122.

Wei, Y., & Liu, X. (2006). Productivity spillovers from R&D, exports and FDI in China's manufacturing sector. *Journal of International Business Studies, 37*(4), 544–557.

Williams, H., & Lumas, P. (1981). The relation between energy and non-energy inputs in a developing economy. *Journal of Industrial Economics, 30*(2), 113–122.

Williams, H., & Lumas, P. (1984). Economies of scale for various types of manufacturing production technologies in an underdeveloped economy. *Economic Department and Cultural Change, 32*(3), 401–412.

Wing, C. C. K., & Yiu, M. F. K. (1995). Firm size and performance of manufacturing enterprises in P.R. China: The case of Shanghai's manufacturing industries. *Small Business Economics, 9*, 287–298.

WITS, World Integrated Trade Solution, Trade Statistics by Product. https://wits.worldbank.org/

World Bank. (1993). *The East Asian miracle*. Oxford University Press.

Wu, Z. B., Yeung, G., Mok, V., & Han, Z. (2007). Firm-specific knowledge and technical efficiency of watch and clock manufacturing firms in China. *International Journal of Productivity Analysis, 107*, 317–332.

Xiaohua, L. (2007). China is a big industrial manufacturer but with low efficiency. China Economist, 122–135.

Yadav, I. S. (2007). Firm size and growth: The Indian experience. *The ICFAI Journal of Industrial Economics, 4*(1), 37–48.

Yasar, M., & Paul, C. J. M. (2009). Size and foreign ownership effects on productivity and efficiency: An analysis of Turkish motor vehicle and parts plants. *Review of Development Economics, 3*(4), 576–591.

Yasar, M., Rejesus, R. M., & Mintemurz, I. (2004). Is there evidence of creative destruction in the Turkish manufacturing sector? Lessons from a cross-industry analysis of aggregate productivity growth. *Applied Economics, 36*, 1937–1945.

Yay, G. G., & Keçeli, S. (2009). The intersectoral linkage effects in Turkish economy: An application of static leontief model. *Panoeconomicus*, *3*, 301–326.

Yeoh, P. L., & Roth, K. (1999). An empirical analysis of sustained advantage in the US pharmaceutical industry: Impact of firm resources and capabilities. *Strategic Management Journal*, *20*(7), 637–653.

Yoo, S.-L., Kim, D.-J., Lee, S.-M., Kang, W.-G., Kim, S.-Y., Lee, J. et al. (2019). Improving patient access to new drugs in South Korea: Evaluation of the national drug formulary system. *International Journal of Environmental Research and Public Health*, *16*(2), 1–15.

You, T., Chen, X., & Holder, M. E. (2010). Efficiency and its determinants in pharmaceutical industries: Ownership, R&D and scale economy. *Applied Economics*, *42*(17), 2217–2241.

Young, A. (1991). Learning by doing and the dynamics of international trade. *Quarterly Journal of Economics*, *106*(2), 369–405.

Zahid, S. N., Akbar, M., & Jaffry, S. A. (1992). Islamabad technical change, efficiency, and capital-labour substitution in Pakistan's large-scale manufacturing sector. *The Pakistan Development Review*, *31*(2), 165–188.

Zhang, T. (2010). Environmental performance assessment of China's manufacturing. *Asian Economic Journal*, *24*(1), 45–68.

Zhang, S., Ondrich, J., & Richardson, J. D. (2003). *The link between trade and income: Export effect, import effect, or both?* [Working Paper, Department of Economics, Syracuse University]. faculty.maxwell.syr.edu/jondrich/PapersOnLine/shuo.jan.dave-10.pdf

Zhang, X. G., & Zhang, S. (2001). Technical efficiency in china's iron and steel industry: Evidence from the new census data. *International Review of Applied Economics*, *15*(2), 199–211.

Zhang, Y. C., & Li, S. L. (2009). High performance work practices and firm performance: Evidence from the pharmaceutical industry in China. *The International Journal of Human Resource Management*, *20*(11), 2331–2348.

Zhang, Z., Jia, M., & Wan, D. (2009). Allocation of control rights and cooperation efficiency in public-private partnerships: Theory and evidence from the Chinese pharmaceutical industry. *International Journal of Health Care Finance & Economics*, *9*, 169–182.

Zhengyu, Y., & Suyun, Y. (2011). Is China's manufacturing technical efficiency cost-push? *China Economist*, *6*(1), 92–101.

Zhou, Y., Xing, X., Fang, K., Liang, D., & Xu, C. (2013). Environmental efficiency analysis of power industry in china based on an entropy SBM model. *Energy Policy*, *57*, 68–75.

Zivot, E., & Andrews, D. (1992). Further evidence of the great crash, the oil-price shock and the unit-root hypothesis. *Journal of Business and Economic Statistics*, *10*(3), 251–270.

Zoltan, A., Morek, R., & Yeung, B. (1996). Productivity growth and firm-size distribution. Milken Institute Publication: Research Reports, Santa Monica, CA, http:/www.unio.org—Sales *Publication* (2005). *Indian Manufacturing Industry: Technology Status and Prospects, United Nations Industrial Development Organization*, 47 pages.

Index

Printed and bound by CPI Group (UK) Ltd, Croydon, CR0 4YY

20/01/2025

14629234-0001